The English hou seventeenth & eighteenth centuries

Rose M. Bradley

Alpha Editions

This edition published in 2019

ISBN : 9789353600617

Design and Setting By
Alpha Editions
email - alphaedis@gmail.com

THE ENGLISH HOUSEWIFE
IN THE SEVENTEENTH &
EIGHTEENTH CENTURIES

A KITCHEN IN THE 18TH CENTURY.

THE ENGLISH HOUSEWIFE
IN THE SEVENTEENTH &
EIGHTEENTH CENTURIES

BY

ROSE M. BRADLEY

Every wise woman buildeth her house : but the foolish
plucketh it down with her hands.

PROV. xiv. I.

LONDON
EDWARD ARNOLD
1912

PREFACE

NOT so long ago I opened an admirable book on domestic economy in which I found it stated that, "scientific training can alone save the sorely taxed housewife to-day from becoming a slave to her domestic responsibilities."

It is a misleading and unattractive statement and one which certainly does not convey the writer's real meaning. There are no doubt housewives at the present time who, filled with a laudable desire to leave the world a little better than they found it, grudge every hour which is spent upon the proper care and management of their own households. Hemmed and pressed on every side by the ever-increasing demands of external work, social and political, they may protest that their own homes must be conducted upon a purely scientific basis with the minimum outlay of time and strength on the part of the mistress. These are however, we believe in the minority. An immense amount of outside work may or may not be done by the modern woman ; but as a rule she has the intelligence to know that the personal touch, the little original methods in which one housewife may differ from another and so lend a distinctive charm and interest to her own surroundings, are worth far more than the most scientific training and the more or less mechanical

v

257896

perfection thus achieved. The relations between mistress and servants, upon which the whole happiness of a household alike for its members and its guests must depend, can be achieved by no purely scientific axioms.

Three hundred years ago, the great lady whose education was at least as good as, if not a great deal better than our own, thought it by no means beneath her to devote the greater part of her time to the care of her household. True, there were no committee meetings, no public platforms on which she could raise her voice on behalf of any cause in which she happened to be interested. She claimed no rights, for she was content with her affections and her duties, which comprised not only her own numerous family, but that much larger one on her husband's land, as well as the poor at her gates. She began life young and her span of years in comparison to our own was short, and perhaps this was one of the many reasons why she found her own sphere sufficiently satisfying.

We have travelled a long way since the days of the learned Tudor ladies and the competent and intelligent housewives of the early Stuarts. The struggle for the Higher Education of Women strenuously and successfully carried out in the nineteenth century, meant in reality little more than a re-building in modern form of an edifice which had crumbled slowly and surely under the influence of the Puritans, and could regain no foothold in the pleasure-loving days of the Restoration, nor in the stultifying early years of the century which followed. In the latter half of it the women of intellect, of whom there were many, owed their erudition rather to their own enterprise than to the instruction received in those refined academies for young ladies where superficial accomplishments were considered the hall mark of gentility.

When, with much pain and difficulty, the new educational edifice for women was reared some fifty years ago it was inevitable that the pendulum should swing a little far, and that the more homely duties of our sex should have fallen for some years into lamentable disrepute. Now that we are re-awakening to the value of house-wifery knowledge, scientific or otherwise, as an asset in women's education, a plausible effort is being made to arouse those "homespun" instincts in the girls which were certainly not encouraged in their mothers. There is still much to be done to complete the work of which our immediate predecessors in the last century laid the foundation stone and built, as it were, the main structure. Some of us may find it in our hearts to hope that while the libraries of this educational edifice are kept at a high standard, and the kitchens are furnished in a manner worthy to attend upon them, time and inclination may yet be found for the further embellishment of the drawing-room. But for this perhaps, the pendulum must again swing back a little.

In the following pages I have tried briefly to trace the domestic life of the English lady from a period shortly before the outbreak of the Civil War until the accession of Queen Victoria. My intention has been to give some picture of her immediate surroundings, her domestic duties, her occupations, expenses and pleasures. In describing her home and its fittings I cannot pretend to any expert knowledge of detail in the matter of architecture, or furniture, etc., a general impression is all that it is within the limits of this book or my own powers to convey. But if it carry with it any of the fragrance which, in these utilitarian days, seems always to linger in the atmosphere of a leisurely and picturesque past, it will, however inadequately, have achieved its object.

My warmest thanks are due to those who have most kindly given me access to their unpublished family papers, including diaries, accounts and recipes which are invaluable as illustrating the domestic life of the time. To Lady Bosville Macdonald of the Isles for the accounts and inventories of the Bosville and Osbaldeston households ; to Mrs. Jacomb Hood for her great-grandmother, the Baroness de Hochepied's diary ; to Colonel Frewen, C.B., for the use of his great-aunt's recipes and accounts ; and to Mrs. Way for the account books of her ancestor, Baron Hill, and his descendants. I have also to thank Lady Sackville for permission to include Lady Betty Germaine's recipe for her famous Pot-Pourri at Knole ; Mrs. Evelyn for the portrait of Mrs. John Evelyn, at Wotton House ; Lady Algernon Gordon-Lennox for the photograph of her herb garden at Broughton Castle ; Sir Albert K. Rollit for the description of the original herb garden at St. Anne's Hill, Chertsey ; and Mr. Frank Schloesser for valuable advice and assistance. My thanks and acknowledgments must further be given to Margaret, Lady Verney, and to her publishers Messrs. Longmans, Green & Co., for permission to make extracts from the "Verney Memoirs"; to Mrs. Dorothea Townshend for the same permission with regard to her "Life and Letters of the Great Earl of Cork" and her "Letters of Endymion Porter," and to her publishers Messrs. Duckworth & Co., and to Mr. Fisher Unwin respectively ; also to the Scottish History Society for permission to quote from Lady Grisell Baillie's "Household Book," and to Mr. Lane, of the Bodley Head, for the use of quotations from "The Memoirs of Lady Fanshawe."

Wherever possible I have gone to the original sources, but there are many comparatively modern books to which I must express my indebtedness, notably: "The Autobiography and Correspondence of Mrs. Delaney," edited by Lady Llanover (Richard Bentley & Son); "The Journals of Mrs. Papendiek," edited by Mrs. Delves Broughton (Richard Bentley & Son); "A Foreign View of England in the Reigns of George I. and George II.," edited by Madame van Muyden (John Murray); Jeafferson's "Book about the Table" (Hurst & Blackett); "The Growth of the English House," by J. Alfred Gotch (Batsford); and the many useful handbooks to the Victoria and Albert Museum.

Lastly I have to thank Mr. Guy Laking, C.V.O., for facilities to study the exhibits at the London Museum, Mr. Lenygon for admission to his show-rooms, and many kind friends whose advice and encouragement have been of very real assistance.

ROSE M. BRADLEY.

GREYCOAT GARDENS,
  September, 1912.

OTHER AUTHORITIES

"The Publications of the Camden Society"; "Home Life of English Ladies in the Seventeenth Century" by the author of "Magdalen Stafford"; "A History of the Cries of London" (Charles Hindley); The Sussex Archæological Society's Collection; Traill's "Social History of England"; "Social Life in the Reign of Queen Anne" by John Ashton (Chatto & Windus); and many others.

CONTENTS

LIST OF ILLUSTRATIONS

The English Housewife

in the

Seventeenth and Eighteenth Centuries

INTRODUCTION

THE RETURN

IN the fresh sunshine of an early summer morning
a little grey lady stole across the lawn in front
of the Manor House. She was very small, and
her feet made no impression as she passed over the
soft velvet of the turf. She was also very dignified,
and it was easy to see that the place belonged to her.
No one need have any doubt about that. Had she
not lived here for three hundred years? She herself
did not know about time, but she fancied she must
have had a very long sleep, and she knew dimly that
there were other people here now, but they were her
people all the same, just as the place was hers.

She moved in her own small and stately fashion
down the walk between the cut yew-trees. The sun
was high, and it was quite time that she visited the

fish-ponds. She must see how the young carp were
fattening. The Squire would be back presently, and
there might be company. But here a little surprise
awaited her. The fish-ponds were there indeed, two
straight, narrow pieces of water, just as she had always
known them, but what was this? On their surface
floated a mass of flat green leaves from which peeped out
many flowers—pink and crimson and great white ones
with yellow centres, opening gloriously to the sunshine.
These must be surely some strange new food for
the fish ; one of those horticultural experiments
which came from Holland. But would the fish like
it ? She greatly doubted it. Meantime, where were the
carp—all those new young carp, a present from a
neighbour in the next county of Sussex, and the
Sussex carp were always to be depended on? Not a
sign of them. She bent down a little nearer, and her
own pale, bewildered little face looked up at her from
the water. There she saw the glint of something small
and gold, and then another whisking in and out
among the lilies. Very small and very gold they were.
The little lady shook her head. The Sussex neighbour
had disappointed her sadly this time ; and all that stuff
with the flowers would never fatten them fit for the
table. Well—she must seek out her steward and speak
about it.

Meantime there was her herb-garden to look to. She
had been away so long. Surely the lavender must
be nearly ready for cutting ; it was time to gather
her rosemary for drying. How glad she would be to
tread once more the bed of thyme under her little feet
and smell its crushed fragrance! She turned back
across the greensward. Here it would be, behind

the low beech hedge so carefully clipped and cut. But
no, the hedge had gone. Well, there had been some
severe winters; no doubt it had died, and perhaps
the rose-hedge might do as well, roses did no
harm in a herb-garden. But as she came nearer, the
little lady opened her eyes very wide indeed. There
indeed was her lavender, cut neat and hedge-wise,
and still covered with flowers; there was also rosemary,
but not enough of it, she thought, rosemary being so
invaluable in the stillroom. She hardly thought about
the lavender or the rosemary at all, however, for within
the little inner hedge she could see nothing whatever
but roses—a perfect riot of them. Clusters of tiny
roses, red and pink, trained over a long arch, something
like the pleached alleys of her memory, and which
stretched away to the other end of the garden, to
where once had stood the little arbour of wych-elm
where she had been used to rest herself. That had
gone now, and the roses covered everything. There
were roses she had never seen or heard of—flaunting
golden creatures which nodded at her from the bed
where her borage and fennel should have been; great
white beauties which had usurped the place of her
cherished southernwood, and everywhere the old-
fashioned roses of her own memory, delicate monthly
roses and the big, fat, cabbage variety. Yes, she had
loved her roses too, but in their proper place. Surely
this ramping fashion was a great extravagance—so
much rose-water could not be needed; and where were
the herbs?

The Squire's lady of three hundred years ago passed
her hand over her eyes and sighed. She remembered
now that they were her children who were living here,

and young people will have vagaries. Her only son
who had lived to grow up had always been wild ; she
had heard that he was a great friend of that too merry
monarch Charles II., but that was after her time.
The dull, hard days of the Commonwealth had driven
her away among the shadows. And these were his
children, or his children's children, she did not know
—anyhow, they were also hers.

She went back and stood on the broad gravel sweep
in front of the Manor House, and this gave her great
confidence.   Here it still stood with its gables and
mullioned windows and twisted chimneys, just as she
and her lord had built it so many years ago.   The
improving hand of Time had mellowed the grey,
weather-beaten stone, and the sun no longer twinkled
on little diamond panes in the window ; but this was
her house as she had known it, and she could not
see the new wing to the south.   Her initials entwined
with those of the Squire were still there over the heavy
porch—where they had stood together so often.   Here
she had watched her husband ride away to join the
King's army, and here they had proclaimed their
boy's coming-of-age to the assembled tenants.

These thoughts gave the little lady courage.   She
slipped into the house and up the wide oak staircase
to her own bedroom.   It was still there, though strangely
altered.   The heavy, carved-oak bedstead, which had
been her pride, remained, but the curtains of thick crewel
work on linen, which had kept herself and her maids busy
at their needles and embroidery-frames through many
long hours of the Squire's absence, had been taken from
the bed and hung at the large opened windows.   The
truckle-bed, where her maid Moll was wont to lie some-

times when the lady felt ill or lonely and her lord was
away, was gone. In its place was a luxurious sofa,
which even her great grandchildren could hardly have
known. Cushioned and springy, it was a contrast indeed
to the day-bed upon which she had sometimes thought
it a luxury to dispose herself. The elegant toilet-table
and large mirror were certainly new, and just a little
shocking to her. Could her son be so rich that his wife
could have her table covered with gold and silver and
crystal toilet ornaments, fit in her day only for the
greatest in the land ? But she had heard of terrible
extravagance not so much later.

The poor little lady was getting tired and confused ;
she did not like the large porcelain bath, with its
glittering brass taps in the inner chamber, where in oak
chests and hanging cupboards she had been used to keep
the more sumptuous portion of her wardrobe. She did
not at first know what the bath was for, but when she
understood she was distressed. It was not safe to bathe
too freely, but was a habit to be practised with care.
Had not Mrs. Alice Thornton nearly perished on her
wedding-day from having washed her feet the night
before, and that in mid-winter ! In the bottles of salts
and bath powders she found something vaguely familiar,
and sniffed them daintily. Something of the sort was
made in her still-room, and fortunately she could not
read the labels which proclaimed them the products of
Harrod's or Bond Street.

Now she wandered through the corridors, through the
saloons full of wonderful polished furniture in strange
woods and designs, of cabinets filled with china ; dainty
elegant chairs which could not be safe to sit on, un-
dreamt of in her day. But there was much of her own

still left ; the solid oak table in the dining-hall, the great
oak presses which put to shame, she thought, the fanciful
gimcracks of the later time. Her own beautiful Van
Dyck portrait smiled down at her. Instinctively she put
her hand up to her neck and wondered where her
pearls had gone to. Then she remembered the fine
silver tankards and flagons which had stood on the press
below, and which had gone to raise soldiers for the King.
She smiled up at the handsome cavalier in his suit of
armour and his deep lace collar, and he smiled back
at her reassuringly. For his sake she had been a very
brave little lady, and he had been proud of her. She
remembered how rudely Cromwell's soldiers had thrust
her aside when they searched the house for arms and
treasure, which, thanks to her ready wit and courage,
they never found. She had been alone in the house then
with her little children, so many of whom lay in the
family vault up in the church yonder.

She began to feel lonely now ; she had seen no living
soul in the house or gardens, perhaps because in her
heart she had not wished to ; the place was to be once
more her own. But at this moment the heavy oak door
was pushed very slowly open and a tiny child in a white
frock came cautiously in. Very slowly it came, stepping
over the slippery polished boards—a strong, determined
little boy of two years old, with a hint of curl in his short
yellow hair, and blue eyes set wide apart which stared at
her without a trace of shyness. Such a boy had been
her firstborn—her John, whose splendid silver porringer
had gone into the melting-pot with all the others to help
his sovereign, and whose young life had been snatched
from her before he was four. This one looked healthy
enough, but you never knew. She wondered how many

of his brothers and sisters were already in that old vault up on the hill.

But the child was now standing in front of her, planted solidly upon his two feet and a slow smile spreading over his chubby face. Her John would have looked at her just like that, but he would not have been quite so sturdy.

Then the small boy spoke. " I'm John," he said, with a pretty self-importance.

The little lady stared. Ah! had she not known it all the time? This was John, her own little John, come back to her, cropped it is true like a Roundhead and without his satin petticoat, but her son and nobody else's. She held out her arms to him in a strange forgotten transport of happiness. John suddenly turned shy and hid his face in his fat hands.

But at that moment a terrible sound, an insistent, repeated, shrill sound, pierced its way through the adjoining corridor. John, quite undisturbed, took courage to peep through his fingers at this wonderful little lady who was so like the pretty picture up there. But she had vanished, frightened out of her brief and shadowy existence. How could she know it was only the telephone bell ?

CHAPTER I

THE TRAINING OF THE HOUSEWIFE

IN the opening years of the seventeenth century the self-respecting English lady preferred to absent herself from the dissolute Court of James I. and his Danish Queen, and to live in comparative seclusion on her husband's estate in the country. Here she could attend to the education of her daughters, administer her household, and entertain her guests in a manner fitting the dignified traditions of her own upbringing in the great days of Elizabeth.

When Charles I. came to the throne the Court was speedily swept and garnished of its worst licence, and a purified atmosphere of home life and the example of domestic happiness were offered by the King to his subjects. But, none the less, the ladies stayed in the country. Even those whose husbands held posts at Court were in many cases content to go up to Whitehall and make their curtsey and return again to their own exclusive surroundings.

Possibly a certain suspicion of the French Queen, of her alien charm which to insular minds has always been suggestive of a frivolous upbringing, and a more definite and far greater dread of her papistry, convinced them that the country was still the safest place in which to train and educate their young daughters.

The education of women continued to be regarded seriously under the early Stuarts, though it is doubtful whether the high standard of the Tudor ladies was maintained, except in select circles. We know that the ladies of Queen Elizabeth's Court had a sound knowledge of Greek and Latin, and could usually speak French, Italian, and Spanish quite fluently. In Holinshed's "Chronicles" Harrison tells us that "they read the Holy Scriptures and histories of our own or foreign nations. They wrote volumes of their own or translated other men's into English or Latin. The younger ones played the lute and the cithern."

It was, however, still the fashion in good families, and especially in the country, for the girls to learn from their brothers' tutor, and in this way they would as a matter of course receive a classical education. Later in the century, when schools such as "Mrs. Priest's genteel establishment for young ladies at Chelsea" began to open, deportment, drawing-room accomplishments, and a smattering of French became of far greater importance to the young person who was presently to make her curtsey to the "Merrie Monarch" than a sound and educative knowledge of Greek and Latin. The Puritan influence as a whole was unfavourable to women's education. We find Sir Ralph Verney endeavouring to dissuade his little god-daughter, Dr. Denton's Nancy, from acquiring too much learning. Nancy, however, has her own views, and saucily replies that she means to outreach him in "ebri, grek, and laten." Let us hope that she also paid a little attention to her spelling, but judging by the letters of her contemporaries, this seems to have remained for long a matter which was governed entirely by caprice.

Certainly, to our ideas, instruction began painfully

early in those days. As soon as they could walk, the children's nurse was expected to teach them to read from their horn books. Here the precious printed page was enclosed in a horn frame with a brass or wooden handle, and carefully preserved by a piece of talc on either side from destructive little fingers. It was a practical plan and one to which we owe the survival of many specimens of these early lesson-books among the treasures of museums or the priceless relics of a cherished past in old country houses, but it also limited the child's first explorations in the new field of letters to the sides of the one page, which must have added not a little to the weariness of these early lessons for both nurse and pupil. One horn-book, however, no doubt succeeded another only too rapidly, to be presently replaced by a bound volume.

The mental achievements of the infant prodigies of these days suggest that the Puritans may have had some reason as well as prejudice for discouraging female education, and that insanitary conditions, a curious diet, and medical treatment compounded of superstition and ignorance, were not the only causes which contributed to the appalling infant mortality of the time. John Evelyn's little son Richard is almost too familiar an example to quote. But when we are told that at the age of two and a half he could read and pronounce English, Latin and French; that at four he could write a good hand, was learning Greek, and amused himself with demonstrating the problems of Euclid; that at five he "disengaged" his godparents as he now understood his own duty after a complete mastery of the Catechism, we cannot wonder that this poor little child, this "incomparable hopeful blossom," did not reach the age of six !

And there were girls who were not far behind him. A pathetic instance of the rigorous training of mere babies in this age has come down to us in the description of the death-bed of the little Princess Anne, a daughter of Charles I. She is said by the chronicler to have been a very wise little lady "above her age" and she died when she was not quite four years old. "Being told to pray by those about her at the last, 'I am not able,' saith she, 'to say my long prayer'—meaning the Lord's prayer— 'but I will say my short one. Lighten mine eyes, O Lord, lest I sleep the sleep of death.' This done, the little lamb gave up her spirit." How much, one cannot but wonder, was this much-loved baby a victim of premature religious and mental development, and the over-anxiety of devoted parents for her future welfare !

Mrs. Lucy Hutchinson, on the other hand, appears to have been one of those who was not at all the worse for her strenuous education. She boasts that as little Lucy Apsley she could read English perfectly by the time she was four, and "having a great memory was carried to sermons, and while I was very young could remember and repeat them exactly, and being caressed the love of praise tickled me, and made me attend more heedfully." Her father had her taught Latin, and she mentions this as though it were no longer the invariable rule in Puritan households even as early as 1625. "I was so apt," she tells us complacently—and indeed this armour of self-complacency may have gone far to preserve her—"that I outstripped my brothers who were at school, although my father's chaplain that was my tutor was a pitiful dull fellow." Accomplishments of all sorts she despised, and she "absolutely hated" her needle, which must have been a sore trial to her housewifely mother and no small inconvenience to herself in years to come. She appears, indeed, to have been a sad little prig, for when other children were reluctantly brought to visit her, she "tried them with more grave instruction than their mothers, and plucked all their babies to pieces." No wonder she was not popular with the well-regulated little girls, her contemporaries, who loved their dolls with true maternal tenderness and were training to be those accomplished housewives who so well adorned the seventeenth century. Later in life Mrs. Hutchinson relates of her mother-in-law, with an appreciation which no doubt had its roots in certain youthful reminiscences, that "notwithstanding she [old Mrs. Apsley] had her education at Court, she was delighted in her own country habitation, and managed all her family affairs better than any of the homespun house-wives that had been brought up to nothing else"!

Book learning was by no means the whole of a little girl's education at this period. If she learnt her horn-book at her nurse's knee, she was also taught to sew her sampler by the same teacher at an equally early age. How surprised would she have been could she have looked forward three hundred years, and seen the tear-stained efforts of her impatient, sticky little fingers framed and glazed, in the rare cases where such early specimens have survived, treasured by her descendants, or more probably by comparatively recent purchasers who have given fabulous sums for them at Christie's. On the sampler they were instructed in all those intricate stitches with which in their own married homes they were to embroider their curtains and bed quilts and hangings and chair covers and the little caps for their babies.

Foreigners professed to be shocked at the severity of English parents towards their children, but as a matter of fact much of the formality of the previous century had already disappeared, and in spite of over-pressure in some cases and an over-conscientiousness in their moral training, there is no reason to suppose that the children who lived in the country did not have very happy lives in the seventeenth century. They played their games much as our own do at the present day. Tom Tiddler's Ground, Hide-and-seek, and Barley Bridge. They were constantly with their mother, and no letter from a wife to an absent husband was complete without some pretty reference to the little ones, or a carefully written enclosure from the child itself offering its duty.

Mrs. Angela Porter's letters are familiar to most readers, but we get through them such a charming glimpse of the value set upon the children of those days that we cannot resist quoting from them. She was the mother of Endymion Porter, a devoted servant of Charles I., and his children were left under her care at his country home on the Cotswolds while he attended Charles, then Prince of Wales, on his journey to Canterbury to meet the Royal bride, Henrietta Maria. Mrs. Porter writes to assure her son of his children's welfare, Endymion being then in attendance at Whitehall. She reminds him that the situation is healthy and that they have every care. " In reference to what you say regarding their food, you must know that they have here butter and cheese in abundance. They have also very good cows, and before the children came they killed a sheep once a week and sent it to market, for beef they do not kill on account of the heat, and veal and lamb sometimes they buy in the market; other times they kill when the cows breed. . . . I will inform you respecting everything, but I must now go and see my little ones to bed." The arrangements for provisioning this household are a little mysterious to modern notions, but there is no doubt about Mrs. Porter's grandmotherly sentiments, which are still more prettily expressed in another letter: "I wish you could see me sitting at the table with my little chickens one on either side ; in all my life I have not had such an occupation to my content, to see them in bed at night and get them up in the morning."

The great Lord Cork, in the midst of his money-making and his many political and other preoccupations, always found time to think of his little motherless girls. He chose suitable presents for them, and the silk or stuff for their frocks, nor, on their visits to him, did he forget to tip them a golden angel apiece, which we can believe pleased them even better than the piece of white damask for little Mary's summer gown, procured at considerable trouble from a great ship which had arrived with merchandise off Kinsale. Much later in the century, in writing to Lord Russell from Tunbridge Wells, where she was drinking the waters, Lady Russell tells him that she and her girls celebrated his birthday with a red-deer pie for supper and drank his health in a sack posset.

From their earliest years the mother gave her little girls a careful religious training, and as they passed all too soon out of the nursery, she personally superintended the instruction they received from their innumerable masters. She herself, or the gentlewoman who assisted her, would teach them to spin, to do all manner of elaborate needlework, and to cultivate those housewifely arts which were to play so important a part in their daily lives.

Lady Fanshawe, in her Memoirs, gives us a delightful account of her own upbringing, both at the town house in Hart Street and at Balls in Hertfordshire, where she obviously much preferred to be.

Her mother, the wife of Sir John Harrison, seems to have been a very perfect example of a devoted wife and a most tender mother, an example which her daughter most assuredly never forgot in the difficult years which followed Lady Harrison's early death. In addition she gave her an education "which was with all the advantages that time afforded, both for working all sorts of fine works with my needle, and learning French, singing, lute, the virginals, and dancing" (the Classics, we notice, are not mentioned); "and notwithstanding I learnt as well as most did, yet was I wild to that degree that the hours of my beloved recreation took up too much of my time, for I loved riding in the first place, running, and all active pastimes; in short, I was that which we graver people call a 'hoyting girl'; but to be just to myself, I never did mischief to myself or people, nor one immodest word or action in my life, though skipping or activity was my delight."

It is a charming and a natural picture of a high-spirited girl, whose buoyant character and education alike fitted her to face the hardships and perils which were to be her portion as the wife of the Royalist Ambassador during the Civil Wars. Her first taste of the trials which awaited her came after her mother's death, when she and her sister were summoned by their father to follow him to Oxford, where the Court then was. She gives a sprightly description of her experiences: "We that had till that hour lived in great plenty and great order, found ourselves like fishes out of the water . . . we knew not at all how to act any part but obedience, for, from as good a house as any gentleman

of England had, we came to a baker's house in an
obscure street, and from rooms well furnished, to lie
in a very bad bed in a garret, to one dish of meat,
and that not the best ordered, no money, for we
were as poor as Job, no clothes more than a man or
two brought in their cloak bags." She seems to have
met these first misfortunes in a brave spirit, and she
certainly found consolation, for it was here, amid "the
perpetual discourse of losing and gaining towns and
men," and with the sad spectacle of war and sickness
before her eyes, that the "hoyting girl," peeps of whose
"hoyting-ish" qualities appear subsequently with good
effect, married Richard Fanshawe, at that time Secretary
of War to Prince Charles, afterwards Charles II.

It was no mercenary marriage which took place that
May day in the little church at Wolvercote, near Oxford,
for the young couple started life with just £20 between
them, but a great deal of love, which was to carry them
safely through the changes and chances of their twenty-
two years of married life.

So many mothers, unhappily, died young in those
troublous days that it was perhaps the consciousness
of an overshadowing fate which induced them to begin
their children's training at such tender years, and even
so they were too frequently called upon to leave their
girls at an age when they most required their care and
solicitude.

It would be difficult to overestimate the loss to the
young Verneys when the happy family life at Claydon,
to which we get such a pleasant insight in the first
volume of the Verney Memoirs, was sadly interrupted
in 1641 by the death of Margaret, the second of a remark
able trio of wives in that family. Margaret Verney,

wife of Sir Edmund, could indeed be ill spared. Not
only had she her own large family of children to care
for, a daughter-in-law and grandchildren under her own
roof, but there were many other young people, connections of the family, who constantly made Claydon
their home, and found in her an unfailing and
sympathetic friend. She must indeed have been a
woman of remarkable tact and discretion, for the old
Lady Verney had until her death shared the London
house with them, and having herself been a notable
manager in her day, she naturally expected to be
consulted and to give her opinion on every domestic
detail that arose. It may have been some consolation
later to her family that, by her comparatively early
death, Margaret Verney was spared much suffering,
for in the following year, 1642, the King set up the
Royal Standard at Nottingham, and Sir Edmund, a
devoted Royalist, perished at Edgehill. Meantime, her
son Ralph's wife, Mary, who seems to have been
scarcely less competent or less lovable than her
mother-in-law, did her best to step into the breach,
to be a good daughter to Sir Edmund and a kind
and careful sister to the motherless girls who were
left.

But the troubles of the Civil Wars, which poor Mary
was not to survive, were close upon them. In 1643 Sir
Ralph, although a Parliamentarian in his sympathies,
was exiled for refusing to take the oath of the Covenant,
and went with his wife to France. Small chance had his
sisters, the youngest of whom, Betty, was only ten years
old, of a decent upbringing. There was no money to
pay for masters or governesses, little enough presently
for marriage portions. Left to the care of faithful

3

servants in a house which was perpetually subject to invasion by "rude soldiers," they were able, no doubt, to pick up a certain knowledge of housekeeping, but all the other branches of education must have been entirely neglected.

When Mary Verney came over to England some three years later to try and settle Sir Ralph's affairs, and went down to Claydon to make an inventory after the sequestration, she was much distressed with the state of things she found there. Everything in the house had naturally fallen into a sad state of disrepair, and there was no order or discipline for the children. Four of her sisters-in-law were by now married, and there remained only Mary and Betty, whom she complains in her letter to her husband have "noe breeding." She adds that Mary has managed to acquire some housewifely arts, but is "extreme clownish," and she suggests that Ralph should manage to afford her a few dancing lessons.

In the seventeenth century girls were constantly married when they were barely in their teens, and the wonder is that there was time, even considering how young it began, for the elaborate education which was considered necessary for the future housewife. The marriages were carefully arranged for them by their parents, but as money played a paramount part in the negotiations, it is a little surprising that the majority of those of which we hear seem to have turned out so well. The Verney girls were not among the most fortunate, but, as we have seen, their chances had been poor, and judging by the correspondence between husbands and wives which has been preserved, especially during the Civil Wars, with their pretty beginnings of

" Dearest Hart," followed by all the little intimate details of daily life, bespeaking a sense of trust, friendliness, and mutual affection, the wives seem on the whole to have been happy in their lot.

The extreme youth of the bride and the heavy burden which house management entailed upon her, often made it necessary for the young couple to live for a time in the house of her husband's father, where no doubt her education as a housewife was carefully continued. Such an arrangement does not seem to have been attended by as much friction as might be expected. Lady Falkland, Judge Tanfield's intelligent little daughter, was one of the few of whom we hear who was unfortunate in her new home, for, married at fifteen, her mother-in-law, alarmed no doubt by her intellectual attainments, shut her up in one room and took away all her books so that she was reduced to making verses. Such a course of treatment was both unfair and foolish, for when Lord Falkland came home and gave her a house of her own the young wife showed herself to be " careful and diligent in the disposition of the affairs of her house of all sorts ; and she herself would work hard, together with her women and her maids, curious pieces of work, teaching and directing all herself." This was considered the more remarkable as "those that knew her would never have believed she knew how to hold a needle."

The Dowager might well have had some excuse for apprehension, if not for exercising such severity, for later in life her daughter-in-law showed herself much fonder of her books and her reflections than of the practical details of existence. We are told that her hair was curled and her head was dressed while she read and wrote, and that the women who dressed her were obliged to walk round the room after her and pin on her clothes while she was seriously thinking on some other business. None the less she took good care of her children as long as they were with her, but her alienation, the result of so much thinking, from Protestantism, and her retreat into the Church of Rome at a time when religion was too closely interwoven with politics for such a course of conduct to be tolerated, ultimately separated her from her husband and family.

Had these ladies who early in the seventeenth century were bringing up their young daughters in the dignified seclusion of their country homes, foreseen the dangerous and difficult days which lay before them, their training, judging by the results, could hardly have been upon better lines. Not the least of their trials were the long weeks of suspense which wives had to endure while husbands were away fighting upon one side or the other, to which was added that extra bitterness often the lot of women during civil war, in the knowledge that a brother was fighting against her husband.

Not infrequently, moreover, were they called upon to themselves assume military powers of organisation in the defence of their own homes. Lady Digby's defence of Corfe Castle is one of the most remarkable episodes in history, and Lady Derby's defence of Lathom House for nearly a year against the Parliamentary troops while Lord Derby was in the Isle of Man, is scarcely less interesting. This indomitable lady was, in truth, Commander-in-Chief of her small forces. She rejected all conditions; saw to the feeding of her soldiers herself, and four times a day she was present at public prayers attended by the two "little ladies," her children. In the same year, 1643, on the other side, Lady Brilliana

Harley was besieged for six weeks in the castle of Brampton by the Royalists while her husband was away fighting for the Parliament. Lady Brilliana was perpetually an invalid, and accustomed to divide her attention between her own symptoms and the welfare of her "dear son Ned," who was also away with the army at this juncture, so it is greatly to her credit that she defended her home with so much prudence and valour. Her doctor from Hereford came to her assistance and was much needed, for the cook was shot by a poisoned bullet, and a running stream that furnished the village with water was poisoned by the enemy. On October 9, 1643, she writes pathetically to Ned, " I have taken a very greate cold which has made me very ill these two or three days, but I hope the Lord will be merciful to me in giving me my health, for it is an ill time to be sike in." She died a few days later.

Even the indomitable Lady Sussex, a neighbour and close friend of the Verneys, known as "the old men's wife" for having married three elderly earls in succession, admits, though in her usual lively vein, that she is having a trying time at Gorhambury, with the difficulty of getting her rents and the danger of being attacked and plundered by the Royalist soldiers. " My fear," she says, "is most of Prince ropperte, for they say he hath littell mercy when he comes." She has piled up the doors with wood, and if she escapes plundering " i shall account it a great maircy of God."

But there were other and more insidious foes than either Royalist or Puritan soldier, which lurked constantly in ambush, ready to spring at any moment and rob the home of its dearest possession. As yet there was no defence against the smallpox, no class was free from

its dread invasion, and the plague, of which there were
in this century several terrible visitations, came near
enough to the gates of the Manor House to make the
Squire's lady tremble.

But it seldom occurred to her to take refuge in flight,
and it was here that the women, and especially the wives
of the clergy, showed a heroism worthy of all honour.
We hear of a vicar's wife in a remote parish in Derby-
shire who sent away her young children, and though she
was in delicate health stayed with her husband and
tended and nursed his parishioners until she herself
was numbered among the victims—and she is only one
instance.

The spelling of these ladies may have been fanciful,
but there is no question that they repaid their early
training by an extraordinary fearlessness and self-control
in the face of danger. Hardships, loss of money, and
nerve-wearing anxiety found them always at their posts,
and doing their duty with a surprising absence of
complaint or murmuring. It may be argued that we
only hear of the more courageous, and that three
centuries ago nerves were made of stouter material than
they are at present. This is quite true, but it is none the
less incontestable that the simple devotional upbringing,
the unquestioning obedience exacted in youth, the high
standard of duty expected in married life, against which
there seems to have been no thought of rebellion, did
a great deal for the women of England before the
Restoration.

"Our English housewife," said Gervase Markham in
his "Country Contentments" published at *The Bible* on
Ludgate Hill, in the first half of the century, "must be
of chaste thought, stout courage, patience untyred,

watchful, diligent, witty, pleasant, constant in friendship, full of good Neighbourhood, wise in Discourse, but not frequent therein, sharp and quick of speech, but not bitter or talkative, secret in her affairs, comfortable in her counsels, and generally skilful in the worthy know-ledge which do belong to her vocation." A Counsel of Perfection, perhaps, yet one which proves that the standard of a lady's attainments in those days was of no mean order, and that as much was expected of her mental as of her purely domestic qualities!

And what, may be asked, became of those who did not marry, who after all this careful training never had the chance of exercising their housewifely skill in the ruling of their own establishments? Happily of these in the upper classes there were not many, for lamentable as it may appear, the fact remains that there was really no place for them, or at all events no place which gave them any suitable position.

In these days the single lady if she has money can do anything that she pleases. Even if her means be limited she can probably have her flat in London or her cottage in the country where she may at least enjoy the privilege of independence, and if necessary she may follow an honourable profession. She will probably have strong views of her own and will work whole-heartedly for some cause, political or social; while "slumming" is always within the reach of the most meek in spirit. If the making of a fourth at the bridge table or the other claims of Society do not appeal to her, it is permitted her, when the need for excitement becomes paramount, to carry a banner through the streets of London on behalf of some feminine grievance, real or imaginary. At the least she may live in dignified seclusion, holding

decided opinions about her garden, and finding an outlet
for her energies in the demands of her relations or
of her immediate neighbours.

But for the lady of the seventeenth century whose
money had been insufficient or some other disability
had hindered from matrimony, there were none of these
resources. It would have been highly improper for her
to have a home of her own, and she must needs live
under the roof of some more fortunate sister or relation
or even friend, and if she had strong views upon any
matter, it would probably be wiser for her to keep them
to herself.

It was customary for the mistress of a house to have a
gentlewoman to help her in her domestic labours, and
such a post offered a natural occupation for an unmarried relative or friend, whose position was often not
much better than that of a superior lady's maid.

Even before their marriage, if they had no homes, and
in the hard and troublous times of the Civil War, girls
not infrequently accepted an offer of this description.
Thus Sir George Strickland's daughter was my lady's
gentlewoman to Lady Sussex. Doll Leake, the charming, elusive Irish girl who flits in and out of the pages
of the Verney Memoirs, first in her gay and petted youth
at Claydon and later in those selfless but suffering years
which preceded her comparatively early death, lived for
a time in the same capacity with Lady Vere Gaudy and
her daughter, the Lady Mary Feilding. Doll had a
little money, saved from the wreck of her Irish home,
which it was Sir Ralph's constant anxiety to invest to
the best advantage—a difficult matter in those days.
She may have had reasons of her own for not marrying,
for she was a high-spirited girl who would not have

been too easily satisfied ; but as it was she found her happiness in giving ungrudging service to any member of the Verney family who needed her.

It speaks much for the discipline of the women of the age that such an arrangement could have been found tolerable for long to either party, but it must also be remembered that there was practically no choice, and the consciousness of the inevitable may sometimes produce in the least accommodating of us a disposition to make the best of things.

Matters, however, did not always run quite smoothly. Penelope Lady Osborne gave her niece, Pen Stewkeley, a very poor time as her gentlewoman. Pen complains that my lady only wants her to wash up her old crape and such-like work, for Lady Osborne was, like the dame described in the "Worth of a Penny," subject to the disease of being penny wise and pound foolish. She was thrifty to discomfort in private that she might make a brave show in public, and while in her will she bequeathed her silver plate and valuables to rich people, she contented herself with leaving her brass and pewter to her needy relatives, and to the gentlewoman the old clothes that the latter had helped to mend !

Jane Wright, on the other hand, sister-in-law to the parson of the neighbouring parish of Chicksands, was well content to be gentlewoman to Lady Dorothy Osborne and to relieve her of those household cares for which, preoccupied as she was with a difficult love affair, she seems to have had no especial aptitude. We, at all events, owe Jane Wright a debt, since she set her young mistress free to write those charming letters to Sir William Temple which have been and must ever be the delight of so many readers.

CHAPTER II

THE COUNTRY HOUSEWIFE

THE country housewife three or four hundred years ago would have held up her hands in amazement at the notion that the woman's sphere could be desirably widened.

Scarcely less absolute than her lord and master, and probably more despotic in her relations with her subjects, she ruled supreme over her servants, her house and all those offices which contributed to its proper provisioning.

In those days a country house in England, whether great or comparatively small, was a little kingdom in itself, supplying its own needs without much help from the outside world. It is true that there were the weekly markets or fairs at the neighbouring towns, to which the farmer's wife would ride in between her panniers laden with butter, eggs, and chickens, and where every sort of commodity was to be bought, both for use and for show, from horse-gear to wedding-rings, and these were occasionally patronised by the gentry.

Also the increase of trade with the Dutch and the opening of commerce with the East in the seventeenth century had introduced many foreign luxuries which it was possible for the well-to-do housewife to order the carriers to bring down from London. But it was still considered more convenient and self-respecting to provide the ordinary requirements of an establishment on the premises. Among the many rules laid down by Markham for the conduct of his housewife, he says that her diet must be wholesome and cleanly, to "proceed more from the provision of her own yard, than the furniture of the Markets."

To be responsible for the "wholesome and cleanly" diet not only of the Squire, his family and innumerable guests, but also of the vast army of servants and retainers which in those days was essential to even a moderate establishment, meant that the lady of the house must be a really able administrator, who not only had to superintend, but also take an active part in the labours which contributed to its upkeep. The woman's sphere was no mere figure of speech. The Memoirs of the time give us a picture of immense and arduous industry, and there is every reason to suppose that the seventeenth-century housewife invested her duties with a dignity in no way inferior to that assumed by the modern woman in her self-appointed work for the public welfare.

Of all the ladies of this period none, perhaps, conformed to Markham's standard of conduct better than Mary, wife of Mr. John Evelyn, of Sayes Court, and later of Wotton. She was the daughter of Sir Richard Browne, the British Ambassador in Paris, and the fact that she had been brought up in France no doubt gave her a decided advantage socially. Her manners and powers of conversation were superior to those of the English bride from the country, however careful had been the latter's training. Mary Evelyn had been accustomed to act as hostess in her father's house in Paris, and at Sayes Court she entertained Sir Richard's

friends as well as those of her husband, from the highest
to the lowest, including many learned men and divines.
She was an admirable hostess, full of genuine and
intelligent sympathy for her guests. Graceful and
charming alike in mind, manners, and person, she may
well stand as a very perfect example to the English lady
and the English housewife of all ages.

Her domestic talents were highly valued and solemnly
referred to by her husband. Mrs. Evelyn "was never
lavish or profuse, but commendably frugal; so that I
profess in the presence of God I never knew a better
housewife. She never delighted in the company of
tattling women, and abhorred as much a wandering
temper of going from house to house to the spending
of precious time, but was ever busied in useful occupations," these "useful occupations" including, among
other things, "the care of cakes, stilling, and sweetmeats."

Of her singular charm and intelligence, however, we
get a much better impression from her own letters than
from the stilted praise of her serious, scholarly husband,
who, after the fashion of his day, lays greater stress upon
her moral and domestic qualities than upon the superiority of her intellect. Mary tries to adopt the same
attitude; she does not consider that "women were born
to read Authors or censure the Learned. . . . The care
of children's education, observing a Husband's commands, assisting the sick, relieving the poor, or being
serviceable to our friends, are of sufficient weight to
employ the most improved capacities amongst us."
Such a view may shock some modern sensibilities, but
there is no reason to imagine that Mary hugged her
chains if, as is improbable, she knew she was fettered,

MARY EVELYN, WIFE OF JOHN EVELYN OF SAYES COURT AND WOTTON.

to the exclusion of other interests. She was a great
reader, a good linguist, and had considerable artistic
skill, working in her few moments of leisure at her
enamel and other paintings. After an excellent criticism
of Dryden's new play, "The Siege of Granada," in a
letter to her friend, Mr. Bohun, she adds, "This account
perhaps is not enough to do Mr. Dryden right, yet it is
as much as you can expect from the leisure of one who
has the care of a nursery." Writing to the same corre-
spondent on another occasion, she apologises for apparent
neglect : "Do not impute my silence to neglect. Had
you seen me these ten days, continually entertaining
persons of different humour, age, and sense, not only at
meals, or afternoons or the time of a civil visit, but
from morning till night."

A gift for friendship was not among the least of Mrs.
Evelyn's charms. No little service or commission for a
friend or neighbour was ever to be considered troublesome, and nobody's feelings were ever to be injured by the
slightest appearance of neglect on her part. In a letter in
which she describes how she has been attending a wedding in London, she protests that this must not account
for her silence, " Neither can I charge the Housewifery of
the Country after my returne, or treating my neighbours
this Christmas, since I never find any business or recreation that makes me forget my friends."

The indulgence of grief was not one permitted to the
mothers of this age, who reared so comparatively few
of their many children. When Mary Evelyn, a girl of
unusual promise, whose bright intellect and sincere piety
made her the joy and pride of both her parents, died
of smallpox at the age of nineteen, Mrs. Evelyn must
continue her daily round of duties as usual, and though

her agony can be gauged even in the restrained language
of her letters, she admits that as a Christian she must
not murmur.

In a very few words this incomparable lady sums up
the whole simple duty of a mother and the mistress of a
household as it was understood in those less complicated
days, and as she so charmingly performed it : " Jack
studies and ruminates ; the girls make a noise ; and I lend
a little time to any one that seems to want it.   How well
I pass the hours in which I am not serviceable to
others, I am no good judge."

The country housewife's day in the seventeenth century needed to be long indeed if she was to accomplish
one-half of her multifarious duties, and early rising was
the universal habit.   Prayers were read seldom later than
six o'clock in summer, and sometimes before sunrise in
winter.   Most of the larger houses had their own chapels,
and during the troublous days of the Commonwealth
and the Restoration it was not unusual to find a priest
or minister whose position was uncertain, living under
the protection of the squire, reading the prayers, saying
grace at his table, and educating his children.   In other
instances prayers were read in the village church, which
of course was totally unwarmed, and considering the
dress of the period must have proved a severe test of
the hardihood of the congregation.   There were probably
not a few ladies who regretted the abolition of the ugly
but protecting ruff of an earlier fashion.

We hear little of breakfast until a much later period.
There was no cup of hot tea or coffee to return to ;
such luxuries were rare even in the middle of the century.
A pint of home-brewed ale or a cup of sack would have
been a poor substitute to the shivering housewife had

she ever tasted any better comfort. She may have preferred a cup of fruit syrup of her own making and a
little of the famous manchet, to which there is such
constant reference.

Judging by the following recipe, a manchet was a dish
of some substance : "Take a bushel of fine wheat flower,
twenty eggs, 3 lb. of butter ; then take as much salt
and balm as usual; temper it together with new milk
pretty hot, then let it lie the space of half an hour to
rise, so you may work it up into bread and bake it ;
let not your oven be too hot."

It appears, however, that it was considered both
healthier and more refined not to break the fast at all
before dinner, which might be at any time between
11 a.m. and noon. Sir John Harington, in his "Schoole
of Salerne," or a Diet for the Healthful, written 1625,
entreats his adult readers not to overeat themselves, and
he even objects to a fixed hour for meals on the grounds
that nature so soon makes a habit ! As late as 1693
people who lead "a fitting kind of life" are earnestly
cautioned by another authority against breaking their
fast, also against beaver, beaver being a "drynkynge"
taken about three in the afternoon, and still called
by that name among the labourers in some parts of
England. Evidently Mr. Wodehouse had his proto-
type in all ages, but the Mr. Wodehouse of Miss Austen's
century would have shaken his head sadly could he
have seen the dinner which the most abstemious of his
ancestors permitted himself.

No doubt life in the country was, except of course in
time of war, monotonous and regular, and when people's
nerves were not perpetually set on edge by the complicated demands of modern civilisation, they could go for

longer without food and they would certainly eat a great
deal more when they sat down to it.   Also Nature has, as
Sir John Harington affirmed, made habits, and the habits
of their degenerate descendants would, perhaps, have
shocked the stalwart ladies of the Tudor and the Stuart
reigns no less than the contemplation of their midday
menu may offend our fastidious palates.

With her large keys, the insignia of her office, hanging
from her waist, the first duty of the country housewife
when she had said her prayers, and had or had not
refreshed herself with a cup of sack and a taste of
manchet, was to see to the feeding and tending of the
poor at the gate.

Of these there was often a considerable number;
yesterday's broken meats were carefully preserved for
the purpose, and it was rare indeed that any tramping
vagabond was turned away without receiving some kind
of rough hospitality. The closing of the monasteries
had cast this burden upon the individual, and the
mendicancy fostered by the pious compassion of these
religious houses had by the beginning of the seventeenth
century, owing to scanty wages and the high price of
corn and other necessities, greatly increased. Labour
before the Civil Wars was plentiful ; there was no lack
of employment, and the landlord was prospering greatly
by these same high prices, due largely to the fall in
the value of precious metals, but it did not occur to
him to raise the wages of his labourers. Rather he
preferred, mainly through the good offices of his lady,
to exercise a benevolent despotism, to practise a magnificent pauperisation, and, in the spirit of the Act of
Elizabeth, that first attempt at a Poor Law passed in
1601, to supply work insufficiently paid to the able-

bodied ; to attend to the immediate needs and necessities of the women and children on his own estate, and to relieve and succour the infirm and old.

Nobody need starve and nobody need take any thought for the future, nor for the bettering of his condition, which was wretched enough. From an economic point of view such a state of affairs was no doubt reprehensible, but there is this to be said for it, that the relations between the classes seem to have been singularly happy and mutually confiding.

The Lady Bountiful played her part with genuine interest and pious fervour, and the uneducated masses, ignorant of the rights and equality of man, were satisfied to be dependent.

Lady Fanshawe's mother, Lady Harrison, is spoken of by her daughter as " very pious and charitable to that degree that she relieved, besides the offals of the table which she constantly gave to the poor, many with her own hands daily out of her purse, and dressed many wounds of miserable people, when she had health, and when that failed, as it did often, she caused her servants to supply that place." One great lady actually built a covered refuge to shelter her poor while they waited for their broken meats, not only at her gates in the country but also outside her house at Chelsea.

The rest of the housewife's morning must be divided according to the season among her innumerable labours. In these she would be assisted by her gentlewoman, and the little girls, when not detained by their studies with the tutor, would follow and watch with large-eyed interest the performance of those duties for which they themselves must before very long be responsible. The lady presents a pleasing picture as she goes about her

business, stately and dignified in the simple fashions
which she owes to the good taste of that French queen
whom she yet views with underlying suspicion. For her
working hours she wears perhaps a plain, literally homespun material with a plain or panniered petticoat, a
pointed bodice laced up the front, with a wide collar
or folded kerchief about her shoulders, and wide, short
sleeves finished with deep lawn cuffs to match the collar.

Whatever the time of year, the cool stone dairy, with
its array of earthen and pewter pans must first be visited,
the supply of milk, cream, and cheeses inspected and
apportioned to the various offices. Outside the house
the herb and the kitchen gardens must claim her attention. She must see that the fish-ponds are properly
stocked with carp and perch and those other coarse fish
with which the table of the country squire, removed far
from the sea-coast, must be kept constantly supplied.
She must make sure that the pigeons, the poultry, and
the rabbits are being fattened in sufficient quantities
to fill up the corners of an ever-hospitable and well-
covered board. Indoors, in the butteries and the
kitchens, there is the cooking and baking to be personally superintended by the really careful housewife.
The venison must be watched that it hang exactly the
right time to make it savoury for her lord ; the hams
and bacons must be cured and hung up in the cavernous
chimneys to be duly smoked. The modern housekeeper,
who writes her weekly stores list, or who orders such things
across the counter, may well sigh for these home-made
luxuries, but she can console herself with the thought
of her infinitely diminished responsibilities, and responsibilities of a kind which have become distinctly less
popular since the days of Mrs. John Evelyn.

From one of the least grateful of her labours, the salting of meat for use in the winter, one which brought many cases of scurvy in its train, the housewife owed her deliverance to the Dutch early in the seventeenth century. It was these ingenious people who, among other agricultural benefits, introduced the cultivation of winter roots into England, thereby making it possible to have fresh meat the greater part of the year, instead of only in the months when fresh fodder was obtainable.

It was from the Low Countries also that hops were introduced a century earlier, and by now home-brewed ale had become the staple drink of England. Brewing being an indoor industry was considered suitable to women, and the men took no further part in it than to carry in the grain. "The art, skill, and knowledge of malt-making," we are told, "even from the fat to the kyln, it is only the work of the housewife and the maid-servants to her appertaining." It is she who must choose the grain and the situation of the malt-house, which should "stand upon firm, dry ground, having prospect every way, with open windows and lights to let in the wind, sun, ayre . . . both to cool and comfort the grain at pleasure, and also close sheets or draw-windows to keep out the frost and storms, which are the only let and hindrance for making the malt good and perfect." The arrangement of the furnace and the floors, the bedding of the kiln, and finally the drying of the malt were equally dependent upon the housewife's judgment, and this could only be acquired by experience.

In the summer months the stillroom would naturally absorb a large share of her thoughts and attention, and in that brief period when the fruit is ripening there would

be much to be done. It is here that she might be found
with her gentlewoman or her maids through the long,
hot afternoon, while the young people played bowls
yonder between the clipped yews, and her husband
gossiped of the latest news with his friends. If he were
not too old-fashioned and fastidious he would smoke his
pipe of tobacco, which, as well as his potatoes, he owed
to that broken-hearted gentleman Sir Walter Raleigh
whose fate had only just become matter of history.

But meantime, towards noon, the great bell had rung
for dinner, and no one who came to that well-covered
board had earned his food more conscientiously than the
lady of the house. Even here, however, there was small
respite from her duties. When she had seen her dishes
carried in in the right order, she must carve for the
entire assembled company before she could seat herself
among the other ladies at the head of the table and
attend to the demands of exhausted nature.

In the dark winter afternoons the ladies would help
the maids to spin the wool, or the flax threads for the
beautiful linen which would be laid away in oak coffers
for the use of future generations. The weaving was
done in the cottages, which meant a small but certain
wage to the women on the estate.

In the evening the mistress of the house, dressed in
her silk gown with the short jacket and the falling lace
ruffles, the stomacher and full skirt of the same colour
and material, might be found bending over her
embroidery frame or working that old English crewel
work on coarse linen for curtains, or the elaborately
embroidered bed quilts, with their bold designs, so many
of which have happily survived the centuries.

Young Edmund Verney's wife Mary, who was at

times mentally deranged, was induced to seek distraction in embroidery. Her father-in-law, Sir Ralph, was anxious, very wisely, that she should be interested in her household business, the regularity of which he hoped might help to keep her mind balanced. Even though she did not do it very well, she was to be commended for it, and needlework was the first and easiest step in the right direction. Doll Leake, who, with her usual unselfishness, went for a time to look after her, writes that Mary is hard at work embroidering hangings for a big green bed. Doll sorts the silks and crewels for her and helps her with the intricacies of "rosemary" stitch. She gently criticises the pattern Mary has chosen, in which she thinks there is altogether too much work. "There is certain birds and flyes and other crepers which I know not, and frute which I do not much like, but it is a very fine thing though they be left out." The birds and "flyes" and other "crepers" have become familiar to us in that handsome Jacobean design, and we do not like them the less because, like Doll, we know not the originals !

We do not hear much of supper at this period. It was obviously a much less important meal than the midday dinner, consisting probably of broth or stews, or something even lighter. We may hope that, candles being home-made and not therefore to be wasted, the housewife's labours concluded early.

The day usually closed as it began, with prayer, but even so, before she retired to rest she may have had one further duty. In a large household there would be constantly an invalid or some old person who required a comforting "nightcap," which it would be the mistress's pleasure to prepare. For this the caudle or posset-pot

would be produced, its comfortable rotund body of
Lambeth, Delft, or Fulham, or some other ware, not
unlike that of its first cousin, the later teapot, but with
the spout standing more upright.   One of the most
interesting relics in the London Museum is a pair of
caudle cups in Lambeth Ware, dated 1660, made on the
occasion of the Coronation of King Charles II., with his
Majesty's portrait in blue upon the rough cream ground.

A caudle for a sick body as recommended at this
period consisted of a lemon posset drink, thickened with
the yolks of eggs and sweetened with sugar.

A posset of sack, claret, or white wine which would
better have suited the taste of the old gentleman of the
household, was a more elaborate concoction.   " Take
twenty yolks of eggs, with a little cream, strain them,
set them by, then have a clean-scoured skillet, and put
into it a pottle of sweet cream, and a good quantity of
whole cinammon.   Set it a-boiling on a soft charcole fire,
and stir it continually.   The cream having a good taste
of the cinammon, put in the strained eggs and cream into
your skillet, stir them together, and give them a warm,
then have in readiness some sack or other wine in a deep
bason or posset cup, good store of fine sugar, and some
sliced nutmeg.   The sack and sugar being warm, take
out the cinammon, and pour your eggs and cream very
light into the bason, that it may spatter in it, then strew
on loaf sugar."

This last service accomplished, the lady of the house
would be at liberty to retire to her low-beamed chamber,
where in winter a log-fire would be burning on the brass
dogs in the great hearth, and after a brief toilet and
seemly devotions creep into her oak four-post bedstead,
with the coat-of-arms carved handsomely at her head,

and draw the curtains tightly round her. Let us hope
that she followed the excellent advice of Sir John
Harington : " Put off your cares with your garments,
whether they be public or private, so that you may sleep
better, but resume them in the morning."

It is not to be supposed, even in this Golden Age,
however, that every woman was a born housewife.
Some, like Mrs. Hutchinson, acquired the art with
difficulty, and there were some who apparently did not
acquire it at all. The eccentric Duchess of Newcastle,
whose mind was given rather to philosophical speculation
and the writing of plays than to more workaday matters,
vindicates herself with considerable humour against the
charge of neglect of her household duties.

Her neighbours, excellent Marthas themselves, who
could not appreciate the light-hearted manner in which
this Royalist lady of intellect bore her financial misfortunes and ignored her housewifely cares, told her that
her maids were spoilt with idleness, since she never
remembered to give them orders. Goaded into action,
the Duchess sent for her governess or gentlewoman, and
bade her " Give orders to have flax and wheels bought,
for I with my maids would sit and spin. The governess,
hearing me say so, smiled to think what uneven threads
I would spin, 'for,' said she, 'though nature hath made
you a spinster in poetry, yet education hath not made
you a spinster in housewifery, and you will spoil more
flax than get cloth by your spinning.'"

The Duchess, slightly discomfited but undaunted
by this verdict, gave herself up to solitary reflection,
and presently remembering that in her girlhood she
had seen her sisters make flowers, and had even made
some very badly herself, again summoned the governess

and told her to buy several coloured silks, for she was
resolved to make silk flowers. Once more the governess
was forced to be discouraging, and to suggest to her
mistress that such toys could be bought in the shops
much cheaper and very much better than she could
make them. Lastly, the Duchess bethought herself of
the duty of preserving, since the fruit hung fresh and
ripe upon the trees, but was reminded that she neither
ate sweetmeats herself nor gave banquets. " Besides,"
added this conscientious and unrelenting governess,
"you may keep half a score of servants with the money
that is laid out in sugar and coals which go to the preserving only of a few sweatmeats."

At length, in full agreement with the gentlewoman,
and no whit humiliated, her Grace decided that the
neighbours might say what they liked, that the maids
would complain more if they were kept to work than
when they had liberty to play, and besides " none can
want employment while there are books to read." So
the graceless Duchess returned thankfully to her writing.
" My thoughts," she complains with conscious virtue,
"although not my actions, have been so busily employed
about housewifery these three or four days as I could
think of nothing else ! "

She certainly managed to let herself off " mighty
easy," as she herself would have expressed it, where her
housekeeping duties were concerned. The Duke, either
by choice or necessity, for he seems to have had no
influence over his wife's vagaries, was a very frugal
man. "He makes but one meal a day, at which he
drinks two good glasses of small beer, one about the
beginning, the other at the end thereof, and a little
glass of sack in the middle of his dinner; which glass

of sack he also uses in the morning for his breakfast
with a morsel of bread." His supper consists of an egg,
and a draught of small beer." For herself, she is satisfied
with a little boiled chicken, and her drink is most commonly water. Such plain living and high thinking was by
no means the universal rule, however, and the Duchess
of Newcastle was looked upon as a very scandalous person
by the good housewives of the seventeenth century.

A good notion of the manners in which the country gentry lived at this time may be gleaned from their accounts.
These were usually kept by the master of the house
in his diary, but sometimes merely upon sheets of paper.
So precious was the paper, apparently, that among these
accounts which have been preserved we constantly find
the bills of different tradesmen upon one piece of paper.
Thus Captain Bosville of Gunthwaite Hall in Yorkshire,
member of the Long Parliament for Warwick, kept the
bills of his own and his wife's dress, his housekeeping
and various items, on two pieces of parchment paper.
The bills are receipted in different handwritings, for
apparently no tradesman presented his own bill upon
his own sheet of paper, but was content to make it
out on whatever was offered him.

They are here transcribed exactly as they are arranged
in the original, and in considering the prices we must
remember that the value of money at this time was about
four or five times what it is at the present day.

FOR THE WORSH. CAPTAINE BASVIL HIS BILL FOR YOUR MINT
CODLING COLLER CLOTH SUIT.

13 *of Decembr*. 1648.	lb.	s.	d.
for 2 yds. ¼ of cloth to a suit at 25s. a yard	02.	16.	3.
for 2 yds. ⅛ of scarlet coullor Taffatie to lion the doublet and face the pocckets and Lienens at 6s. 6d. a yard	00.	16.	3.

	lb.	s.	d.
for 1 yd. of peach Coller Taffatie to the Roufs on the sleuf hands and to the gloufs and face the gloufs...	00.	06.	0.
for dimitie to lion the hose	00.	05.	0.
for callicoo to the hose	00.	03.	0.
for 3 oz. of silver lace to the gloufs and sleuf-hands at 4s. 8d. an ounce	00.	14.	0.
for Canvis and stiffening	00.	04.	0.
for poockets hoocks and eyes	00.	02.	4.
for gallone and Lupe Lace	00.	01.	6.
for 4 dozen ½ of brest bouttons	00.	01.	6.
for drawing of the suit	00.	01.	4.
for 2 trumpoynts	00.	00.	8.
for 3 doson of poynts and ribon to the hose... ...	00.	18.	0.
for 6 yds. of read and mingled skie couller Ribon and red riben to the hose...	00.	03.	0.
for silk	00.	02.	0.
for 3 yds. ½ of scarlet couller Riben to bind the Lienens	00.	01.	6.
for Making the suit and gloufs	00.	15.	0.
same is ...	07.	11.	7.
received in part ...	2.	05.	0.

Rest due 5. 11. 1.

On the back :—

Receved in foul of this bil the some of 5 lb. 11s. by me Receved
ANDREW VAULEY (?)

Mr. Vauley and Joseph Higher acquittances.

						lb.	s.	d.
for a shoulde of muton	0.	2.	4.
for a breast of veal	0.	2.	6.
for a quarte of lam	0.	2.	6.
for bread	0.	0.	4.
for oranges and lemons	0.	1.	6.
for milk	0.	0.	1.
for buter	0.	0.	7.
for broth	0.	0.	3.
for ale	0.	0.	2.
						00.	10.	03.

	lb.	s.	d.
for laces	0.	2.	0.
for a comb	0.	0.	10.
for gloves	0.	1.	4.
for gloves	0.	4.	4.
for thrid	0.	2.	8.
for going by road	0.	1.	00.
for a coach hir	0.	1.	00.
for ale and bread	0.	0.	2.

Feb. the 26th, 1654.

Received then of William Bosseville Esq., the sum of eleven pounds four shillings in full of this bill of all deeds and amounts from the beginning of the world untill the day of the date hereof of Febry. received by me

JOHN CALES

acquitai[ne].

On the other side of the paper, in the beautifully neat, but rather illegible square handwriting of the seventeenth century, is a bill for Mrs. "Bossvill's" dress. There were no dressmakers in those days, the more ordinary garments being made at home, but the services of a tailor were requisitioned for the best gowns, the lady providing all her own materials.

Mrs. Bossvill hir bill feb. 20th, 1654.	£	s.	d.
Imp⁰. for Stais for ye silke dress and wastcoate ...	00.	04.	00.
for Silke and Galone	00.	01.	06.
for lynings for the bodis and sleevs	00.	02.	03.
for bordering and binding	00.	02.	02.
for Colored Taffaty	00.	05.	00.
for fassenings for the sleeves and Cuffes	00.	00.	06.
for making of ye sute	00.	10.	00.
for Silke and Galome	00.	02.	03.
for sleev linings	00.	01.	06.
for 3 yards of Ribboning	00.	01.	06.
for houkes and eye	00.	00.	03.
for making of ye Coat	00.	08.	00.
for stais for ye blacke wastcoate	00.	03.	06.

	£	s.	d.
for Silke and Galome ...	00.	01.	04.
for one yard of black Calico ...	00.	01.	04.
for linings for ye bodis and sleeves ...	00.	02.	03.
for fassenings for ye sleevs and cuffes	00.	00.	03.
for making of the sute	00.	09.	00.
for silke for ye 3 mantolls	00.	01.	04.
for linings and Galome for ye littell Sleevs	00.	00.	08.
for making ye mantolls and sleevs ...	00.	05.	00.
for 2 yards and one quarter of red lase ...	00.	18.	00.
for silke and galome for the peticoats	00.	02.	00.
for 2 yards of Ribben ...	00.	00.	08.
for making ye piticoats	00.	02.	06.
for 2 jerkits	00.	10.	06.
for 2 demmety wastcoats	00.	03.	04.
for 3 yards of Taffaty Ribbon	00.	01.	06.
some is	04.	14.	04.
	1.	8.	4.

for 3 dozen of Candolles ... 0. 14. 0.

4. 12. 4.

£5. 6. 4.

CHAPTER III

THE HOME

NO picture is complete without its frame, and we can hardly arrive at a satisfactory idea of the housewife of a long-past day, and her innumerable avocations, without a glance at the house which sheltered her, and its furnishings. "There is his chamber, his house, his castle, his standing bed and truckle bed."

By the middle of the sixteenth century, the Englishman's house was ceasing, very literally, to be his castle. Defence against his enemies, which had found stern expression in the battlemented walls of Gothic castles, in the moat and the drawbridge, in the portcullis, in the rare and narrow windows and the iron-clamped doors, was no longer the first consideration.

Already in the fourteenth and fifteenth centuries, domestic arrangements had shown a tendency towards improvement. There was a greater desire for privacy, more room was allowed for sleeping accommodation, and Chaucer tells us of the "chambers" and "bowers" which had begun to supplement the great hall as living rooms.

But the sixteenth century brought a great revolution in domestic architecture. In the reign of Henry VIII.

England was already awaking to the glorious possibilities
to which she was to attain in the spacious days of
Elizabeth. The Renaissance, otherwise the Italian
influence, was at work in the building of houses, as in
every other form, both of artistic and practical activity.
The dissolution of the monasteries had thrown a great
deal of magnificent church property into secular hands,
and in the beautifying and adapting of this to their
own uses, men thought more of pleasure than defence.
Hampton Court was built by Cardinal Wolseley with no
thought but that of providing himself with a sumptuous
and convenient home, and Knole, acquired by the
Crown, was enlarged and beautified with little idea
of self-protection. By the reign of Elizabeth, arable
farming had become extremely profitable, and the county
gentlemen were greatly enriched by the sale of the
fleeces of their flocks. The prosperity of the upper
classes encouraged prodigal expenditure, and building
as shown by the example of Bess of Hardwick was the
fashionable mania.

In considering the aspect and situation of a house, Dr.
Andrew Boorde, in his " Dietary of Health," 1542, says :
" The air must be pure, frisky and clean ; the foundations
of gravel mixed with clay. The chief prospects should
be east and west, or north-east and south-west ; never
south, for the south wind doth corrupt and make evil
vapours." Wind was to be avoided at any cost, but
damp was looked upon as a necessary and unimportant
evil ; so, as we know, all the houses of this period were
placed well down in a hole.

The greater houses of the Tudors continued to be
built with outer courtyards ; no longer, however, with an
idea of safety for the living rooms, but rather with a

desire for warmth and with a view to symmetry, although
the decorative roofs and chimneys were invariably of
different heights, the Dutch precision of a later day
being yet distant.

In the architect Thorpe's plans of the Elizabethan
houses preserved in the Soane museum, we see that
the great hall lay, as a rule, between the offices and
the living rooms, forming the cross-stroke in the letter
H, while the porch added later the projecting stroke
which was supposed to transform it into the letter E.
This, was not however, until the entrance to the hall
had been transferred from one end, behind the
"screens," to the centre. The great hall was still the
main feature of all houses large and small, even when
the daïs in the Bay window, devoted to the use of the
family and noble guests, gave way to the "privee" parlour,
where they might dine in greater seclusion, this in
time being superseded by the great chamber or dining-
room.   Henry VIII. apparently, rather discouraged this
fashion of the lord dining apart from his retainers, and
referred with some asperity to those who "do much
delight and use to dyne in corners and secret places."

None the less the desire for secret places continued
and presently developed the great chamber, the parlour,
and the withdrawing room, all approached by a broad
oak staircase with heavily carved newels, which sometimes had a dog gate at the bottom to prevent the straying
of hounds to the upper regions. Foreign workers had
told of the handsome staircases of French châteaux, and
the idea was quickly seized upon by the English architects
and the narrow stone or brick corkscrew staircases of the
Middle Ages were discarded.

Near the kitchens and butteries and servants' quarters,

was sometimes a winter parlour where the lady of the house could sit and superintend her maids at their spinning, or be within reach if difficulties arose over the preparation of the dinner. It must have been chilly work for her sometimes pottering backwards and forwards across the stone hall from one end of the great house to the other. She would have rejoiced when the dirty habit of strewing rushes went out of fashion, and the floors were covered by strong leather, or in the more sumptuous apartments, with carpets brought from India and Persia. Wide fireplaces with chimneys had superseded the hole in the floor which may still be seen in the great hall at Penshurst, with the ventilating outlet to let the smoke out, or the detached fireplace standing against the wall which had hitherto been the alternative.

These large fireplaces with their handsome dogs and andirons, large enough, many of them, to contain a priest's hole of concealment in the chimney, felt no doubt draughty to the old men among the retainers who would sit on the settles on either side. At all events we hear a complaint that " when everyone made his fire against a reredos in the hall where he dined and dressed his meat, our heads did never ache, now our tenderlings complain of rheums, catarrhs and poses."

The multiplicity of windows, also a novelty, called forth some disparaging comment from old-fashioned people. But as these were at first of small leaded panes and few enough of them were made to open, they could not have been a much more serious inconvenience than the unglazed windows, where linen steeped in oil had to be used sometimes to keep out the cold air. In those days a wooden shutter to be closed over the window at night was part of the traveller's habitual luggage, which

reminds us of a habit of certain members of a fast
vanishing generation of our own day, who carried their
black calico blind about with them to exclude the light,
and were almost as much offended as surprised when
they found one already provided !

The influence of Inigo Jones, who came to England
with Anne of Denmark, made itself felt in a more personal element in the great houses of the rich. With the
Stuarts we find a more pronounced sense of comfort and
elegance apart from mere luxury, which was ceasing to
be such a novelty, in the domestic arrangements. Bacon
describes the houses of the wealthy as converted into
" delicate and rich cabinets daintily paved, richly hanged,
glazed with crystalline glass, and all other elegancy that
may be thought of." It is not difficult, with the help of
such houses as Knole in Kent and others before us which
still retain the contemporary furniture and fittings, and
from the inventories of those which no longer exist or else
have been entirely modernised, to picture the interiors of
the great houses of the seventeenth century.

For warmth the walls were either panelled, the linen
scroll pattern having given place to the small panelling of
the Stuart period, or else were hung with splendid
Flemish tapestries according to the Tudor fashion ; with
velvet or silk hangings, or with tapestry woven of
coloured worsteds or flax. In the decoration and furniture the Renaissance influence made itself felt no less than
in the architecture. Sometimes the oak panelling was
painted as on the staircase at Knole, and constantly it was
very richly carved. More especially was the elaborate
carving to be found in the houses of rich merchants
whose travels abroad had enabled them to see more of
foreign artists and their work, and to import the latter.

The timbered roof of the great hall was superseded by a plastered ceiling, sometimes extremely elaborate with pendants hanging from it, sometimes of chaste and simple design. Over the chimney-pieces in the living rooms were fine carvings in stone or wood, the family coat-of-arms or a medallion in the centre panel with pilasters on either side being a favourite device.

Lord Cork gave orders that the chimney-piece in his parlour at his new house of Stalbridge was to reach up close to the ceiling with the Boyle coat-of-arms, "complete with crest, helmet, coronet, supporters, and mantling and footpace, fair and graceful, in all respects, costing £10."

Being rich enough to indulge his passion for bricks and mortar in the most sumptuous manner, he agreed with the plasterer to ceil with fret work, "my study, my bed-chamber and the nursery at Lismore and to wash them with Spanish white." The plasterer became a person of considerable importance owing to this prevailing fashion of decoration. He had his own livery company and a royal charter had been granted to him even in the reign of Henry VIII.

Heraldic glass also became very fashionable at this period, the coats-of-arms being combined to record marriages between great houses or even, in some instances friendships. After a visit from Queen Elizabeth, the Tudor rose with the entwined initials E.R. would almost invariably blossom forth on a prominent window in the house, whose hospitality the great Queen had accepted.

The heraldic idea was also extended to the fine wrought iron backs of the fireplaces, where the owner's coat-of-arms constantly composed the decoration, if scenes out of the Bible were not preferred. This was often the work of foreign artists, the English smith's work being at this time rather in abeyance. So rare, indeed, had English ironwork become that iron locks were regarded as choice personal possessions to be left as valued legacies in wills, and a house in London which had locks in it could certainly command a higher rent than one without.

But after all it is not in these greater houses of the land, built, many of them, in Elizabeth's day with the chief object of entertaining the sovereign, and whose builders vied with one another in extravagance, that we get the best impression of English life in the Tudor and Jacobean periods. These great houses, overloaded outside with Renaissance detail and crowded inside with costly foreign furniture and carpets and hangings, with ebony and ivory cabinets, with embroidered satin beds and Indian coverlets, beautiful as they are and priceless possessions not only to their owners but also to the nation, are not essentially English in their characteristics. It is rather in the old manor houses where there has been neither means nor opportunity for this prodigal expenditure, but where each bears the stamp of its original owner, that we may acquire some more intimate knowledge of the daily life of our forefathers.

Many of these, alas ! have been pulled down or rebuilt in a tasteless age, others have perished by fire, but there are, happily, yet many that remain, with their graceful gables and twisted chimneys, their diamond-paned windows, their roomy stone porches, standing among old world gardens and sunny orchards, an enduring testimony to the best and most solid traits of national character.

The knight or squire whose forbear had originally received his certain circuit of the ground, granted by the King to him and his heirs after him, took an active and personal interest in the building of his house, not only for his own sake, but for that of the generations to follow.

From motives of economy these manor houses were usually built out of the material which lay nearest to hand.   Thus we find black and white half-timbered houses in the neighbourhood of forests, in parts of Sussex, Kent, Cheshire and other places.   The plaster used in Kent and Sussex came from the chalk of the down country; bricks were used where there was clay, and stone in the vicinity of quarries.   Only the really rich could afford to import Caen stone.   Granite was the solid material employed where obtainable and, in the eastern counties, flint was mixed with the brick.   The actual building of these smaller houses was usually done by the village craftsmen and masons, who were less affected by foreign influences and carried on a certain local tradition of taste.

The innumerable windows, bays, oriel, mullioned, latticed and dormer, which increased so much in size and number under Elizabeth, were to prove so heavy a burden when Charles II. introduced the window tax, that many had to be bricked up.   Meantime, the small leaded panes, white glass being still rare, were filled up with glass of many shades from bottle green to amber.   This was no doubt the origin of the shocking "bottle-end" panes with which the modern suburban builder proudly adorns the upper panes of the windows in his Queen Anne villa !

We have a description of Sayes Court, the property of Sir Richard Browne, Evelyn's father-in-law, a typical lesser manor house of the period.   "A long, low house, two storeys high, with mullioned windows and pointed gables.   Adjoining it was a small garden; the stables were attached to the house; and near was a barn, constructed entirely of beams of chestnut wood. An old orchard lay on one side, bounded by one of the garden closes." Here there is little mention of the famous garden which, no doubt, did not greatly interest the officers of the Commonwealth except as land to be seized, any more than it would the officials in charge of the Land Tax, and those who were responsible for the futile attempt to enforce Form IV. in our own day.

There is a description of the interior of Sayes Court in a survey of the Manor before its sale by Parliament: "The ground floor consisted of one hall, one parlour, one kitchen, one buttery, one larder with a dairy house, also one chamber and three cellars. In the second storey, eight chambers, with four closets and three garrets." It is an official rather than an inspiring description of the old manor and its grounds at Deptford, but it also gives a greater suggestion of comfort and compactness from the housewife's point of view, than the sculleries, the meat houses, the bolting houses, the "spiceries" and "trenchers," "pewters," and "brushes," which were all in addition to the ordinary offices of the great houses, and, for the good maintenance of which she would be responsible.

Wotton, in Surrey, which belonged to Mr. Evelyn's brother and which he afterwards inherited, is a good example of the Tudor-Jacobean Manor house, especially in domestic arrangements. These have naturally suffered some modification, but there are a number of out-houses in close proximity to the spacious kitchen, which may be identified as the brewery, and the bakehouse or "pastry." In some houses there were also a dry larder, a wet larder, and a surveying room or service room which may, here as elsewhere, still be distinguishable, though put to more modern uses.

In what is now the servants' hall at Wotton and may possibly, before the present dining-hall was built, have had a more dignified use, there still remains the long solid oak table for the servants.   In front of the wide fireplace is a smaller table carefully protected by a rounded wooden screen with a seat attached to it, and here, in a certain privacy and shielded from draught, sat the steward and superior retainers, and possibly at one time, the family itself.   Over the mantelpiece is a carved wooden garland, the work of Grinling Gibbons, whose dramatic discovery by the author is related by John Evelyn in his diary.

In "a very convenient apartment of five rooms together, besides a pretty closet which we furnished with the spoils of Sayes Court," lived John Evelyn with his wife and family, until his brother's death placed him, for the last few years of his life, in possession of the entire property. We have all, in old houses, met with the inconvenience as well as the charm of those little rooms opening one out of the other, but to their original occupiers, who had no overweening love of privacy, they seemed merely pleasant and convenient.

The entwined initials of the squire and his wife, with the date of its completion, is often to be found carved in the heavy stone porch over the doorway of the old manor house, and the personality of the squire and of his lady still seems to pervade the old wainscoted rooms, the grey walls, and the cobbled courtyard, which no modern atmosphere nor modern improvements can wholly banish. Ightham Mote, of an earlier date, is one of the few which still has its moat of running water, but

by the seventeenth century the moat and the gatehouse
had both as a rule entirely disappeared.

In Evelyn's lament for the simpler ways of home life in
the country before the Restoration, he speaks of the
sturdy oaken furniture of the house which lasted one
whole century. " The shovel board and other long
tables, both in hall and parlour, were as fixed as the
freehold, nothing was moveable save joint-stools, the
black jacks, silver tankards and bowls." If he could see
the " sturdy oaken furniture " now, after a lapse of more
than three centuries as sturdy as when he himself used
it, he might well feel that he had understated the case.
He wrote at a time when walnut was beginning to
supersede oak, and his knowledge of wood, no doubt
told him of its much less durable quality. Many of us
are still sitting upon the straight upright chairs of
Charles II., with their cane seats and backs, and
walnut frames, carved often with the crown and the
Tudor rose, and we know to our cost that the worm has
made much greater inroad on their stability than he
could achieve on the black oak of the earlier century.

The Stuarts, however, expected and obtained greater
ease and greater elegance in their ordinary house-
furnishing. Chairs were scarce in Elizabeth's day,
and Evelyn, in speaking of old-fashioned furniture,
makes no allusion to them. The straight, low-backed,
arm-chairs of Henry VIII. are not suggestive of comfort,
and in the houses of the rich, the Tudor chairs were
X-shaped, a design imported from Italy. The oak joint
stool being portable was greatly in use and, for more
sumptuous purposes, there were stools covered with silk
and brocade copied, no doubt, from the French *Tabourets*,
and which later, covered with the same material as the

other hangings, became an inevitable part of the bedroom furnishings. But the Stuart housewife had many varieties of chairs, all very wide in the seat and straight in the back. Sometimes the seats were covered with tapestry or needlework, sometimes they were of solid oak and later of cane, but cushions seem always to have been plentiful.

Cromwell made an effort to revert to the uncompromising chair of the sixteenth century and to banish ease and beauty of form wherever possible, but the Restoration lost no time in restoring such luxuries and conveniences as already existed and adding others. The long day chair of walnut wood, with its adjustable back, came into being at this time, and, well cushioned, if less luxurious than a Chesterfield, would not have been uncomfortable. Children's high chairs on much the same pattern as our own, with a little shelf for their toys or porringer, were made of walnut and earlier of oak, as were the very solid and comfortless looking cradles with the heavy overhanging hoods in which, well protected from any dangerous possibility of fresh air, the babies were put to slumber.

The shovel board table admired of Evelyn, had already given place in most houses to the solid handsome Elizabethan table with its lemon-shaped carved legs, and very often an inlaid surface. In some cases these were draw-tables which, by an ingenious mechanical contrivance, could be extended for purposes of hospitality.

There were tapestry table covers, or carpets as they were called, on the familiar oak gate tables which were also much in use, of all sizes. There were also good solid occasional tables standing about for backgammon and chess board, less easily overturned and certainly less graceful than their mahogany successors.

With the sturdy oak and carved walnut furniture, with the striped Turkey carpet, the velvet cushions, the wainscoted or "old-fashioned tapestry" hung walls, the leaping fire of logs under the carved stone mantel, the shining brass or silver andirons, the great brass scuttles and the silver sconces, the parlour of our forefathers must have presented a warm and comfortable appearance, and one that might justly rejoice the heart of the housewife as she sat at her spinning-wheel or her embroidery frame on winter evenings.

England was certainly a cleaner country then than now, but there were always the damp fogs, and already the fumes of sea-borne coal increasingly burnt, to tarnish the brass and silver and dim the polish on the furniture. Linseed oil and plenty of elbow grease were bestowed upon the latter, while there were no patent polishes to eat into the former, which must also depend upon energetic rubbing.

In the carved oak chests familiar to us all the housewife kept those of her own clothes, which there was not room to bestow in the little closet intended for that purpose through her bedroom. The household linen was also stored here, and even sometimes her money and valuables until the banking system was introduced into England by the Dutch at the end of the century. Even the modern housewife often finds these same oak chests standing about in halls and on landings of considerable use for storing things away in. But they have now sunk to the level of superior "glory-holes," for those indiscriminate possessions which she does not quite know what to do with, which she has not the strength of mind to destroy, and which it is a relief sometimes to put away and forget altogether.

One of the most important pieces of furniture to the mediæval housewife and which survived to be greatly used in Tudor and Jacobean houses was the "livery" cupboard. This was originally merely an oak stand with open shelves much like a modern dinner waggon, and was used for the server to set down the dishes upon before taking them to the board. Later, however, the shelves were closed with perforated panels to let in the air, and they were used as the receptacles for the broken meats set aside after dinner for the use of the poor. In the kitchen it would originally have been called a dresser, but transferred to the dining-room and the perforated doors added, it was called a "livery" from the French word *livrée*, defined as the delivery of a thing that is given, a word that survives now chiefly in connection with the clothes of our men-servants.

"Liveries," as they were called, were also sometimes served out "for all night"; for with supper at five and no other meal until the dinner the following mid-day, the weakly might suffer hunger. A livery cupboard on a small scale was even occasionally placed in bedrooms much as a thoughtful hostess of to-day provides her guest with a biscuit tin. There is a record of a seventeenth-century lady who left her "posted sett worke bedstead and livery cupboard to it" to her daughter, and it is suggested that the cupboard probably formed a portion of the pannelling of the bedstead. The idea is not attractive when we consider the probable nature of the provisions placed there accompanied possibly by a measure of ale, but the ladies of that age were presumably neither sensitive nor afraid of mice.

Then there was the court cupboard, to the uninitiated
looking much like a livery cupboard, but holding a place
of superior importance on the daïs in the dining hall and
intended to hold the gold and silver plate of which before
the civil war there was a great deal in use, and which was
rightly regarded as a valuable investment. The plate
was ranged upon a series of shelves which were supposed to vary according to the rank of the owner. In
the course of the seventeenth century the shelves were
replaced by a cupboard of which the panels were closed
and beautifully carved, and it found its way into the
great parlour and was used as a repository for all sorts of
treasures.

The development of the sideboard out of a mere
trestle which afterwards became a long low cupboard, and
of the Jacobean chest of drawers out of the oak chest
which first had a drawer placed under it, and was
presently hoisted upon turned and twisted legs and
continued to grow in height and ornament until it became the Tallboy of the eighteenth century, makes an
interesting study in evolution for those who care to
pursue it. This may be done very profitably in the
Victoria and Albert Museum, or in such a house as Knole,
where much of the furniture and fittings from the sixteenth and seventeenth centuries have been so carefully
preserved.

The heavy, low four-post bedstead was naturally one
of the most important features in a Tudor or Jacobean
ménage. Its elaborately carved back was sometimes
fastened into the panelling of the wall behind, and its low,
heavy ceiling was supported by the massive carved posts
actually standing away from the bed, so that it was as
solid and fixed as any of the other furniture so much

admired by Evelyn. The head of the bed was often
adorned with the monogram of husband and wife or the
family coat of arms and much rich Renaissance decoration,
this being occasionally inlaid or in gesso work instead of
carving. Some of these bedposts were surmounted with
the four Evangelists, but as time passed there was a
tendency to replace the Evangelists with strange grinning
monsters, which we cannot think were conducive to
pleasant slumber. Naturally these beds were hung with
curtains which could be tightly drawn at night or in case
of illness so as to exclude as much as possible of light
or air.

In the course of the seventeenth century another type
of bedstead was introduced from France, and few of the
larger houses were without one or two of these, as the
means of the owner allowed. The frames and posts were
made all in one and were of beechwood, and they were
very much taller than the oak bedsteads. The tall slender
posts, the tester, the cornice and ceilings were all upholstered with the same material as the curtains, quilt, and
valence, as were the two stools which stood at the foot of
the bed, and this was sometimes very gorgeous. We
read of a green and gold bed of a " parcelgilt bed with
hangings and quilt of tawny taffety," and velvet and
satin were quite ordinary materials. The most magnificent is that occupied by James I. at Knole, which is hung
with gold and silver tissue.

The best bed was invariably left to the widow and was
a very sacred possession, since here her many children
had been born and her husband had died.

There were plainer oak bedsteads in Jacobean days,
which had neither posts nor ceilings but neatly panelled
low backs, and they must have been infinitely more

wholesome and comfortable for the occupants than those of their richer neighbours, but were no doubt considered extremely chilly. There was also the truckle bed for the body servant or retainer, which could be packed for travelling and was pushed under the larger bed to be out of the way in the daytime.

There was one other bed which has happily disappeared, and which was no doubt the pride as well as the burden of the seventeenth century housewife. This was the "mourning" bed, hung entirely in black, probably black velvet, not even the sheets in the case of a widow being permitted to be white, and the walls of the room and all the furniture were draped in an equally gloomy fashion. It is difficult to conceive of anything better calculated to deprive the bereaved of all reflections of a consoling character than this barbarous fashion. It was not until the close of this century that a young widow in the country was permitted to have a white sheet because she was ill and could not bear the black cloth !

Mourning was and continued to be a very expensive matter, since it was the custom to send it to all intimate friends as well as to near relations. Lady Sussex with the great good sense she displayed in practical matters twice refused " blakes " [blacks] from the Verneys during the Civil Wars because she knew they could not afford it and alleging as her reason that she was living quietly at Gorhambury and seeing nobody. It was also the habit to lend the mourning bed round the family and among neighbours, for it was not to be supposed that every household could boast so proud a possession.

The bedding of those days, made of feathers or flock produced and cured on the premises in the country, was a great care if proper attention were bestowed upon it.

It required to be constantly renewed at all times, aired in
the sun, and the heavy mattresses perpetually shaken up
and beaten to prevent them from getting lumpy. Whether
the bed staves of which we occasionally hear mention, and
which we see at a later date in Hogarth's pictures, were
used for the latter purpose or whether they were merely
a means of assistance to elderly, rheumatic folk in
ascending mountainous beds or descending therefrom
remains an open question.

If we pass from the furnishings of the greater mansions
to the more modest of the manor houses, it is instructive
to glance at the manner in which a Sussex country
parson furnished his new rectory at Horsted Keynes in
the middle of the seventeenth century.

He bought of William Clonson, upholsterer itinerant,
living over against the Crosse at Chichester, but who
comes about the country with his packs on horseback :—

	£	s.	d.
A fine large coverlett with birds and bucks	2.	10.	0.
A sett of striped curtaines and valance	1.	8.	0.
A coarse coverlett	1.	2.	0.
Two middle blankets	1.	4.	0.
One beasil or Holland tyke or bolster	0.	13.	6
For the parlour chamber I bought of Mr. Hely in London a bed with purple rug, curtaines etc., which cost me altogether	20.	16.	7.
I bought of Thomas Booker 2 sheets for 9s. and of Widow Langley 2 more fine sheets, for which I am to pay 18s.			

His brass he bought at the Ship in Grace Church
Streete, London :—

	£	s.	d.
A paier of brass andirons	1.	2.	0.
A paier of iron dogs with brass heads	0.	5.	6.
Shovell and tongs with brasses	0.	4.	6.

	£	s.	d.
A warming pan	0.	7.	6.
2 brass kettles weighing 37 lbs.	2.	9.	2.
A Latten candlestick for my Mayd Mary ...	0.	1.	6.
Of Edmund Barret at Lewis a clock, for which I payd £2 10s.			

Pendulum clocks were only invented in this year to supersede the old water clock, so the parson was of an enterprising as well as extravagant disposition. He made up for this, however :—

"For 3 yards and ¾ of scarlet serge, of which I made the library cupboard carpet, besydes my wastcoate made thereof 15s. !"

About the same time, however, he has an outburst of generosity and presents his patron with "a faire silver tankard," which came to £10. 15. 3., "paid for engraving his and wife's arms and for a cabinet given to Mistress Anne daughter £1. 5."

This extravagance may have been encouraged by the fact that he had just made a small sum of money by selling six cocks at Shrove-tide, from which it is to be inferred that he encouraged cock fighting.

Turning his attention once more to his furnishing he pays 10s. for the round table standing in his great parlour "and for a wooden chair to sit upon in my study which I bought in Crooked Lane 3s."

He also buys some scarlet serge for a waistcoat to be trimmed with "galloone" and red silk buttons, in the same breath, as it were, that he subscribes £1 to the collection for the building of London after the Fire. Indeed he seems to have been a very sporting parson and a generous one, and deserves better treatment from those

he benefited than the last pathetic item in his accounts
suggests :—

"I bought in London a portmantle costing 5s. 6d., and
a male pellion 1s. and a locke key to the portmantle 6d."
This portmantle and all that belonged to it I lent to my
cousin Lewen which he never returned." We can
imagine the childish joy of the simple gentleman in the
"portmantle" with a lock, a rare luxury. Words
apparently failed him with regard to the conduct of
"Cousin Lewen"!

CHAPTER IV

HOSPITALITY

BEN JOHNSON in an address to Penshurst thus eulogises the accomplished hostess whose house was kept perpetually at such a high standard of perfection that the King and Queen could pay a surprise visit to her in her absence and find all in order for their entertainment :

> " Her linen, plate, and all things right
> Though she was far : and every room was drest
> As if she had expected such a guest."

Barbara Gamage, the Welsh heiress, who had married Robert Sidney, Viscount de l'Isle, Chamberlain to Queen Anne of Denmark, and who became the grandmother of Sacharissa, was not only a notable housewife but possessed the equally valuable art of choosing gentlewomen and servants upon whom she could confidently rely to fulfil their duties when she herself was "far."

The entertainment of royalty was the most important and arduous duty of the great lady of Elizabethan and early Jacobean days. As we have seen, several of the more magnificent Tudor mansions were built with this purpose in view and to gratify the Queen's almost childish love of paying visits. The bed Elizabeth slept in, the room she occupied, the shoes or the gloves she left behind her are cherished with pardonable pride by the descendants of her many entertainers, and these not being always among the most wealthy must sometimes have found their sovereign an expensive and exacting visitor.

But hospitality to all who chose to demand it, to the lowest as well as to the highest in the land was the first virtue to be practised by the country housewife. In days when there were few inns, none in country places fit for the accommodation of ladies, when roads were bad and coaches heavy, and several nights had constantly to be spent in the course of a single journey, a friend's house was the natural halting place.

And friends were by no means the only visitors. Officials of all sorts, travelling the country in the course of their duties, such as judges on circuit, expected to be entertained in the larger houses. Suites of rooms were specially built for visitors who, if they were people of any consequence, brought in their train an immense number of servants and retainers. The lady of the house had to be ready to provision a large or a small party often without longer notice than the sight of the first pack-horse, mounted manservant, or the coach itself turning in at the bottom of the avenue. We can imagine the perturbation, the fluster and the bustle as word of the invasion was passed through the household.

The more primitive days of entertaining when the guest brought his own bedding were over. The Stuart hostess was expected to provide all such necessities for her guest, though there was no prejudice about over-crowding, and the servants, except those body servants who slept on a truckle bed in their master's or mistress's room, probably " lay " where they could.

Housemaids would be sent scurrying off with hot brass warming pans for the great four post bedsteads ; wood fires would soon be blazing up the chimneys, and the fine lavender scented holland sheets and pillow beeres, kept aired we'll hope and ready, would be fetched out of the oaken coffers.

The food was a more complicated and serious matter, but here also the experienced housewife would not be found wanting. Her store-room would be carefully stocked from the nearest market, and the reserves of her larder, supplied by the squire's park and pasture were considerable. Venison would be hanging in the summer and autumn, and there would be no lack of meat nowadays even in the winter. There must be fresh fish procured from the ponds, and of poultry and rabbits there would be plenty, though not perhaps of the tenderest since they must be eaten immediately after being killed. Quantity, however, appears to have been at these impromptu entertainments the first consideration, and the housewife must have been thankful for the game season when her larder was additionally stocked with pheasants and all sorts of wild birds as well as hares. The garden could be relied upon in summer to supply all fresh vegetables and fruits, of which there was also a constant interchange between neighbours in order to obtain variety, new sorts being brought from foreign countries. Meantime, her orders hastily transmitted to her gentlewoman or more trusted servant accustomed to these invasions, the housewife would be standing beside the squire in the porch ready to welcome the occupants of the coach or coaches, as they lumbered heavily up to the door.

We may be sure that, in the well-trained and carefully

educated country lady of those unhurried days, her guests would find the sincere and sympathetic welcome and the undivided attention which they would certainly expect. Possibly her mind may have wandered forward as to the fitting entertainment to be provided for them when they should be refreshed by food and change of raiment. Did she, as would many a modern hostess under less trying circumstances, venture to hope that the ladies at all events would be thankful to rest in their chambers after travelling since daybreak in a springless coach upon the roughest roads, or even on horseback ? Perhaps her thoughts would run on to the little masque, which might be performed by her young people later in the afternoon, or she would reflect, with a sigh of relief, that there was always the bowling green for the gentle-men, and gossip and embroidery for the ladies ! More probably she thought of none of these things, but merely that it was pleasant to welcome friends or relatives, or even strangers. If they came from London they would have fresh news to tell of the King and his increasing difficulties ; of the French Papist Queen and her pretty children ; of the newest fashions, or the latest vagaries of the Roundheads. And if they did but come from the other side of the county, there was still news other than that brought by the carriers and sold with the goods in the market.

But the greetings over, the housewife must hasten back to the kitchen to see to the proper ordering of the dinner and to the seating of her guests in the dining-room or the hall according to their social position.

An account has been preserved of the ceremony, and it is nothing less, of the daily dinner at Raglan Castle, which gives us an idea of the manner in which the

A CAVALIER LADY IN WALKING DRESS.

household and guests, as well as the vast army of
retainers and servants were seated at the greatest
houses in the land.

There were two tables in the dining-room, at one
of which sat the Earl himself, his family and guests
of his own rank : they were waited on by gentlemen
and the pages, gentlemen's sons for whom the Book
of Nurture instructing them in manners had been
written in the preceding century. At the other table
sat the knights and honourable gentlemen, my Lady's
gentlewomen and any other gentlewomen who were
living in the house or had come as guests, and these
were served by footmen. In the hall there were three
tables. At the first of these, presided over by the
steward, sat the comptroller, the secretary, the master
of the horse, the master of the fishponds, the tutor and
such gentlemen who were guests and were under the
degree of knight, and these were waited on by footmen
and plentifully served with wine.

At the second table, which was served from my
Lord's table and with other hot meat, were the gentleman server, with the gentlemen waiters and pages to
the number of twenty-four or more. The third and
last table was presided over by the clerk of the kitchen,
and here the yeomen officers of the house were fed.
There were two tables in the housekeeper's room for
the Ladies' women and for the chaplain and any stray
gentlewomen strangers that did not appear below stairs.
Such an inviduous arrangement must inevitably have
led to a good deal of heart-burning on the part of
those ladies and gentlemen who considered themselves
superior to the housekeeper's room. In addition there
were butchers, keepers, brewers, bailiffs, ploughmen, a

tailor, saddler, plumber, farrier, falconer, and all the vast army of men who were necessary to do the work of a large self-depending estate in the country.

The imposing ruins of Raglan which still remain may give us a pretty clear idea of the feudal state maintained in the country by the Marquis of Worcester in the seventeenth century, but all the patriarchal magnificence came finally to an end when the Castle surrendered to Sir Thomas Fairfax in 1646.

For the ordering of a stately banquet of the period, it was the business of the Clerk of the Kitchen to arrange the meat in due order at the dresser, and to hand each dish to the server, who in his turn must deliver it over to the gentlemen and yeomen waiters to bear to the table. An incompetent marshaller of dishes is likened to "a Fencer leading a band of men in a rout, who knows the use of a weapon, but not how to put men in order."

In the ordinary squire's house, however, this was the duty of the lady or her gentlewoman, and considering the innumerable dishes which composed each of the two courses of a banquet, her task was sufficiently heavy.

First the sallets must be marshalled in their proper order—the grand sallet, the green sallets, the boiled sallets—then some smaller compound sallets. Then follow the fricasses, collops, rashers, etc. The boiled meats which come next in order are to be accompanied by the broths, both simple and stewed. The simpler kind was in fact the water in which the joint or joints had been boiled with a handful of herbs added, while richer material of meat, calves' head or fish would be included in the stewed broth. All sorts

of roast meats would next be placed on the table,
beginning with the inevitable chine of beef or a sirloin
and leg of mutton, leading on to veal, a pig, or capons,
a goose and a swan. It is curious that no arrangement
seems to have been made for keeping these many
dishes hot, nor the plates either, which to our ideas
suggests an unappetising accompaniment of tepid grease.
Room on the table must be found for the hot baked
meats, fallow-deer in a pasty, chicken or calves'-foot
pie ; also for the cold baked meats, pheasants, a turkey,
goose, woodcock, etc., and the first course concludes
with the favourite carbonadoes, both simple and compound. It must be added that fresh water fish "soused"
are to be served with the sallets, fried fish with the
fricasses, fish "stewed hot, but dry," among the roast
meats, sea fish, if obtainable, among the baked meats,
and broiled fish among the carbonadoes. The table
needed to be solid indeed for all these dishes had to
be placed upon it at the same time, and, it must be
noticed, not merely in the order mentioned.

The arrangement of the table with a view to effect
was quite as important then as now, though the effect
to be obtained differed very considerably from that of
present-day standards. Before every trencher should
"stand a sallet, a fricase, a boyld meat, a roast meat,
a bak'd meat, and a carbonado, which will both give
a most comely beauty to the table and a very great
contentment to the guests !"

The second course, another amply satisfying meal in
itself, was to consist chiefly of poultry : first the lesser
wild fowl, mallard, teal, snipe, etc., and then the lesser
land fowl, pigeons, partridge, raite, chicken, young
pea-hens. Then come the great wild fowl, bittern, crane,

bustard and such like, and the greater land fowls,
peacocks (which, however, even now were beginning to
be regarded rather as a decoration than a delicacy),
pheasants and gulls—the classification may seem curious.
The second course closed with hot baked pies and
tarts of marrow bone, quince and other luscious
material, and cold baked pies of red-deer, hare, gammon
of bacon, roe and wild boar, etc.

Pies were a very favourite dish in the seventeenth
century, and the cooks of the period were evidently
good pastry makers. Humble pie, made out of the
"umble" or "umbles," livers, hearts and entrails of
animals, was by this time reserved for the lower tables,
where the retainers and unimportant guests had to eat
"humble pie." A surprise pasty out of which leapt
live creatures was still an amusement at the tables
of the great, and considered "a pretty dish to set before
a king." There is no doubt where the nursery rhyme
had its origin.

To return to the banquet, however, the table for the
second course was as yet by no means sufficiently
loaded. "*Quelquechoses* and all made dishes which rely
on the invention of the cook are to be thrust into
every place that is empty and so sprinkled over all the
table." We must not forget the "Marchpanes," the
marzipan of modern German confectionery, the preserved fruits and comfits of every kind, as well as fresh
fruit, according to the season, which by some culinary
lawgivers of the period were considered of the first
importance since "they occupied the first place, the
second and the last," that is to say they helped to
adorn the table throughout the meal.

Figures and devices, originally made of sugar or

pastry, and later of painted cardboard known as Warners and Subtleties, were another form of decoration which, surviving from the mediæval dining-table, flourished abundantly under the Stuarts. They merely represented the desire for colour which now finds a more graceful expression in flowers, and the same explanation may be found for the prodigal use of saffron, cochineal and other dyes used in the concoction of food for the old English table, a fashion which survived far into the nineteenth century.

Master Robert May, *chef* to Sir Kenelm Digby, the most fashionable cook of his day, who considered that in his own sheltered person the art of cookery in England alone survived the Commonwealth, was most ingenious in devising these "subtle diversions." One of the artist's greatest triumphs was designed for a Twelfth Night supper. A man-of-war, made of pasteboard, was to be floated in a great charger on a sea of salt in which were to be eggshells full of rose-water. On another large charger was to be a stag made of paste and filled with claret : while on yet a third was to be a paste-board castle complete with portcullises, gates and drawbridges. The castle and the ship having real trains of gunpowder were to fire at each other while the ladies pelted one another with the eggshells full of rosewater to conceal the smell of the powder. An arrow being withdrawn from the stag, its life blood, in the shape of claret wine, would flow freely. At either side of the stag's charger were to be large pies which, upon being carefully cut would let loose live frogs and live birds respectively, the latter flying at once into the candles and extinguishing the lights. We are told that "with the flying birds and the skipping frogs, the one above the other beneath" much delight and pleasure was caused to the whole company. We can at least believe that the diversion caused the ladies "to skip and shriek," but our sturdier forefathers took their pleasures with courage, and Master May adds complacently that such contrivances "were formerly the delights of the nobility, before good housekeeping had left England."

Gervas Markham sets down in his Country Contentments what he considers to be a "more humble feast or an ordinary proportion which any good man may keep in his family for the entertainment of his true and worthy friends." This was to consist for the first course of "sixteen dishes of meat that are of substance, and not empty or for shew." The first dish was to be the shield of brawn with mustard which had rather superseded the Elizabethan pottage at the beginning of a meal. We need scarcely capitulate all the dishes that followed. They included beef, both boiled and roasted, a " Pigge rosted," a goose, swan, and turkey, venison, a "kid with a pudding in the belly," an olive pie, a couple of capons, and lastly the inevitable custard or meat pie. And to these full dishes may be added the usual sallets, fricases, *quelquechoses* and devised paste, which make the full service no less than two-and-thirty dishes, which is as much as can conveniently stand on the table and in one mess." After this the second and third courses, but there were usually only two, may be added at discretion and on the same principle of fulness in one-half of the dishes and show in the other.

This was the *petit diner sans cérémonie* or something like it which the country housewife was expected to

prepare for her casual guests. No wonder that supper
seems to have been a negligible quantity!

Under Robert May's portrait in the frontispiece of his
famous book are the following lines :—

> "What would'st thou view but in one face
> All hospitalitie, the race
> Of those that for the gusto stand
> Whose tables a whole ark command
> Of Nature's plentie, would'st thou see
> This sight, peruse May's book, 'tis he."

The Country Housewife was certainly expected to
command "a whole ark," but she was not always
expected to provide quite such large banquets. Each
course in a dinner of ceremony had from sixteen to
twenty dishes, but Robert May also provided a bill of
fare for every month in the year in which only six dishes
were considered sufficient for one course. In winter
they began with eggs and collops, to be followed by the
inevitable brawn and mustard; and in summer by
"Musk Mellons," the prerunner of the slice of melon
often served as a prelude to dinner in these days, which
was succeeded by pottage; buttered brawn, not to be
entirely omitted, coming at the end of the second
course.

The Christmas dinner of the country squire was
probably less elaborate than that recommended by
this fashionable cook for his greater patrons. This was
to begin with "oysters at the entry"; in each of the two
courses there were to be twenty dishes, of the kind
described above, and oranges and lemons were to be
served between the courses. Among the dishes, as mere
items, were a sirloin of roast beef, a turkey stuffed with

cloves and mince-pies, but no plum pottage—plum pudding had not yet made its appearance. The first course includes the "kid with a pudding in his belly," as suggested by Markham, and concludes, of course, with custard, but it is noticeable that there is no mention of fish until a sturgeon is introduced quite at the end of the second course.

Fish being still a dish eaten under compulsion on fast days, was not as yet particularly popular at banquets, which may account for its late appearance on the menu on such a festive occasion.

Here is a dinner of ceremony for Fast Day :—

FIRST COURSE.

Oysters if in season.
1. Butter and Eggs.
2. Barley Pottage or Rice Pottage.
3. Stewed Oysters.
4. Buttered Eggs on Toast.
5. Spinach Sallet boild.
6. Boild Rochet or Gurnet.
7. A jole of Ling.
8. Stewed Carp.
9. Oyster chewits.
10. Boild Pike.
11. Roast Eels.
12. Hadducks and fresh Cod or Whitings.
13. Eel or Carp Pie.
14. Made dish of Spinach.
15. Salt Eels.
16. Souc'd Turbut.

SECOND COURSE.

1. Fried Soles.
2. Stewed Oysters in Scallop Shells.
3. Fried Smelts.
4. Conger's Head boild.
5. Baked Dish of Potatoes or Oyster Pie.
6. A Spitchcock of Eels.
7. Quince Pie or Tarts royal.
8. Buttered Crabs.
9. Fried Flounders.
10. Joles of Fresh Salmon.
11. Fried Turbot.
12. Cold Salmon Pie.
13. Fried Skirrets.
14. Souc't Conger.
15. Lobster.
16. Sturgeons.

At least there was a large choice !

Robert May precedes all his Bills of Fare with the sad announcement, "As used before Hospitality left the

Nation," but this was in a late edition, revised probably
during his seclusion under the Commonwealth, when he
had small hopes that his sun would ever rise again.

With hospitality on such a lavish scale, the mistress of
a large house, even before the financial pressure of the
Civil War, sometimes found it difficult to make her
housekeeping money cover all her expenses. The great
Lord Cork, when he moved to his new house at Stalbridge in 1638, being then a widower, entrusted his
housekeeping to the joint efforts of his daughter, Lady
Barrymore, and his daughter-in-law, Lady Dungarvan.
He allowed them £50 a week in addition to the produce
of the lands and woods at Stalbridge and "powdered"
(salt) beef, salt salmon, bacon, and stalled oxen brought
from his estates in Ireland.

The £50 proving insufficient, the sum was considerably increased, but divided counsels not conducing to
economy, combined with the fact that neither of the
young ladies was an experienced housekeeper, they still
found it impossible to make both ends meet. Apparently
they judged it wiser this time to keep their difficulties to
themselves, and it was not until they were making the
annual move from Stalbridge that it was discovered that
they were in debt to bakers, brewers, vintners, and
graziers, to the extent of £700! When, a year later, it
was further revealed that a ton of claret wine, costing
£18, had not yet been paid for, Lord Cork, who, rich and
generous though he was, was also extremely punctilious,
was justifiably very much shocked, and probably found
it expedient to make a change in his housekeeping
department. Only two or three years later, in 1642, the
old Earl writes of his beleaguered conditions at Lismore,
his place in Ireland, where his garrison, consisting of

fifteen companies, were subsisting mostly upon salt beef,
barrelled biscuits and butter, with only water to drink.
It was as well his extravagant daughters were not there
to share this frugal diet, and it is pathetic to read of his
efforts in these hard times to give them the handsome
Christmas presents that they were accustomed to.

Scotch hospitality was naturally no way behind the
English, though still rather mediæval in its details. We
hear of a princely banquet where the servitors waited
with their hats on, and where a basin of rose-water was
placed before each guest to wash his hands. The dinner
was followed by beer cup and strong waters ; singing
boys sang the Grace and the Paternoster ; there was a
coup of ale and a collation before bed, and a stirrup-cup
at parting. In England also there was plenty of drink to
wash down the long dinners, but this chiefly consisted of
French wines, claret, and burgundy, which were imported
exceedingly cheaply, Rhenish wine, Spanish wines, canary
sack, and, of course, the home-brewed ale, which was,
however, kept on occasions, for the lower tables. A
certain standard of sobriety was still maintained in the
country at this period, and the squire after a convivial
dinner could generally be trusted to ride home in
safety.

After the Civil War, hospitality became a very heavy
tax, especially upon the smaller households. There were
few squires who were not seriously impoverished by the
loss of possessions and the heavy taxes which had been
laid upon them. Yet ways and means must be found, for
hospitality was still ranked as the first virtue. So they
continued in a more modest fashion to entertain one
another, and their poorer neighbours, and to recommend
each other a suitable physic to be taken afterwards ! On

any special occasion, the welcoming home of a bride, or the visit of a guest of distinction, neighbours were ready enough to help with presents of game, fish, fruit, etc., and one bride's popularity was gauged by the amount of venison she received in her first year of housekeeping.

The Puritans did their best to put a stop to feasting and junketing. Christmas Day was not to be observed, and the mince pie was looked upon by the fanatic as idolatrous. Happily their influence did not extend far into the country, and the national love of good cheer and conviviality survived in spite of Roundhead dogma.

Mrs. Walker, the admirable wife of the Rector of Fyfield, chaplain to Lord Warwick, had an established system of entertaining. At Christmas she fed the whole parish, rich and poor, old and young, for three consecutive days at the Rectory, and to a housewife, who probably only had a few country wenches to help her, this meant a good deal. On the anniversary of their wedding day, she and Dr. Walker entertained their more exalted neighbours, among whom was their patron the Earl of Warwick and his wife Mary, daughter of Lord Cork. Lord Warwick always supplied the venison for this great occasion, and no doubt the Countess found many good things to contribute from her kitchen and her still-room. At one of these dinners of high degree there were "three coroneted heads, and others of best quality, next to nobility!" We can well imagine the honest pride of good Mrs. Walker in her company, but the chief dish on her table was one of pies, as many in number as the years which she had been married and all made with her own hands.

Mrs. Walker was a most devoted wife and helpmeet to the Rector, but she very sensibly considered that her

husband's place was in the study and not in the kitchen,
and when he proffered suggestions on domestic matters
she would quietly and kindly set them aside, " I pray thee,
let me alone, trouble not thyself : let me but know whom
thou invitest, and leave the rest to me." She was a
magnificent housewife and a most benevolent despot in
the village, where her frown was equivalent to Jove's nod,
but where she was loved even more than she was feared,
owing to her immense kindness. The morning after her
more important entertainments the good lady's door
would be beseiged by her humbler parishioners come, on
one excuse or another, to beg her advice, and invariably
sent away laden with the very substantial crumbs which
had fallen from the rich man's table.

People did not much mind how they were crowded
together in those days at any family gathering, especially
for Christmas festivities. Relations were convinced, as
they sometimes are now, that because they were relations
they had the right of entry to a house whether they were
invited or no. " I entended you no trouble, but did
believe that I might crowd in among the rest of the
company," was an excuse no doubt frequently offered
by married sisters and cousins to the distracted host and
hostess, who had already been forced to put up beds in
the drawing-room, and who, even in those days of open
house, were coming to the end alike of their resources
and their forbearance.

A house-party at the Stukeley's, at Preshaw House,
reminds their friend Dr. Denton of the miracle of the
loaves and fishes, for there are sixty-five visitors to be provided for and only one guest-chamber—and yet it is
done ! One sprightly young woman determined not to
be done out of what promises to be a cheery gathering

in the drab days of the Commonwealth writes to her host
that she will certainly come, since she and all the other
virgins "can lie together," his convenience or that of the
other and invited "virgins" not for one instant being
considered !

CHAPTER V

THE KITCHEN AND THE INVENTORIES

HAVING seen the menus of the banquets and the heavy dinners which it was the housewife's duty to provide, it may be of some interest to investigate her kitchen; to find out how some of these strange dishes were prepared and the utensils which she had at her disposal.

In the early days of English architecture the kitchen had stood quite detached from the rest of the building. This was a precautionary measure against fire and was incidentally most effective in avoiding the smell of cooking, if such a detail were thought of, but it is an arrangement which also suggests tepid dishes and every other domestic inconvenience.

In Tudor and Jacobean houses, the kitchens, butteries, dairies and all other offices pertaining, were, as we have seen, part of the establishment and placed together at one end of the hall, behind the "screens" and well under the housewife's supervision. The stone-floored kitchen with its high raftered ceiling was usually large in proportion to the house, and gave plenty of room for the cook to harry the army of scullions which was necessary to assist in the preparation of such large meals. Women cooks were now employed in moderate houses, but, in the greater establishments then, as now, men still ruled the kitchen.

There were no lack of cookery books in England. "The Forme of Cury" produced by the cooks of King Richard II. containing recipes for dishes of all descriptions, suited to narrow means as well as to princely establishments, was followed by many others. The reign of Elizabeth, when the extension of trade introduced a larger choice of foreign luxuries and opened the way for more elaborate culinary efforts, was particularly prolific in these, and there were many more in the seventeenth century. Cookery is very much mixed up with physic in these curious manuals, and, indeed, the accomplished housewife was expected to have an equal knowledge of both, since the need of the one frequently followed hard upon the other. The housewife in the country, however, probably preferred her own recipes and those handed down to her by her mother and grandmother before her, and of these there was a frequent interchange among friends and neighbours.

Meat seems to have been eaten in great quantities, and before the Civil War and to a much later period it was remarkably cheap. We have seen the modest sums paid by Captain Bosville for his meat in Yorkshire during the Commonwealth, and we may compare them with some items in the papers of Baron Hill, a Chancellor of the Exchequer, living in Somersetshire. In 1638 he paid

	s.	d.
For a breast and legg of mutton...	2.	0.
For a legg and loyn of mutton	2.	0.
For a Bushel of Wheat	5.	6.
For rootes and cabbidge	0.	6.
For a rabbit...	0.	7.
7 oz. of China (could this have been tea?) · ...	7.	0.
1 oz. of rhubarb	0.	4. etc.

Wheat was dear but it was to grow still dearer, for in 1658 we find it in Sussex selling at 7s. 4d. the bushel, a prohibitive price for the poor man. The Civil Wars, however, interrupted English trade less than might have been expected. The wages of the day labourer rose slightly and the price of food, as a whole, did not immediately increase to any considerable extent. The conquest of Jamaica in 1655, created a new and important trade with our Colonies, and sugar—presently to be so heavily taxed—became a prosperous industry and could at least be obtained freely in the market. This was an item of considerable importance to the housekeeper when so much preserving had to be done for the table, and when the knowledge and fear of gout was not so perpetually before her eyes.

If we could peep into one of the old kitchens and see it arranged as it was three hundred years ago, we should not find the same shining array of pots and pans and dish covers which adorn its walls and shelves to-day. Earthenware was the ordinary material for kitchen utensils with occasional vessels of wood or brass or pewter. There is a good collection of domestic appliances in the London Museum, where we may see cooking pots, butter-pots, "traps," fuming pots, pipkins, skillets, jugs, mugs, tigs or dishes and candlesticks, all of quaint design. Slip ware, as it was called, was fashionable in the seventeenth century and came largely from Wrotham in Kent. This was red ware decorated round the edge with a thin cream or brown mixture of clay, forming a rough geometrical pattern, and glazed with a yellow glaze. There were still in use also the green glazed vessels of the sixteenth century, and there were red Toft dishes with the pipeclay wash on the inner surface, on which was roughly painted the name of the maker, or sometimes that of the person for whom the dish or "tyg" was intended. Certainly the kitchen lacked nothing in picturesqueness and colour in its furnishings, if it could not yet boast the smart array of copper and enamel which the French cooks were later to introduce into England.

In the museum at Kensington Palace we may also see the long iron two-pronged fork with which the cook would fish his meat out of the broth to see how it was getting on.

In the Middle Ages a great deal of cooking had been done in the pot, stews and boiled meat being popular. These savoury messes were less expensive, and also required a great deal less attention from the cook than a roast, which must be constantly turned and basted and the dripping collected. But no menu of Tudor or Jacobean times was, as we have seen, complete without several roasts, and the turning of the spits or broaches was a duty which had hitherto devolved upon some aged retainer or wandering vagabond who was glad enough to earn a few groats and keep himself warm at the same time.

In the Tudor kitchens a dog was ingeniously trained to turn the "roaster," by running round the inside of a wheel upon the same principle that a captive squirrel revolves in its cage. To incite him originally to this form of exercise, the poor dog had a hot coal applied to his heels—a penalty which was repeated if he showed any desire to slacken—and when we consider the size of the joints in those days, he must have been often both hurt and astonished at the length of this uncomfortable run. The poor turnspit, with his long body and crooked but powerful legs, continued at this sad and arduous duty in many houses until far into the eighteenth century, when he was relieved by the invention of the smoke-jack.

Naturally for roasting a great deal more fuel was required than for the pot, and very thankful the housewife must have been when coal was obtainable for this purpose. Cooking of any sort with only charcoal or wood or turf must have been a slow business. In the seventeenth century coal was increasingly used as house-fuel ; but at any distance from the sea, except near the pits, it was still a luxury. The coal was all sea-borne, and in London came entirely from Newcastle, and the coal-owners not being allowed to deal directly with the ship-masters who carried it, the inevitable middle-men made it very dear. In 1638 the price was 19s. per chaldron in winter, and 17s. in summer, which, compared with modern prices, does not seem excessive, if we do not remember the much higher value of money. The woodmongers who sold it in London were accused of giving short measure by means of shrinking the sacks, and one great lady in the country who, considering the state of the roads and the difficulty of porterage, should have been glad to have any at all, complains loudly of the "very bad coles" that have been sent her.

Whatever the fuel that was burnt on those wide hearths, there must have been plenty of it to roast the huge pieces of beef, the quarters of sheep, and the birds of every size and variety which were hanging on spits all at the same time before the fire. No wonder that each kitchen usually boasted two fireplaces and ovens, besides, in some houses, the "pastries"—a separate office where a vast amount of confectionery was prepared. The slovenly fashion of putting the joint or bird in the oven would have shocked our grandmothers not a little, and their grandmothers and great-grandmothers a great deal more.

One old book of the time gives instructions how to roast "a chine of Beef, a Loin of Mutton, a Lark and Capon at one fire and at one instant." The beef must be previously parboiled more than half through; the capon must be spitted first "next the hand of the turner," then the chine of beef, then the lark, and lastly the loin of mutton, "and place the lark so as it may be covered over with the Beef and the fat part of the loin of Mutton, without any part disclosed"; the capon and loin must then be basted with cold water and salt, and the chine of beef with boiling lard. When the beef is almost done, the mutton and capon shall be wiped with a clean cloth all over, and then basted with sweet butter. Lastly, when "all be enough roasted, with your knife lay the Lark open, which by this time will be stewed between the Beef and Mutton, and basting it also with dredge altogether, draw them and serve them up."

The pottage of Elizabethan days was still to some extent in favour, and continued to be so until the introduction of what we call soup. The plainer kind, made of "those ordinary wholsome boyl'd meats which are of use in every good man's house," was a most useful dish, for it "can as well feed the poor as the rich," and consisted merely of beef, or more preferably mutton, boiled with a quantity of herbs. There were many richer and more elaborate kinds, however, and the "Plain Savoury English Pottage" taken from the Closet of Sir Kenelm Digby, Kt., Opened, is a remarkably inclusive compound, and one which appears to be more savoury than plain !

" Make it of Beef, Mutton, and Veal ; at last adding a Capon, or Pigeons. Put in at first a quartered onion or two, some oatmeal or French barley, some bottome of a Venison pastry-crust, twenty whole grains of Pepper ; four or five Cloves at last, and a little bundle of sweet herbs, store of Marigold flowers—you may put in Parsley or other herbs." Indeed, it seems according to these old recipes that the cook might put into these pottages practically anything he chose so long as the mess was sufficiently rich and tasty for his master's seasoned palate. Esau's mess of pottage might have been something of this nature.

Sir Kenelm Digby was as fond of trying new recipes in cookery as he was of experiments in physic. Most of the latter and a good many of the former were tried on behalf of his beautiful wife, Venetia, who died of consumption. He is said to have given her capons fed with the flesh of vipers, but all his most alarming as well as his more rational remedies proved unfortunately of no avail.

In his "Closet Opened" are a number of recipes borrowed from the ladies of his acquaintance ; among them is Lady Fanshawe's barbarous manner of fattening her poultry. She caused them to be made drunk with ale, so that they might sleep after a meal and then wake and eat again. She also caused a candle to be kept burning over the coop all night, so that the misguided creature might think it desirable to feed all the twenty-four hours round, with brief intervals for drunken slumber. Barley boiled in water, milk, and strong ale was to be its food, and ale was to be placed in the water-trough. By this means the unhappy bird was to be fattened in a fortnight, and we can only hope its enforced debauch did not last longer.

Pies of all sorts were greatly in request. Every beast that walked or swam or flew, fish, meat, poultry, venison, could be safely enclosed in pastry, separate or all together, and adorn the odd spaces on the table or be sent as a very welcome present to a friend in London. But, as may be seen from the following recipe, a pie was not quite the simple matter in those days that it is now. "To bake a chicken pye, after you have trust your chickens, then broken their legs and brest bones, and raised your crust of the best paste, you shall lay them in the coffin close together, with their bodyes full of butter: then lay upon them, and underneath them, Currents, great Raisins, Prunes, Cinamon, Sugar, whole mace and salt: then cover all with great store of Butter, and so bake it: after powre into it the same liquor you did in your Marrow-bone pye, with yolkes of two or three Eggs beaten amongst it, and so serve it forth." The liquor referred to is white wine, rose-water, sugar, cinnamon, and vinegar mixed together! Thus prepared, the poor chickens in their "coffin," as the pie-dish was realistically called, can have been scarcely recognisable. The idea, however, was usually to disguise what might have been recognised as unpalatably plain food.

The roast bird must have a *sauce piquante*. For a chicken a sauce is recommended by Robert May as follows :—"Slict oranges, a little white wine, rose water, beaten mace, ginger, some sugar, and butter. Set them on a chafing dish of coals and stew them. Then have some slices of manchet round the dish finely carved, and lay the chicken, being roasted, on the same ;" or a simpler one consists of sliced onions, claret wine, gravy, and fat boiled up ! For a pigeon he recommends, "Minced onions boiled in claret wine almost dry, then put to it nutmeg, sugar, gravy of the fowl, and a little pepper."

Mrs. Woolley gives a recipe for a lamprey pie, a lamprey being a fish which, if it has not disappeared from modern waters, has certainly done so from modern kitchens. "Take your Lampreys, pull all the pith that runs along the back, and all the black, then wash them clean: season them with pepper and salt, make the crust of your pie very thick and put good store of butter in the bottom. Then lay in your lampreys with some large mace, then more butter and some white wine, so bake it very well, then fill up the pye with melted butter and keep it to eat cold."

Carp and eel pies were very frequent, and probably the best means of preparing such coarse fish. Tarts appear to have differed from pies only in that the pastry was twisted or tortured into patterns. The dish prepared for a pie or tart was called a *trap*, and only became a *coffin* when covered with the paste. The material which was to go into it—fish, flesh, vegetable, fruit, eggs, and milk, and what not—was referred to as the *tartee*. There were, of course, fruit pies and tarts of every description —"apricock," pippen, codlins, or quodlings, a name applied to super-excellent cooking apples, being among the most popular fruits for this purpose. The "quod-lings" were considered more tasty by some people if mixed with whole cinnamon, sliced ginger, and a little musk and rose water. Mince pies were a very old English Christmas dish made originally in an oval shape to represent the manger. The mincemeat was made very much like our own, except that a great quantity of meat was used as well as suet, and it was sweetened with rose-water, as were most of the con-

fectionery dishes of this period. There being no
brandy to preserve it, it was probably made fresh for
the occasion, which will account for the further
difference that pippins are mentioned in the recipes
instead of apples.

The *Carbonadoe*, of which Gervase Markham made a
point in the arrangements of a banquet, was a dish, he
tells us, "brought out of France," and was made of meat
broiled upon coals. For this a broiling-iron or Plait-
iron should be used (the cook who uses a gridiron is
greatly censured) with "hooks and pricks," so that the
meat can hang close before the fire with the hot plate
behind it, "and it will be ready the sooner." Breast
of mutton, half-boiled, might be cooked in this way,
or the legs, wings, and carcase of any bird, or indeed
any other sort of meat, so that it has been partially
roasted or boiled first ; and lastly, "the uttermost thick
skinne which covereth the ribs of beef, and is called the
Inns of Court-goose, and is indeed a dish used most for
wantonnesse, to which may also be added the broyling of
Pigs-heads, or the brains of any fowl whatsoever after it
is roasted and dressed." Giles Rose, the fashionable
cook of a rather later period, who probably scorned old
Markham's precepts, decided that cutlets of pork could
be carbonadoed very well upon a gridiron, and would
make a very dainty dish for supper mixed with stewed
onions and verjuice !

The *Quelquechose* was, as its name announces, another
French dish, and was made of a great many materials.
Eggs, cream, currants, cinnamon, cloves, mace, salt,
ginger, spinach, endive, and marigold flowers, to which
might be added the further delicacy, " Pigge's Pettitoes,"
well boiled, and all were fried together with butter. The

Quelquechose was, in fact, not far removed from a Compound or Grand Sallet. The sallet or salad appeared in every menu in the seventeenth century, and was largely eaten by the lower classes as an antidote to the salt food on which, being unable to afford fresh meat, they subsisted in the winter. John Russell, in the "Boke of Nurture," solemnly warned his readers against "grene metes" and "frutes raw," and by a good many they continued, probably with some reason, to be thought unwholesome. John Gerarde, of the "Herbinal" fame, says that lettuce should be boiled to make it more digestible, but as a whole, a spring salad was recommended to be taken until such time as the summer vegetables were ready. There were the Simple Sallet and the Grand Sallet, the boiled, baked, and pickled sallets.

The Simple Sallet was only one herb or vegetable, such as young lettuce, boiled carrots, chives, or radish roots, served simply on a fruit-dish with vinegar, salade oil, and sugar. The Compound Sallet was a mixture of "young Buds and knots of all manner of wholesome Herbs at their first springing," mixed together, such as red sage, mint, lettuce, violets, marigolds, spinach, etc., and to these were added on great occasions blanched almonds, raisins, figs, capers, olives, currants, and slices of oranges and lemons. All the ingredients of our salads were in use and a good many others, including rose and violet leaves. Fish, and flesh, and bird were also added to the Grand Sallet, but mayonnaise sauce was not yet invented as a finish.

Towards the close of the century John Evelyn produced his *Acetaria*, a tract upon the proper ingredients to be used in a salad and its preparation. In this he distinguishes between vegetables intended for the pot

and those which should only be eaten raw. His great
knowledge of horticulture and his own fine taste in
gastronomy ensured the advice of so learned a gentleman being received with respect and attention, and his
instructions are practically the same as those which are
followed in salad making and salad dressings at the
present day. The "sauce,' he says, must be a careful
mixture of mustard, oil, and vinegar, with or without
the hard-boiled yoke of a new-laid egg, and the only
salad bowl to be contemplated must be of "porcelaine
or of the Holland Delft Ware," silver or pewter being
most undesirable on account of the "sauce." Wood he
does not mention, probably because in his day wooden
vessels seldom appeared upon a gentleman's table.

Judging from the old journals of the time which have
been preserved, the accounts, as we have seen, were
usually kept by the husband, so much money being
allowed at intervals to his wife for the housekeeping.
The same custom apparently prevailed in Scotland, the
home of good housewifery, for Lord Fountainhall's
journals are full of such items. "Given to my wife
two dollars," a dollar, worth about five shillings, being
used in Scotland in the seventeenth century for household and other payments. "Then given hir to buy
shoes, linnen, and other things with five dollars. Then
given to my wife to buy turkies a dollar." Money was
also given to his wife to buy meat to entertain the
"Gossips" when they visit her at the birth of the child.

Apparently the lady did not feel it incumbent upon her
to keep any separate account of her expenditure, although
it is true that Lady Bosville's housekeeping items do
appear upon the back of her dressmaker's bill, though
whether in her own handwriting we cannot say. In the

diary of the Sussex parson, who was deprived of his
cherished "portmantle" in so unscrupulous a fashion,
there are only the briefest references to his wife at all—
"I gave my wife 15s. to lay out at St. James faire
at Lindfield, all which shee spent except 2s. 6d.,
which she never returned mee," and on another occasion "tobacco for my wife 3d." This does not
somehow suggest that the poor man was blest with
a very sympathetic helpmeet in his careful but also
generous commissariat.

Mr. Pepys, a busy professional man in London, made
an effort to instruct his wife with a view to her assistance
in the domestic exchequer. He notes in his diary that
on a certain Lord's Day "My wife and I all the afternoon at arithemetique, and she is come to do Addition,
Subtraction, and Multiplication very well." Whether
her education progressed to any practical result, history
does not narrate, but we gather from the diary that Mr.
Pepys continued to keep his accounts with the same
admirable care and system. He may complain occasionally that increasing prosperity has also been
"expensive to my purse" in the increased splendour of
living it involved, but he has, as a rule, no reason to
feel anything but complacent at his yearly balance.
"To my accounts of the whole year till past twelve at
night, it being bitter cold, but yet I was well satisfied
with my work; and above all, to find myself, by the
great blessing of God, worth £1,349." At the end of
the following year, 1665, there is an even greater pæan
of pious gratitude. "All the afternoon to my accounts;
and there find myself, to my great joy, a great deal
worth above £4,000, for which the Lord be praised!"

If Mrs. Pepys did not learn arithmetic, however, she

probably knew by heart the number of her pipkins and
skillets, and of her fine sheets and pillow beeres laid away
in lavender. When they had husbands to do it for them
the ladies did not trouble about accounts, judging, perhaps
wisely, that finance was essentially a man's affair; but they
were none the less careful in making and keeping their inventories. In a list of the possessions of a thrifty Scotch
housekeeper we find "a goodly store of feather and nap
beds, cods and codwares (pillowslips), sheets and blankets,
arras work, curtains with servit ribbons, buird (table)
cloths, serviettes, towels, pots (iron and brass), a dozen
plates (pewter), trenchers, a *broken candlestick*, cooking
and brewing utensils, a meikl auld kost etc."

Another Scotch inventory includes a "silver pyke
tooth, a pik lug (for the ear), a timber washstand, a
stretching goose (flat iron), a bullet for breaking coals,
a hanging flowered chandelier for the hall, a broth plate,
and a dozen tin plates." The mention of a washstand at
this date is very unusual; but, on the other hand, there
is no mention in these lists, north of the Tweed, of such
obvious articles as chairs, bedsteads, tables, and earthenware.

Both in Scotland and England, however, the house-
linen was very carefully disposed of in the ladies' wills to
their daughters and daughters-in-law. Margaret, Lady
Verney, entreats her son Ralph to see that his father does
not let any of her household linen be sold. Most of it
she leaves as an heirloom to Ralph, and his son, and
son's son; but certain of the sheets of her own
making are to be divided among his sisters, and were
destined to prove in the future a fruitful source of
dissension.

Lady Sussex, who was a Lee of Ditchley, quarrels

with her brother about her mother's will, and enquires anxiously about a box she has at Latimers, in which there are some very fine sheets "some roght about and with a border of gold and lasede, and cortins and cossin cloths rought all over, whether these must passe by the name of hur linen, for she gives all her linen to two of hur grandchildren not naming her householde linen but in generly hur linen."

No wonder the housewife of old days was precise and not a little jealous over her possessions. Family sentiment and fine thread were alike woven into the disputed sheets and the finely-wrought damask tablecloths. She herself was spinning the thread of another stock for those who came after her. House linen was not bought at "white sales," and within three or four years fit for nothing but to be converted into dust sheets, and preserved, when fine enough, for bandages. In the country even the skillets could not be so hastily replaced, though their cost was certainly not excessive, while the chairs and tables, the stretching goose, and the coal hammer would be expected to serve at least three generations!

CHAPTER VI

THE TABLE

THE ordinary dinner table of the seventeenth century would to our eyes have presented a rather curious appearance in the variety of utensils in use.

The wooden platters formerly used for food had given place, except in the poorest houses, to pewter, and sometimes to earthenware. A magnificent dinner service in pewter is preserved almost complete at Knole. The plates are all the same size as was indeed usual with all dinner services until the end of the eighteenth century. There are two sizes of dishes, one capable of holding the immense joints of beef which were the pride and mainstay of the English banquets, and the other size which is of about the same dimensions as in these days would be used for the Sunday sirloin, was probably kept for the poultry. The enormous soup tureen and sauceboats give some idea of the great number to be served, who would have sat at the long Elizabethan table in the dining-hall.

The cleaning of pewter so that it shone with almost as great a brilliance as silver itself required some skill and experience, and was a matter to which the careful housewife would have given considerable attention. Sir Ralph Verney, left a widower, did not find his dinner service

8

cleaned to his satisfaction. Possibly the French cook he had imported was too great an artist to superintend these details, and he writes for advice to his sister, Margaret Elmes, the clever housekeeper of the family, known by some of her circle as "Madam Spye-fault." She replies : "For your plaites if they are well washed every mealle with woater and brann, soe hott as theare hands can indewar it, then well rinsed in faire woater, and so sett one by one, befoare the fire, as they may dry quick, I am confident they will dry with out spots, for I never knew any sawce staine soe except it bee pickled rabbits, which stand up on the plait a while, so they will stoaine them filthyly . . . This is all the scill I have, which I have set downe att large."

Mrs. Elmes may have been a noted housekeeper, but she certainly went out of her way to make spelling a difficulty. Meantime, we hope for Sir Ralph's sake that he was not exposed to the horror of pickled rabbit standing up on a dish. Having had several years of more delicate French cookery, he would probably have revolted from some of the dishes considered as delicacies by his stay-at-home sisters !

When the devoted servants of Charles I. melted down their silver dinner services in order to raise a troop for His Majesty, he not infrequently rewarded them with a complete dinner service in pewter, which is jealously preserved by their descendants as a very precious heirloom, and handsomely engraved with their coat of arms.

Even where there was a great deal of silver this usually made a brave show upon the court cupboard, while pewter was used on the table, and we hear of pewter being hired for great entertainments much as we might hire plate and linen at the present time.

It is tantalising to read of the trenchers, the plates, the candlesticks, the "faire silver Tankards" which must at one time, at least have covered the dressers, and on very favoured occasion, have so greatly adorned the heavily laden tables of our ancestors. Silver mugs and porringers were very favourite christening presents then as now, but these also only too often had to be sold or go into the melting pot. We read of one generous-minded lady who wisely suggested when money was scarce that the silver porringer she had presented to her godson should be parted with for what it would fetch. Money being scarce, presents of plate were made in lieu of payment, and plate constantly changed hands between friends, presents being passed on as a matter of course, and with no resultant ill feeling on the part of the donors. This handsome Jacobean silver, massive without being florid, much of which disappeared during the Civil Wars, is naturally very precious, and it is not uncommon in country churches to find the "faire Tankards" being used as chalices for the communion table, the gift probably of some dead and gone squire in the neighbouring Manor house.

In the plate list of Baron Hill, the chancellor of the exchequer, we find, in 1636 :—

	£	s.	d.
A paire of wyne Boles	3.	7.	9
A silver posatt Dish	2.	19.	2
A great and little salt weghing 23 oz.	6.	6.	6
A little book of gold	3.	0.	0
A dozen of silver spoons	6.	15.	9
A paire of fruite dishes	3.	6.	9

How many, we wonder, of these treasures survived to the descendants of a loyal servant of the King ?

During the Restoration the professional and upper

middle classes began to accumulate silver as a necessary
adjunct to the table. Mr. Pepys congratulates himself
several times, with no small surprise, upon the goodly
array of plate he has managed to collect, and a great
deal of the handsome silver of this and the succeeding
age has been preserved for the enjoyment of posterity,
money for foreign wars being raised by other methods
than the melting-pot. The silver of Charles II. is particularly rich and splendid. There are porringers and
cups wonderfully chaste and fashioned, and with no
tendency to be florid like the heavy silver of the later
Georges. But with all the richness and beauty there
is perhaps nothing much more interesting in the silver
of this period than the lovely, but perfectly plain dinner
service given by Charles II. to Nell Gwynne, now in
the London Museum. It is said that many of the
Spaniards who were washed ashore after the wreck of
the Armada were silversmiths, and that some of these
settling at Exeter taught their craft to the English
workmen, and thereby greatly improved both their
designs and workmanship. At all events, we may feel
sure that Mr. Pepys had every reason to smile with
satisfaction over the candlesticks and dishes which
were yearly added to his store.

Earthenware utensils also found their way from the
kitchen on to the dinner-table. Lambeth Delft was a
rather superior pottery in imitation of the Dutch which
had a white enamel, and was generally much decorated.
This was largely used for jars of all sizes, for sack,
claret or white wine, and also for mugs, dishes, platters,
posset pots, etc. There are many examples of this
ware in the museums, and at the London Museum on
a capacious mug with blue birds on a white ground

is the following legend : " James and Elizabeth Greene.
A gift is small—Good Will is all." Out of such a mug
James Greene would have drunk his full measure of
home-brewed ale with a hearty relish.   In the same
place is a set of blue and white plates of a rather later
date, each one of which bears a line of a verse intended, but not altogether calculated, to keep up the
spirits of a desponding housewife.

> "What is a merry man
> Let him do what he can
> To entertain his guests
> With wine and merry jests,
> But if his wife doth frown
> All merryment goes down."

In the latter end of the seventeenth century we hear
a good deal of the Fulham ware, founded by John
Dwight of Christ Church, Oxford.   This was a greyish
white stone ware, called at the time "transparent,"
being indeed the nearest approach to porcelain that
had been arrived at in England.   The most remarkable
specimens of Dwight's work which have survived, are
the pathetic recumbent figure of his little dead daughter
clasping a bunch of flowers, at the Victoria and
Albert Museum, and a life-sized bust of Prince Rupert,
at the British Museum.

But we may conclude from the housewives' inventories that there were also many ordinary objects
of domestic interest manufactured of stoneware at
Fulham, for the Elers, the noted potters who are said
to have introduced salt-glazing into Staffordshire, began
their work here with a ware which they also called porcelaine.   It was probably of Fulham ware in its infancy

that Lady Brilliana's fruit dishes were made which she begs her "sone Ned" to replace for her. "All my fruit dishes are brocken. Thearefore, good Ned, if there be any such blue and white dishes as I used to have for fruit, buy me some; they are not of the ordinary metal of blue and white dishes."

Real china dishes were brought to England as early as Shakespeare's time, either taken from captured Spanish ships of merchandise, or else more legitimately bought at Venice, and by the time Cromwell found it expedient to impose a duty upon them, they must have become a regular article of commerce.

Another furniture of the dinner table the seventeenth century housewife certainly owed to Venice, and that was the glass. James Howell, a Welshman, Histriographer Royal to Charles II., started his varied career as steward to Sir Robert Mansel who had acquired rights in a patent for making glass with pit coal in 1615, one of the monopolies of James I.'s reign. His factory was in Broad Street, and he employed Italian workmen with the result that the glass was not unlike Salviati's glass of the present day. Howell travelled for Sir Robert both in Italy and Spain, collecting ideas and material for improving the glass, but from the specimens which have been preserved, many of which were dug up in the London streets, wine bottles, stems of wine glasses, etc., the glass continued to be distinctly Venetian in character, except that the glass is thicker, and the colours more clouded.

When glass began to be manufactured in England no foreign stuff was allowed to be imported except that from Venice, which was carried round the country by itinerant vendors, and we read of three or four glasses being bought at a time in remote country houses. At Knole are preserved some good specimens of flat wine flagons of this clouded glass. There is also a giant which is said to be a Jeroboam, but which would hold quite sixteen of our ordinary quart bottles. However, at the banquets of the period it is easy to believe that this was not at all too much.

At Knole are also preserved other very curious relics of the sixteenth and seventeenth centuries in the shape of two long glass measures for ale. These are called respectively My Lord's Conscience and My Lady's Conscience, and at first sight My Lady's seems to be very much the longer! A closer examination, however, will prove that it is also very much the narrower!

Failing silver, the pewter and earthenware dishes were probably all put on together, and the clouded coloured glass could not have added greatly to the general effect, even upon the shining whiteness of the tablecloth.

Table cutlery until quite the middle of the seventeenth century was distinctly primitive, a spoon and the blade of a knife being the only implements available, freely assisted by fingers. Under these circumstances it was desirable that the hands should be washed before and after food, and a bowl, usually of rose-water, was handed round, or set before each guest, while a serviette was very much an object of use and not of mere ornament. Apparently each member of the company was not always allowed one to himself, but it was handed round with the basin, and was of a size considered large enough to be shared.

The spoon was an instrument of paramount importance, and yet oddly enough the hostess did not feel

compelled to provide one. Each of the guests was
expected to bring his or her own in a case, and in
this custom we may see the origin of the conventional
christening present of silver knife, fork and spoon.
Three or four hundred years ago no present from a
godparent was more welcome than a set of silver
spoons, and to be born with a silver spoon in one's
mouth was no mere nominal privilege, the lower classes
having to be content with those made of wood, horn
or latten (tinned iron). These spoons all had a wide
shallow bowl, and the handles of the silver ones were
usually much ornamented, some with those figures of
the Apostles, which have been so generally copied.

Silver mugs, were an equally useful and favourite form
of christening present while glass was still scarce, for
earthenware was not suitable to the best society.

The wooden handled knives were slim and sharp,
and the lady we hear of, who suffered from an excessive
gentility unusual in that robust age, accomplished a
feat of skilled and accurate gymnastics when she
balanced one pea, or half a pea, upon the blade.

Until the middle of the seventeenth century forks
were a luxury, treated rather as toys, elegant, with
jewelled handles, wherewith the ladies might pick
daintily at their sweetmeats.

In the reign of James I., a Somersetshire squire, of
the name of Coryate, made a grand tour on the con-
tinent, and in Italy he became much enamoured of
the fork already in general use in that country. He
brought it home to England where, however, it was
not at first received with any enthusiasm. He pushed
his cause steadily, however, meeting British prejudice
with true British obstinacy. The fork was derided on

the stage and from the pulpit, but none the less by
the end of the reign of Charles II. few self-respecting
English tables were without them. The carving fork
naturally made the greatest innovation both in manners
and to the meat itself. While there was only a knife,
coverings of paper had to be placed on that part of the
joint which was seized by the left hand. This would
have been comparatively simple in handling a leg of
mutton where there was a bone to lay hold of, but
must have presented considerable difficulties in the
case of a sirloin. No doubt the paper frills which are
still to be seen adorning cutlet bones are a survival
of the means taken by the lady of the house to preserve
her hand in something approaching cleanliness.

With the arrival of the fork, however, all this was
changed ; carving became a finer and more elegant
art, and the napkin little more than an extra decoration
for the table. At fashionable tables under the Restoration, serviettes were folded in the form of birds and
animals, fruits and flowers, and it was considered an
unpardonable breach of good manners to undo these
beautiful structures.

Mr. Pepys when giving a dinner party mentions that
he was "mightily pleased with the fellow that came to lay
the cloth and fold the napkins ; which I like so well as
that I am resolved to give him forty shillings to teach my
wife to do it." We seem to hear this jovial and complacent host calling upon his guests to admire the
fantastic forms before them as well as the newly acquired
plate and the excellent dinner provided, while they sat
against a background of the King's houses, Whitehall,
Hampton Court, Greenwich, and Windsor, with which the
four panels of Mr. Pepys' dining-room were decorated.

A day arrived, a century later, when serviettes were
swept altogether as a needless luxury from the board of the
thrifty housewife, and only returned as an inconspicuous
but necessary adjunct to every meal, at least in middle
class houses, toward the latter part of the nineteenth
century. In his journal to Stella in 1711, Swift says that,
" After dinner we had coarse D'Oyly napkins fringed at
each end upon the table to drink with."   Thomas D'Oyly
at the "Nun" in Henrietta Street, Covent Garden, a seventeenth century linen draper had invented a variety of
linen goods which might be cheap and genteel, and
bequeathed his name to the present minute mat under
the finger bowl, the direct descendant of Swift's fringed
napkin.

Meantime the fork probably made its way very slowly
into houses in the country. When it came it was two
pronged, three pronged, and anything as time went on up
to six-pronged. In the seventeenth century, while they
were still scarce, the handles were probably silver. The
charming green handles and other materials upon which
we now set a proper value belonged probably to the steel
pronged fork of the following century. As late as 1729
the poet Gay begs Swift, when the latter is invited to stay
with the Duchess of Queensberry, not to eat with the
point of his knife, nor to despise a fork with three
prongs. Swift replies in self-justification that at a poor
house forks were only bi-dental, that at Mr. Pope's, it
was impossible, without a knife, to convey a morsel of
beef with the incumbrance of mustard and turnips into
your mouth !

Charles II. was supposed to have greatly improved the
table manners of the English, but foreigners still found
much to criticise. Sorbière remarks that the English

scarcely ever make use of forks or ewers, " they just dip
their hands into a bason of water." Cosmo also finds that
there are still no forks at this period on the English table.
A little later some "Rules of Civility" were translated
from the French for the benefit of the fashionable world.
In these, readers are warned not to wipe knife or fork
on bread or the cloth, but on napkins. They are also
requested not to pick their teeth at table with knife or
fork, and it is added that "some are so curious that they
will not endure a spoon to be used in two several
dishes." Such injunctions and commentaries read
curiously in these days when our nation justifiably prides
itself on its superior table manners, and has not infrequently shuddered from some such lapses as the above at
a *table d'hôte* in other countries.

But to return to our housewife of a rather earlier
period. After she had marshalled in her dishes it was her
still further duty to do all the carving, assisted if the party
were a large one by her gentlewoman or any other lady
present. For this purpose all the ladies sat together at
the head of the table, while the men sat at the lower end.
It was arduous work, but no doubt the housewife made a
virtue of necessity, and felt her position to be entirely
one of dignity. Even after William III. had introduced
the Dutch fashion of setting the sexes alternately, she
does not seem to have immediately relinquished the duty
of carver. In the opening years of the eighteenth
century Lady Mary Pierrepont, afterwards Lady Mary
Wortley Montagu, as a young girl, had to preside at her
father, the Earl of Kingston's table, and not only had to
"persuade and provoke his guests to eat voraciously,"
but to carve every dish with her own hands, carefully
choosing the right morsel for each man according to his

rank, the squires who sat on either side of her not being allowed to offer their assistance. She received instructions from a carving master three times a week, and was obliged to eat her own dinner an hour or so beforehand when the Earl had company.

In the seventeenth century the ladies were equally well instructed, though before the introduction of the fork their work was certainly less delicate. Mrs. Hannah Woolley in the "Gentlewoman's Companion, or a Guide to the female Sex," printed in 1675 at the *Adam and Eve* in "Little Brittain," gives the very curious terms then used for carving with equally quaint explanations. The variety of terms is bewildering, and the embryo housewives of the day must have required to apply their minds to the mastering of them more seriously than they did to the rules of English grammar and spelling. In referring to small birds she was told to "Thigh that Woodcock, Mince that Plover, Wing that Quail or Partridge, Allay that Pheasant, Untack that Curlew, Disfigure that Peacock, Unbrace that Mallard, Spoil that Hen, Lift that Swan, Rear that Goose," and so on. Here is the explanation of how to *Unbrace a Mallard.* "Raise up the Pinion and the Leg, but take them not off, raise the Merrythought from the Breast, and lace it down sloppingly on each side the Breast with your knife." The "sloppingly" is painfully suggestive of what all table processes must have been before the introduction of the fork. If you want to "mince" your partridge, sauce him with wine, powder of ginger and salt, and so set him on a chafing dish of coals to keep warm. Use a quail after the same manner.

Then follow the dramatic directions for attacking the fish. "Chine that Salmon, String that Lamprey, Splat that Pike, Sauce that Plaice, Culper that Trout, Tame that Crab, Barb that Lobster," etc. The terms are practically the same in all the other many cookery books of the period, and must have required much learning.

In 1653, the author of the accomplished "Lady Rich's Closet of Rareties" begs the "ingenious gentlewoman of the period" to use a fork in carving, although the instrument is still a rarity. She also instructs her in the manners expected of a gentlewoman at the table. She must "observe to keep her body straight, and lean not by any means with her elbow, nor by ravenous gesture discover a voracious appetite. She must not talk when she has meat in her mouth, nor "smack like a pig," nor venture to eat spoon meat so hot that the tears stand in her eyes. The author adds that, "It is very uncomely to drink so large a draught that your breath is almost gone, and you are forced to recover yourself. Throwing down your liquor as into a funnel is an action fitter for a juggler than a gentlewoman." She is also reminded to distribute the best pieces first, a most important rule.

The instructions as regards manners remind us a little of the nursery, but in the low countries at this period there was a theory that in the absence of "march panes and such juncates, it's good manners if any there be, to carry away a piece of apple-pie in your pocket." The old-fashioned English nurse would hardly at any time have approved of such a proceeding.

CHAPTER VII

THE HERB GARDEN AND THE STILL ROOM

IN the beautiful old English gardens of the sixteenth
and seventeenth centuries with their formal terraces,
their fish ponds, their bowling greens and cut yew
walks, their mazes and their flower borders, the country
housewife had her own concern.

While the squire and his steward and gardeners saw
to the planting of fresh trees in the orchard, to the
clipping of the yews, the pleaching of the alleys, the
housewife attended to her herb and her kitchen gardens,
the geometrical design of her flower knots and the
husbandry of her bees.

In the garden at Sayes Court, which she inherited
from her father, Sir Richard Browne, while Mr.
Evelyn planted his choice trees and shrubs, the
cedars from Libanus and the mulberries from Lan-
guedoc, his wife gave much personal attention to
her flower and herb garden. The "knots" and
borders were full of gay flowers of the homely
as well as the more rare kind. Roses, violets, stocks
and gillyflowers were there, not only for pleasure,
but for the perfumes to be distilled from them, as
well as for the candied sweetmeats into which
they could presently be transformed for the table.
This was the garden where Abraham Cowley, a near

neighbour, loved to examine his host's horticultural
novelties, where Jeremy Taylor discoursed with poor
precocious little Richard Evelyn, and where Mr. Pepys,
a little bored, a little supercilious, but a good deal
amused, discovered the glass bee-hives, so " you may see
the bees making their honey and combs mighty
pleasantly."

There were many fashions for the planting of the
housewife's garden. William Lawson, early in the
seventeenth century, devoted a considerable space in
his " New Orchard and Garden " to instructing her in
the laying out of her ground, in the sowing and planting
of her herbs and flowers, in the choice of her soil and in
the keeping of her bees. He gives many elaborate
designs and devices for her knots or flower-beds, but
notes that while these must always be square, they
should be bordered about with roses, privet, hops,
rosemary, etc. The passion for box edgings probably
came in a little later.

While Lawson decides that there must be two gardens,
he maintains that there must be certain herbs in the
flower garden, and the kitchen garden must not want for
flowers. The flower garden should be hedged with
lavender and rosemary, and the herbs are to include
roses and violets, which are of use in reviving the senses
both in flowers and water. Lawson was no formalist,
and the kitchen gardens of to-day with their flower-
edged rows of vegetables, and the herbaceous borders,
their tall hollyhocks, lilies and poppies behind, and their
tangle of lower growing flowers in front alike owe
something to the taste and discretion of the seventeenth
century gardeners.

Andrew Marvell in one of his charming garden poems

tells us of another pattern no less attractive for the housewife's garden :—

> " How well the skilful gardener drew
> Of flowers and herbs, this dial new,
> Where, from above, the milder sun
> Does through a fragrant zodiac run.
> And, as it works, the industrious bee
> Computes its time as well as we !
> How could such sweet and wholesome hours
> Be reckoned but with herbs and flowers ? "

The sundial fashion here described was probably rather a fantasy for the gardens of the rich than for the ordinary kitchen garden, but the herbs mingled with flowers were not infrequently planted in circles round the sundial, too seldom now to be found in the modern kitchen garden.   In the corner might be a small pleached arbour where the lady, heated with the effort of stooping to cut her flowers and herbs, might,

> " . . . steal into the Pleachéd Bower
> Where honeysuckles ripened by the sun
> Forbid the sun to enter."

Lord Bacon in his familiar but always delightful essay on Gardens, says that while sweet-briar and wallflowers " are very delightful to be set under a parlour or lower chamber window," and the flowers of the lime tree and honeysuckles " should be somewhat afar off," " those which perfume the air most delightfully, not passed by as the rest, but being trodden upon and crushed, are three, that is burnet, wild thyme and water-mints. Therefore, you are to set whole alleys of them, to have the pleasure when you walk or tread."

This idea of treading upon herbs to bring out their
lean and pungent fragrance seems to have survived into
he eighteenth century. One of the few genuine herb
:ardens remaining in England is at St. Anne's Hill, near
Chertsey on Thames, originally the home of Charles
ames Fox, and now the property of Sir Albert K. Rollit.
Here the garden which surrounds the old Georgian
house, with its cedars of Lebanon on the smooth shaven
awns, the small deer park, and above all the herb
:arden, are very much as the statesman knew them at the
·lose of the eighteenth century. In the herb garden, the
herbs grow in no particular order, and are not raised
above the level of the turf walks, and indeed offer
hemselves to be trodden upon. Here are still rosemary,
borage, thyme, sage, fennel, mint, parsley, rue, lavender,
chives, southernwood, tarragon, savory, hyssop, chervil
and marjoram growing in charming confusion, enclosed
by the' thick, old-world beech and yew hedges which
have been there in all probability as long or longer than
he house itself. The modern herb garden at Broughton
Castle has been laid out with this same idea of crushing
he fragrance from the herbs under foot, and set about
with thick hedges and overshadowed by splendid trees—
t gives us a very good idea of the herb garden of the
past of which it is a careful reproduction.

Under the French influence of the restoration, the
knot of the English gardener gave way to the no less
decorative *parterre* of Le Notre. This was followed by
the Dutch taste of William, which in absurdly exaggerating
the formality and the topiary work of the formal garden,
unhappily initiated the downfall of the latter.

In the singularly artificial age which followed, there
came a demand for what was called Nature, and Pope's

garden at Twickenham was laid out in the natural taste, under the architect Kent's influence. Presently from the mountains of Savoy came that cry for Nature, from the embittered philosopher, who, in his own manner of living, consistently outraged all the laws of that nature which he so ardently proclaimed. So amazing and widespread was Jean Jacque's influence that it actually reached the gardens of England. In an artificial desire for natural effects, the straight dignified walks between clipped yews were transformed into twisted paths of no purpose. The fish ponds became serpentine pieces of ornamental water. Mellow brick walls were replaced by Ha-has and the sunk fence. The grottoes beloved of Pope sprang up in unexpected places with their ugly decorations of shells and looking-glasses. Artificial mounds and "scattered clumps that nod at one another" adorned the rich man's garden, and the ladies found little room left for their flower beds, flowers being indeed the last consideration.

This era of destructive taste had been initiated by Kent before the days of Rousseau, but the worst offender was his successor, known as "Capability" Brown on account of his unfortunate habit of seeing capabilities in every old world garden for successful transformation into the much admired "park-like" scenery! Happily the fashion did not last long enough, or was not sufficiently universal, to destroy many of the more beautiful gardens of England both great and small, which have survived to be the joy and pride of succeeding generations.

Through all these changes and chances, however, from the square garden of the Middle Ages with its strong enclosing walls or thick-set hedges, until towards the close of the eighteenth century, when it became

THE HERB GARDEN AT BROUGHTON CASTLE.

merged in the kitchen garden, the herb garden held its own.

To the seventeenth century housewife, her herb garden was a matter of very vital importance. A knowledge of the uses of the different herbs, for medicinal no less than for culinary purposes, being an important part of her education. Where doctors were few and at a considerable distance, she must be responsible for the "care of the family touching their health," and not only of the family, but of all her poor dependents in the village. She must know "how to administer many wholesome receipts and medicines for the good of their healths, as well as to prevent the first occasion of sickness." She had several books to instruct her, and was further aided by the experience and wisdom of her elders, a generous absence of scientific knowledge, and an unlimited faith on the part of the patient in the very remarkable cures to which the latter was occasionally subjected.

Of these books John Gerard's "Herbinal" was perhaps the most famous. John Gerard was for twenty years gardener to Lord Burghley and helped him to lay out the magnificent gardens of Theobalds, and he also introduced many new flowers into England. Later he became a master in "chirurgerie" in London, had himself a famous garden of simples in Holborn, and another granted to him near Somerset House on condition that he allowed Queen Anne of Denmark the use of his herbs. Early in the century followed Gervase Markham's comprehensive book of "Country Contentments," and later, Nicholas Culpepper, described as a gentleman student in physic and astrology published his little book of medicines made of English herbs.

A perusal of these books and others of the same period

shew us that every age has its own fashion in diseases as well as in remedies, and perhaps the fearsome cures applied by the ladies of the seventeenth century were not much more alarming to their victims than the experiments of modern science may be to-day. Of their efficacy we can say less : it was rather a question of faith being strong enough in most cases to sustain the human frame through its more ordinary maladies, and, as a consequence of the survival of the fittest.

Even where doctors were in attendance the housewife constantly acted as dispenser with the herbs of her own garden. The housekeeper at Claydon had a wonderful "purginge drink as she made for the maids and the upholsterer," to which the doctor refers with respect and admiration, but suggests that some burdock seeds or root should be added. The upholsterer was unfortunately given too much of the potent draught and was like "to make a dye of it," but survived to cherish we should imagine a wholesome dread of Mrs. Westerholt's remedies. In a day, however, when bleeding was the first and most obvious remedy resorted to, when bleeding cups were made in every variety of metal and ware, and when to be bled twice a year—in the spring and the autumn—was considered as desirable as it is sometimes thought now to take a tonic, all doses were of proportionate strength and magnitude.

Culpepper who, as we have said, was also an astrologer, had very strong views as to the planets by which the different herbs are governed, attention to which he considered greatly affected their utility. Hops, being under the dominion of Mars, were believed in for cleansing the blood which may be a minor reason for so much ale being drunk.

Lavender is owned by Mercury, and "is of special good use for all the Griefs and Panes of the Head and Braines that proceed of a cold cause. Because Lettuces are owned by the Moon they cool and moisten what heat and dryness Mars causeth—the juyce of Lettuce mixed or boyled with Oyl of Roses, and applied to the forehead and temples, procureth sleep and easeth the Head-ache proceeding of an hot cause." To rosemary he gives a high character for he says being claimed by the sun it is good for all diseases external and internal. The doctor's observations about Basil are so quaint as to be worth quoting almost in full, as shewing the weird counsels upon which our forefathers had to rely for relief in their sufferings.

"This is a herb which all Authors are together by the Ears about, and rail at one another like lawyers. . . . For mine own part I presently found that speech true— *Non nostrum niter nos tantus componere tites.* And away to Dr. Reason went I, who told me it was an Herb of Mars, and under the *Scorpion*, and perhaps therefore called *Basilicon*, and then no marvel if it carry a kind of virulent quality with it. Being applied to the place bitten by a venomous Beast, or stung by a Wasp or Hornet, it speedily draws the Poison to it ; *Every like draws his like.* . . . Hollerius, a French Physician, affirms upon his own knowledge, that an acquaintance of his by common smelling to it, had a *Scorpion* bred in his Brain, something is the matter this Herb and Rew will not grow together, no, nor near one another : and we know Rue is as great an enemy to Poyson, as any grows . . . I dare write no more of it."

The seed of soft rush might be given in wine and water to provoke sleep, but with caution "lest the Party that takes it wake not until the Resurrection." Culpepper explains the proverb, "I care not a rush for them," by saying that rushes are of little account in medicine since every remedy can be made up without them. The housewife certainly had much to learn before she could be trusted to dispense these alarming herbs with safety; if she were wise she probably let such doubtful things as basil and rushes severely alone.

In all the old books there are also minute directions as to the way of gathering, drying, and preserving simples and their juices for syrups, distilled waters, oils and conserves. The right moment for gathering your herb was often of supreme importance. Thus *Rosa Solis*, or *sun-dew*, a little red hairy bog plant, must be gathered (if possible) at the full of the moon, when the sun shineth before noon. Of the leaves of this little plant, which however must not be touched or washed in the process, a comforting cordial could be made, mixed with aqua vitæ, liquorice, dates and sugar. This compound required to stand in a pewter pot or glass for three days and nights, and afterwards distilled through a lymbeck, and mixed with ale should be taken at bed-time, or in the morning fasting. If these directions are faithfully obeyed, the weakest body in the world, or one in consumption, will speedily become strong and lusty, and have a "marvellous hungry stomack."

There seem to have been a diversity of opinion about stills. Culpepper did not approve of a pewter still. He says that waters should be distilled in sand, but as this is difficult to explain in writing he will not attempt it! With the same frankness he admits that he cannot teach the preserving of flowers with vinegar and salt, having no skill in it himself. "I never saw any that I remember, save only cowslip flowers, and that was a great fashion in Sussex when I was a Boy." This learned authority notwithstanding, the preservation of flowers, rose leaves, violets, etc., was very fashionable since these were, as we have seen, necessary to adorn every dinner table, and in this matter the housewife could probably dispense with Mr. Culpepper's instructions.

In the seventeenth century every housewife had her own recipe for preservation against the plague. The *naïveté* of most of these is a very powerful argument in favour of the theory that, pure faith by whatever name it is called, is the most important factor in illness, or at least infection. When Sir Ralph Verney went to town in June 1665, while the plague was raging. "Aunt Isham" tells him to "ware a quill as is filed up with quicsilver and sealed up with hard waxe and soed up in a silk thinge with a string to ware about your neck." This, she affirms is a "sartine preventive" and his horse should wear the same on his head. She also recommends him to have "Lente figgis in a readiness" which should be roasted and mashed together and mixed with Mithredate.

Here is a simple but perhaps more scientific preservative. "Take of Sage, Rue, Briar leaves, or Elder leaves, of each an handful, stamp them and straine them with a quart of white wine, and put thereto a little Ginger, and a good spoonful of the best treacle, and drink thereof morning and evening." "To bite and chaw" the dried root of Angelica, to smell a nosegay made of the tasselled end of a ship-rope, presumably for the sake of the tar, are among the least complicated of the many suggestions for prevention against infection. Fine powdered ivory mixed with old ale and mithridate

and several herbs, was also a sovereign remedy much
recommended. When once the pestilence had declared
itself, resort might be had to a live pigeon cut in two,
applied to the sore, in default of a less unpleasant plaster
of egg, honey, and finely chopped herbs. That the
patient was instantly wrapped in woollen clothes, with
hot cloths or bricks made "extream hot" applied to the
soles of his feet, proves that through all the violent and
fantastic remedies of the day, to which a speedy death
might seem preferable, ran a redeeming vein of good
common sense. The virtues of a mustard plaster were
fully appreciated, though why to the mustard should
have been added vinegar, the crumbs of brown bread,
honey and figs, is not apparent.

Of a certain French lady it was once observed that
"*Elle passe sa vie à faire difficilement les chose faciles*," and
from our superior heights of scientific enlightenment
and convenience it may seem to us that our grandmothers spent a great deal of time in preparing over-
elaborated remedies. We must remember, however,
that they were working in the dark, separated perhaps
from the available medical knowledge of the day by
several miles of difficult roads, and that they were after
all taking more personal trouble, however mistaken
for their patient, whether it were husband, child, servant,
or some poor dependant, than we who to-day can call
in a doctor and trained nurse for the most ordinary
malady, and relieve ourselves of the added strain of
responsibility. True the patient might die of his broken
bones, or more probably they might be beyond mending
before the "Oyle of Swallows," which took nine days to
prepare and was compounded of almost every conceiv-
able herb and other object, except happily swallows,

was ready, but if he were still alive it was no doubt
ultimately soothing, and the housewife had certainly
put her best skill into it.

For the "*Frenzie*, or inflammation of the Caules of the
brain," it was recommended to squirt the juice of beets
up into the patient's nostrils by way of cleansing his
head. He must then be given to drink posset ale in
which violet leaves and "Lettice" have been boiled, "and
it will suddenly bring him to a very Temperate mildness,
and make the passion of Frenzie forsake him." Daisy
roots mixed with salt and other ingredients are recommended for toothache, and this was an instance in
which probably the salt alone would have been at least
as efficacious, but as we know simplicity can only be
attained through a complicated and arduous education.

A deaf person again must wait a fortnight for the oil
which will come out of a gray eel which has been buried
for that length of time in an earthenware pot in a dung
hill, no other oil being considered efficacious."

Such being the attitude of mind, it is no wonder that
when the light of science began to spread the "quack"
was really preferred by many intelligent people to the
genuine doctor. In the case of one little blind girl,
a "mountybank" recommended by Prince Rupert was
preferred to Daubeney Turberville, the oculist of the
day, who had undertaken to cure her. Even Sir Ralph
Verney, a most reasonable person, when told by his
good friend and uncle, Dr. Denton, to drink asses' milk
with sugar of roses, preferred to follow the advice of
a quack, and also, like many another old gentleman
before and since, to do a little doctoring on his own
account. So he begs a friend in London to buy him
a "role of extract of Licoris for 1s."

The visit of a doctor in those days was certainly a serious matter, for he often had to stay in the house two or three days to watch the results of his violent remedies, and being sent for from house to house over rough country, travelling usually on horseback, the country practitioner at all events had an arduous time. He seems, however, to have been well remunerated, and during the Civil War, when money was scarce and lady patients at all events still required his services, handsome presents of plate were a constant form of remuneration.[1]

Human nature is much the same in all ages, and we read of ladies who loved to have a perpetual new doctor with whom to discuss their "disordered spleens," and of one doctor, bolder than the rest, who gave dire offence by begging his patient to take less physic.

Lady Brilliana Harley was most earnest in her injunctions to her son Ned while at Oxford, in the matter alike of his physical and moral welfare. While she sends him "turkey pyes," and "Stokes apells," by the carrier, and insists upon seeing the patterns that the young man has chosen for his clothes, she spends much time in concocting home-made remedies for any possible ailment with which he might be afflicted. On one occasion she recommends him "bolsome" which she considers a most "sufferin" (sovereign) thing, but she is sure he takes too much exercise, which overheats his blood. In the spring her maternal anxiety struggles with her Calvinistic piety as regards fast days, and she

---

[1] Sir Ralph Verney writes to Mary after the birth of a little son in London, that if Dr. Denton should absolutely refuse money, she must lay the amount, £30, out in plate for him, and suggests six trencher plates and a pair of little candlesticks.

writes: "I purpose if it please God to remember you
with some of Bromton dyet against Lent. I wisch
you may not eat too much fisch. I know you like it,
but I thinke it is not so good for you. I hope you have
something over your bed's head." Another time she
sends him some "besser stone," to be taken at night,
and adds the pious hope that "the Lord bless all means
to you."

Ned, a young man at Oxford, probably preferred the
turkey pies to the medical remedies, and cheerfully
accepted the apples, if he felt less grateful for "The
Returne of Prayer," which was concealed in the basket
under them. Presently he feels that the tables may be
judiciously turned, and suggests to his mother, who has
written him perpetual complaints of her ill-health that
she shall be bled, the one remedy which occurs to
his youthful imagination. She replies briefly: "I thank
you for desiring me to be let blood, shure if I were
avers to it, yet you might persuade me," but beyond
this refuses to commit herself.

Her maternal solicitude and jealousy are alike up in
arms, however, when she hears he has been accepting
remedies from other people, and still complains of his
cold. "I believe ye sneezing powder did you noe good,"
she writes with a touch of feminine vindictiveness, "and
let it teach you ye wisdome not to take medicines out
of a strange hand." Not unnaturally she places greater
faith in the two grains of orampotabeley she has herself
sent him, and which must be stirred till it be dissolved.
"Your cousin Frank thinks it will do miracles." On
another occasion she complains that "It pleases God
that I continue ill with my coold, but it is, as they say,
a newe diseas," probably one of the earliest visitations

of influenza. Ned and his mother were, however, the best of friends, and the undergraduate seems to have shown no offence when the gardener was sent to enquire into his welfare at Oxford, and reported him as much grown.

All those who grew herbs for the market reaped a fine harvest during the plague. Rosemary went up from 12d. an armful to six shillings a handful. As a preventive to infection, aromatic herbs were both carried on the person enclosed in jewels worn round the neck, or in pouncet boxes or vinaigrettes. The gold-headed cane of the physician originally held a vinaigrette as a protection, and herbs were also strewn in the churches or in any place of public assembly. There is a curious survival of this habit in the stiff little bouquets carried by the clergy at the distribution of the King's Bounty in Westminster Abbey on Maundy Thursday. When such people as the High Almoner, the Sub-Almoner, the Dean of Westminster, and other dignified clerics had to be brought into close contact with the very poor, it was no doubt considered a wise precaution, or at least a mitigation of possible inconvenience that they should have a bunch of aromatic herbs to apply to their noses !

Mr. Pepys was a great believer in charms. He wore a hare's foot against the colic. He also quotes several rhymed charms, among others:—

For stenching of blood—

> "Christ was of a Virgin born,
> And He was pricked with a Thorn;
> And it did neither bell, nor swell:
> And I trust in Jesus this never will."

Or for a burning—

> "There came three Angels out of the East;
> The one brought fire, the other brought frost.
> Out fire; in frost,
> In the Name of the Father, and Son, and Holy Ghost.
> Amen."

While a touching faith in such charms still existed in the minds of educated people, and Wiseman, surgeon to Charles II., believed in the virtue of His Majesty's Touch for the King's Evil, practical medicine made, under the Restoration, a start upon more modern lines. The Charter was granted to the Royal Society in 1662, and the College of Physicians founded the first idea of a dispensary in 1687. There were Physic Gardens at Oxford, and a famous one at Chelsea, which still exists, but it was the middle of the eighteenth century before active assistance, by the founding of hospitals, was given to the poorer classes. These continued to depend in the country upon the herbs and the nostrums of their richer neighbours, who, in turn, eluded the scientific recommendations of their doctors whenever possible.

But it was not only these alarming remedies which were prepared from the herbs in the still-room. At least as much attention was given to the preservation of the complexion, the care of the hair, the eyes and the teeth, as to internal remedies.

For a "pimpled or saucy" face, an ointment made of roasted eggs and white copperas is highly recommended, and one lady begs another to use myrrh water to prolong an appearance of youth. Southernwood, burnt to ashes and mixed with oil, is what Lady Brilliana would have called a "sufferin thing" for making hair grow; and a drink for "a pearl in the eye" was to be concocted of marigold, fennel, and mayweed mixed with a pint of beer, to be drunk in bed at night, or "next the heart," that is to say, fasting in the morning. For pain in the eyes such simple remedies as celadine and rose-water, distilled by the housewife were permitted, though other and more elaborate messes were earnestly recommended.

Tooth washes were innumerable. Great care seems to have been taken of the teeth, and in a day when a bath was a rare event, requiring much preparation and a doctor's instructions, the teeth were to be washed morning and evening, and even after food. Tooth brushes, in use in Paris by the middle of the century had not yet reached England, but must have been brought over by the exiled gentleman, who returned with the Restoration. In the opening years of the century a famous dentifrice was composed of vinegar, rosemary, myrrh, ammonia, dragon's herb, rock alum, and fine cinnamon, to be all boiled together. Then honey was to be added, and the mixture was to be transferred to a clean bottle, and be used before and after meat. The pill slabs and the earthenware pots for holding all these unguents and accessories to the toilet may still be seen in the museums. If they were less ornamental additions to the ladies' dressing-tables than the glass and silver and gold and tortoiseshell of modern times, they were no less useful.

The distillation of water and perfumes were also of enormous importance. The earthenware still seems to have been considered preferable to pewter for this purpose also. First and foremost there was aqua vitæ, which was in such frequent use in the dispensary that it is perhaps worth quoting one old receipt in full :—

"Take of rosemary flowers two handfuls, of marjoram, Winter savory, rosemary, rew, unset-time, Germander, rybwort, Hartstongue, mounseare, white worme-wood, buglosse, red sage, liverwort, hoarehound, fine lavender, issocrops, penyroyal, red fenell, of each of these one handful; of elicampane roots, clean pared and sliced, two handfuls. Then take all these aforesaid and shred them, but not wash them, then take four gallons and more of strong ale, and one gallon of sack-lecs, and put all these aforesaid herbs shred into it, and then put into it one pound of licorice bruised, half a pound of aniseeds clean sifted and bruised, and of mace and nutmegs bruised, of each one ounce : then put altogether into your stilling pot, close covered with rye paste, and make a soft fire under your pot, and as the head of the limbeck heateth, draw out your hot water and put in cold, keeping the head of your limbeck still with cold water, but see your fire be not too rash at the first, but let your water come at leisure and take heed unto your stilling, that your water change not white, for it is not so strong as the first draught is, and when the water is distilled, take a gallon glass with a wide mouth, and put therein a pottle of the best water and the clearest and put into it a pottle of *rosa solis*, half a pound of *dates* bruised, and one ounce of granes, and half a pound of sugar, half an ounce of seed pearle beaten, three leaves of fine gold, stir all these together well, then stop your glass, and set it in the sun the space of one or two months, and then clarify it and use it at your discretion : for a spoonful or two at a time is sufficient, and the virtues are infinite." So indeed they should be, and it must be remembered that aqua vitæ was, as a rule, only one ingredient recommended in an elaborate mixture of many others.

Perfumes and pomanders of all sorts were in great request. No fine lady's costume in times of plague was complete without a pomander chain. The pomanders were little balls made of various aromatic herbs, liquid aloes, nutmeg, and balm, moulded together with fine wax, and dried in the sun. The housewife also made her own washing balls, which consisted of various herbs and other ingredients pounded into a paste with just enough soap used to stiffen them, and were in common use until early in the eighteenth century when soap itself was introduced as a more convenient substitute.

It was apparently the fashion to perfume the elaborate fringed and decorated gloves which were worn by both ladies and gentlemen. For this purpose the gloves were actually boiled (it must be supposed that the colours of those days were fast) in musk and rose-water, and a mixture of herbs. They were then to be partially dried and rubbed with some stuff called Benjamine, amber-grease and musk ground up with oil of almonds, after which they must be hung up to dry, or better still, run the instructions, "let them dry in your bosom."

The preserving of fruit, and the brewing of home-made wines, of cowslip, elder, etc., kept the housewife and her handmaids unceasingly busy in the summer. Foreign wines also had to be doctored according to taste. So much white wine was drunk as well as being used for cooking and medicinal purposes, and after the journey it constantly had to have extra flavouring added to suit the strong English palates of the seventeenth century.

Mead and metheglin were other popular drinks which were made in the still-rooms. They were both concocted of honey and herbs. Sir Kenelm Digby's recipe for an " excellent white Meathe " is as follows :—

" Take one gallon of Honey, and four of water. Boil and scum them till there rise no more scum, then put in your spice a little bruised, which is most of Cinnamon, a little Ginger, a little Mace, a very little Cloves. Boil it with the spice in it, till it bear an egge. Then take it from the fire and let it cool in a woodden vessel, till it be but lukewarm, which this quantity will be in four or five or six hours. Then put into it a hot tost of whitebread, spread over on both sides pretty thick with fresh barm : that will make it presently work. Let it work twelve hours, close covered with cloves. Then turn it with a Runlet wherein Sack hath been that is somewhat too big for that quantity of Liquor; for example, that it fill not by a gallon. You may put a little Lemon-peel in with it. After it hath remained in the vessel a week or ten days, draw it into Bottles. You may begin to drink it after two or three months. But it will be better after a year. It will be very sprightly and quick and pleasant and pure white."

We wonder whether it was from the same recipe that Lady Brilliana Harley's " litell runlet of meathe " was made which she sent up to Sir Robert, in London, and which had been so especially fancied by her father. " I send it up now," she writes, " because I think carage when it is ready to drincke does it hurt ; thearefore, and please you to let it rest and then taste it, if it be good, I pray you let my father have it, because he spake to me for such meathe."

We must confess that it passes our imagination to

think what the "runlet of pickled cockles" can have been like which on one occasion rejoiced Lord Cork's heart as a Christmas present from Ireland.

Some Irish Usquebagh was sent to Lord Coventry by Lord Cork's orders with the following recommendation : "If it please his lordship, next his hart, in the morning to drink a little as it is prepared and qualified it will help to digest all raw humours, expel wind and keep his inward parts warm all day after without any offence to his stomach."

CHAPTER VIII

THE SERVANTS

BEFORE the Civil Wars, the servant problem was practically unknown. In the Middle Ages the line drawn between the menial and non-menial classes was a much slighter one for, in the greater houses, the upper servants were constantly men of considerable social rank. Gentlemen's sons were sent into noblemen's houses as little boys to be trained in their duties which consisted partly in waiting at their lord's table, and " The School of Vertue and booke of good Nourture for Children," written by John Russell in the preceding century, was full of admirable advice and injunctions as to the children's table manners, and instructions how they were to conduct themselves generally.

But the fifteenth and sixteenth centuries gradually brought considerable economic changes, and in the great days of Queen Elizabeth men had other and far more important pursuits than to occupy themselves solely with domestic administrations.

There were still, however, a certain number of gentlemen retainers. Even in the seventeenth century, Lord Cork had many of his own relations, both male and female, among his upper and confidential servants, and in his own magnificent and autocratic manner he arranged their marriages and provided them with portions.

He drew up very stringent rules for what he calls the government of his family at Stalbridge where a manner of living, which seems to belong rather to the splendid prodigality of a previous age, was still apparently practised.

" 1. Firste, all ye servants excepte such as are officers, or are otherwise employed, shall meet everye morning before dinner and every night after supper, at Prayers.

" 2. That there be Lodgings fitting for all ye Earl of Cork's servants to lye in ye House.

" 3. That it shall be lawful for ye Steward to examine any subordinate servant of ye whole Familie concerning any Complainte or Misdemeanor committed, and to dismiss and put awaye any inferior servant that shall live dissolutelie or disorderlie, either in ye House or abroad, without ye especial command of the Earl of Cork to the contraire.

" 4. That there be a certain number of ye gents appointed to sitt at ye Steward's Table ye lyke at ye Wayters' Table, and ye reste to sitt in ye Hall at ye longe Table.

" 5. That there be a Clarke of ye Kytchin, to take care of such Provision as is brought into ye House, and to have an espitial eye to ye several Tables that are kept either above Staires, or in ye Kitchen and other places.

" 6. That all ye Women Servants under ye degree of Chamber, maydes be certenlie knowne by their Names to ye Steward, and not altered or changed upon everye occasion without ye Consent of ye Steward, and no Schorers to be admitted in ye House.

" 7. That ye officers everye Fridaye night bringe in theire Bills unto ye Steward, whereby he may collect what hath been spent, and what remaynes weeklie in ye House.

" Thomas Cross his orders for ye keeping of ye House, 1638."

The Squire in his manor house, however, did not live in this imposing fashion, and the domestic arrangement of these less exalted people are, on the whole, a more interesting study in the evolution of our own, from which they are not, after all, so immeasurably removed.

In the lesser houses the upper servants were generally chosen from the families of the most respectable tenants. Thus the interests of employer and employed were to a great extent identical, and there is no doubt that a strong tie of mutual affection bound them together. The servants of this age received moral and even physical chastisement with as much meekness as the children, and returned the kindly, if autocratic care bestowed upon them by their mistress with loyal devotion.

Old servants obviously regarded themselves as members of the family. It was in their care that, in some cases, the younger members of a family were left while the Squire and his wife were in exile during the Commonwealth, and the old nurse's letters, sometimes, as in the case of the Verney's, compare very favourably in the matter of spelling and grammar with those of the young ladies themselves.

We find many instances at this period of the servants being remembered in their mistresses' wills. Dame Margaret Verney, Sir Ralph's mother, left Betty Coleman £10 to place her "and pray tak som care toe see her plased with. . . . If cooke is with me give her sum £3 and sum of my worser gowns. . . . Pay the undermaids and poore, before the bigger sums," and we may feel sure that Sir Ralph faithfully carried out these thoughtful instructions. During the Civil Wars, the men not only served their masters but fought for them, and the women stayed and helped their mistresses to protect the home, and when occasion arose there were those who uncomplainingly shared the discomfort of their exile.

We are far from suggesting that such happy relations between mistress and maid do not exist even in the more strenuous and complicated conditions of this century.

Many of us are privileged to know old servants, nurses, in large families most often, or some other devoted man or woman, who has perhaps followed his or her master's changing fortunes, and is regarded as a much honoured member of the family.

Whether the species will not presently be altogether extinct, in the so-called levelling process which is in reality the demagogic uprising of a greedy and still uneducated class in a democratic age, is quite another question.

It is safe to assume that the country housewife of the seventeenth century met the unpleasant side of the "servant question," as we call it, for the first time when she accompanied her husband to France. The French servants disliked the refugees, and they treated their English employers without ceremony, coming and going as they liked in an independent fashion which a good deal astounded their would-be benevolent despots.

Mary Verney, Sir Ralph's wife, was fortunate in being accompanied by her faithful Luce and Besse who, though they did not like foreign fare any better than the average modern English maid, and were a good deal shocked at being given roast meat only one night in a week for supper, and that no doubt of an inferior quality, remained nevertheless faithful to their master's fallen fortunes.

It is a curious fact that these seventeenth century ladies who were so unusually capable in their kitchen, their malt house, their still room and all domestic offices, were quite helpless when it came to dressing themselves or doing their own hair. A maid was the first essential of life to them, just as when in their exile and poverty, they hardly knew where to turn for the necessaries of life, they must send to England for their patches, oris powder and other adjuncts of the toilette essential to feminine self-respect.

The standard of values has altered. The great lady now-a-days might be sore put to it to bake her own bread or send up her own dinner, but under stress of circumstance it would be rare indeed if she could not put on her own clothes, do her hair, at least tidily, and even contemplate her own packing without too much misgiving. If it were not so, it would be improbable that she were a great lady at all!

But while her young sisters-in-law, in the direst poverty at Clayden, quarrelled furiously over the divided ministrations of their one maid, Mary Verney, quiet, courageous and always considerate, also found herself in difficulty. Leaving Besse, who had learned to talk French, in charge of the house, her husband and her little son, Mary took Luce with her when she went to England to take an inventory of Clayden after the sequestration. Luce, who is her personal attendant, is, for a little, doubtful of being able to return to France. What is Mary to do? "I cannot take Besse next to me," she writes to her husband, "because I know she cannot starch, and beside I know she can never learne to dress me," and yet she does not like to put a plainer servant above her, and with only two cannot keep either a fine chambermaid or a gentlewoman. At length a maid turns up, "very good-natured and a gentleman's daughter of £400 a year . . . in a gentlewoman's habit but will not refuse to do anything."

Fortunately she was not put to the test, for with a private fortune of £400 a year, it is too likely that this over good-natured lady would have looked upon a journey to France as a mere jaunt to be enjoyed in the proper spirit. The admirable Luce thought better of her disinclination and returned to Blois with Mary, and remained to support her master through the early days of his widowerhood and, later, to help in the orderly and economical management of his affairs at Clayden. It was Luce who, in the expensive days of the Restoration, when lemons were sixpence apiece, succeeded in getting some at three shillings a dozen, and when hospitality and retrenchment, two difficult conditions to combine, were equally essential at Clayden, looked out the cheapest and best markets in town for fish and foreign fruits.

Lady Brilliana Harley writes pathetically to her husband about the character of a gentlewoman of whom her need is great, " I am toold of a gentellwoman by Dr. Barker—she was bread with my old Lady Manering— she, they say, is religious and discreet, and very handsome in dooing of anythinge . . . if you like it, I would think of having her, for I have nobody about me, of any judgment, to doo anythinge." The poor lady, always more or less of an invalid, was suffering from fever at the time and had already been bled twice without result, and hesitated before a third attempt. " I hope the Lord will direct me what to doo," she exclaims, with her usual pious fervour, and, since there is no further reference to the matter of the gentlewoman, we may hope that, when procured, she proved satisfactory.

Servants' characters, written or personal, were considered at least as important then as now, though in the early days of the century it was not very often that the upper and confidential servants changed their situations. Some of the qualifications required of them were remarkable. Lord Worcester being entrusted by

his wife to engage some men-servants was delighted to
find two footmen who could play the violin. There was
yet another who was a great performer but unluckily
he refused to wear livery !

When Sir Ralph Verney sent down a French man
cook, Michael Durand, to Clayden, he desires that he is to
use his leisure in learning to read and write, and in
baking French Bread in the great brass baking pans.
The cook, however, had no wish to be educated and was
extremely vexed because he was not allowed to shoot
hares for pies in March. None the less this same man
obviously knew his own business and became not only
invaluable to his master but to the whole family circle,
for he was constantly sent to cook a dinner on any
festal occasion. No wedding breakfast or funeral supper,
or Christmas festivity was complete without Misto's
supervision.

Whatever the view of their English maids Sir Ralph
had probably learned to appreciate the superior delicacy
of French cooking during his exile, and we read of him
even sending a " very little footboy " to Blois to learn how
to make pastry and good French fancy bread. Michael
Durand was, it seems particularly clever at fish pies
which were sent as presents to Sir Ralph's friends in
London, but not even he could succeed, apparently, in
making carp pies particularly tasty. During his master's
absence in town he was lent to Aunt Sherard who
was delighted to think that her husband would be so
well fed for the time being, but was a little anxious lest
the Frenchman should be extravagant and "over bold
with the maids !"

When Michael died in 1671, after twenty years true and
faithful service, the Civil Wars had already brought a

certain change into the conditions of domestic service. When the squires re-established themselves in their country houses, retrenchment had to be the first consideration. A tenth of all they possessed was extracted from them by the Lord Protector in 1655, as a security for peaceful behaviour. Happily the tyranny of the major-generals did not last very long, the bill being thrown out by Parliament the following year, but even so, it took a long time for the country gentlemen to recover, even partially, from the financial straits in which the war and the sequestration of their property had placed them. The housewives wrung their hands over the destruction of their cherished possessions, feather-beds eaten up by rats, fire-irons destroyed by rust, and moth in the carpets and hangings, the result both of an empty and neglected house, and of one roughly tenanted by soldiers.

The linen, that most priceless family heirloom, was, in many instances worn out by rough usage. There was the same trouble in the Park, gardens and orchard, where there had certainly been no less destruction. Nurseries of young trees must be planted, rabbits turned out to eat the coarse grass, and it is improbable that the soldiers had left many fat carp in the ponds. For the house repairs, windows, but only those that were necessary must be reglazed, grates renewed, the water pipes attended to, and the cistern cleaned. It is not difficult to imagine the dismay of the squire and his lady, conscious as they were that there was very little money wherewith to make all these necessary repairs.

Poor Sir Ralph Verney had to face these difficulties without his brave and devoted Mary beside him, she having died after her heroic and suffering visit to England on behalf of his affairs.

The old house-keeper at Clayden was not at all satisfied with Sir Ralph's first efforts at housekeeping. She complains that the sugar he has sent down is fitter to spend in the house than to preserve with, and she demands two dozen glasses without brims, of a shape which the poor harassed man can find nowhere in London. No doubt these old servants were tyrants as they would be to-day, but the master and mistress would be thankful in the midst of their difficulties to be re-united to such faithful friends. The retrenchment must obviously be in the employment of fewer " menials," or lower servants, and in less lavish housekeeping.

It was at this time no doubt that country estates ceased to be self-supporting, provisions coming down more frequently from London, or being bought in the markets. We hear even a murmur, where women servants were severely limited of the brewing, and some of the washing being done in the village. Brewing was still and continued for long after, however, to be the work of women, and that a knowledge of malt was a valuable asset may be inferred from the fact that when the justices of Rutland settled the rates of wages in 1610, it was adjudged that a chief woman who can bake and brew, and make malt and oversee the other servants, shall have for her wages about double the sum of one who had not these qualifications. As we have seen, however, the old-fashioned country housewife usually undertook these duties herself.

Even when we consider that the value of money was about five times as high as it is to-day, the rate of wages was low for domestic servants, as also for labourers.

In all the private journals of the seventeenth century, the servants' wages are carefully noted, and they seem to

have ranged from 30s. to £8 per annum. The country
parson's man servant received £5 a year and his maid-
servant £3, and the day labourer in his garden 1s. a day.
This was in the middle of the century, and in the
country, at all events, they do not seem to have risen
perceptibly higher after the Restoration. Lord
Fountainhall in Scotland paid only eight dollars or
about £2 for his child's nurse, to which he added one
dollar to buy a Bible with.

A Sussex Squire, who began his journal in 1683, gives
us a very detailed account of what he paid to his servants,
and other matters. His journal is such delightful
reading, for he was a gentleman with a strong sense
of the humorous, that it is a temptation to quote the
whole, and indeed there must be constant reference to it
for those little details which make up the sum of daily
existence. He illustrates each paragraph with a quaint
and spirited woodcut either of the object mentioned, or
with a characteristic little sketch to indicate the moral
habits or the occupations of those to whom he refers.

In 1685, Abraham Holford came as footman at the
wages of 30s. per annum, with coat and breeches and
hat. Margaret Lawes came as chambermaid at the
wages of 50s. per annum, and Mary Coley as cook at 50s.
per annum. John Hall the coachman, who was destined
to be a sore anxiety as well as a valued and faithful
friend, entered Mr. Burrell's service on July 1, 1685,
receiving £6 a year as wages, and a coat and breeches.
"I gave him 2s. 6d. more," he adds, "for catching
moles." "John Coachman" figures perpetually in these
pages, and always with a neat little drawing of a beer
mug in the margin. For John, alas!—though we have
every reason to believe he was an excellent servant—had

no notion of living soberly. " Paid to John Coachman, in part of his wages to be fooled away in cyder or lottery, 5s." is an example of many such entries that occur. " John Coachman spent money intended for a goose on ale," and on another still more serious occasion, the coachman's casement had to be mended at the price of 2s., he, not having been sufficiently sober to find his way home to bed through the door ! Yet he receives little gifts of money from his master on occasions, such as the birth of Mr. Burrell's only daughter, which points to the friendliest relations, and he died in his service in 1712, from the effect of a fall, being we presume still unregenerate, predeceasing his master by only five years.

In 1698, the Squire notes that he engages a footman in April, Thomas Goldsmith, at 30s. per annum, and a livery coat and waistcoat once in two years, "but being detected in theft, I turned him away on the 21st of August. After a ramble to London, being almost starved, he came again as footman, on March 25, 1703, at £4 per annum, one livery coat and breeches in two years. If he went away at the end of the first year, he was to leave his livery coat behind him." A necessary caution this, in view of his former conduct. What does not appear is why after his previous treatment of his master he was to receive such an increase of wages. We can only conclude that his added years and, we must hope, experience entitled him to more pay, added to the fact that by the reign of Queen Anne the rate of wages was no doubt increasing, and a servant who had once served in London would have acquired an exalted notion of his value.

For his footman's shoes he pays 4s., for making his

waistcoat 2s., stockings 1s. 6d., breeches 3s. 6d., hat 4s. ; the footman's paragraph is illustrated by a clay pipe which may denote a tendency towards idleness. This kind-hearted gentleman, who was such an admirable housekeeper and who pined and died soon after he had handed over the reins of government to his unsatisfactory son-in-law, knew when it was not justifiable to be lenient.

In 1693, " I payed Frances Smith all her wages due to this day, £2, and discharged her, she being a notorious thief." On another occasion he regrets that he had paid Hollybone 4s. "for repairing paling, which was a little too much, for he worked three days but gently !" From this entry we may see that the price of daily labour was rising a little above the 1s. a day of the Commonwealth, and that the British working man had much the same failings as he has to-day.

In the squire's journal we find a reference to a *Bucking*—that is, a general wash which took place once or twice a year. He adds a memorandum like any house-proud lady—" I washed in soap : bought blew, 1s. 'Tis better to buy as we want than by wholesale, and so it is with soap." We are already far removed, however, from the country housewife earlier in the century, who would have been outraged at the thought of buying soap at all.

If the wages were low the servants had many ad-vantages, when they served in the old-fashioned squire's household. In sickness they were nursed as carefully as any member of the family—we hear of one who was moved into the guest chamber during an illness in order that he might have a fire and the best that the house could afford.

And if their bodies were attended to, their moral

welfare received even greater consideration. Mrs.
Evelyn was only one of many ladies who instructed
her servants herself in the principles of religion. In
the Puritan households it is possible that the servants
may have grown a little restive under all the pious
ministrations of their mistresses. Mary Rich, Countess
of Warwick, a daughter of Lord Cork, who, as a young
girl and for the first few years after her runaway marriage, had greatly enjoyed, and no doubt adorned the life
at Court, suddenly became an austere Puritan, and to
atone for past frivolities she devoted herself to her own
salvation and that of her household. She herself
catechised her maids, gave good council to her coachman, and prepared her footman for the Sacrament.

When Tom Coleman, who had served Lord Warwick
for twenty years, lay sick, the remedy his mistress
prescribed was to take her chaplain to pray over him.
In this respect, however, he escaped more easily than my
Lady's niece, Lady Mary St. John, who was attended
during a severe illness by two doctors and four or five
different ministers, who prayed daily with her, but
having, we suppose, stout nerves and a strong constitution, she recovered all the same! We may smile over
the excessive piety of some of these ladies, but we must
not forget that it was such women as Lady Warwick, her
neighbour Lady Maynard, and Lady Godophin who helped
to keep alive the old traditions of feminine purity and
simple goodness in an age when, owing to the inevitable
reaction against the tyrannies of Puritanism, such old-
fashioned virtues were in danger of suffering wholesale
shipwreck.

Whatever the beautiful simplicity of relations between
mistresses and servants in the country might still be,

in London, by the middle of the century, there was a
good deal less tolerance on the one hand and more
independence on the other.   During the Fire of London
Mr. Pepys is deeply incensed against his servant,
Mercer, who, either in a panic or taking advantage of
the general confusion, fled to her mother.   There Mrs.
Pepys found her, and beat her soundly according to the
good old fashion.   The mother, however, did not take
this treatment in good part, and complained that her
daughter was not a 'prentice girl, "to ask leave every
time she goes abroad."   "My wife with good reason
was angry," remarks Mr. Pepys, "and when she came
home bid her begone again," which filled her master
with some uneasiness until he reflected that he and
Mrs. Pepys were at that moment occupied in moving
out their possessions before the advance of the all-
devouring flames, and that if they lost much he would
be "in fear of coming in a little time to be less able to
keep one in her quality!"   Mercer had been previously
described as a "decayed merchant's daughter," and had
been treated with much consideration, so she probably
considered herself, with some justification, in a position
which should have exempted her from a beating.

In 1675, Mrs. Hannah Wolley published, in addition
to her famous Cookery Book, "The Gentlewoman's Companion or Guide to the Female Sex," which was printed
at the Adam and Eve, in *Little Brittain*.   In this she
deplores the ways of "this depraved, later age," and it
is evident that in London, at all events, the servants
were aping the self-indulgent and corrupt manners of
their masters.   Her advice to mistresses, as well as to the
servants, is admirable, and suitable to any century.   "If
you find you have a bad or unfaithful servant (as

now-a-days there are too many, more than ever) whom
you cannot either by fair means or foul reclaim, vex
not nor fret at what you see is remediless, but first
making her thoroughly sensible of her errors, give her
fair warning to provide for herself, and convenient for
your own affairs, and do not, as a great many much
to blame, give too ill a character of her, which will
raise you little benefit, although it may lay the basis
of her utter ruin ; but rather be silent if you cannot
speak good. . . . Though a bad servant, detain not the
wages, nor any part that is justly due, for the labourer
is worthy of his hire." What could be more just or
diplomatic ? It would seem from this that an equivalent to the month's notice on either side was already
expected.

She further recommends the housewife to see that
everything be kept cleanly in the chambers, the beds
often turned, the furniture often beaten in the sun and
well brushed. Her advice that every Saturday an account should be taken of every servant's layings out,
and once a month an account of all the expenses of
the whole house, was probably, as we have seen, more
often observed by the master than the mistress. But
all her recommendations to the servant might very well
have been written to-day.

Laundry-maids are told to be sparing of their soap,
fire, and candles, and to entertain no charwoman unknown to the lady of the house. Housemaids are " to
be careful for and diligent to all strangers, and see that
they lack nothing in their chambers." They are not to
displace things by carrying them from one room to
another. They are to help laundry-maids in the morning or on washing-day, and be ready to help the house-

11

keeper or waiting-woman in the preserving and distilling in the afternoon. The "cook-maids," who have high wages, are begged not to "lay them all on their backs, not to covet to have the kitchen stuff for vails, but rather to ask more wages."

The custom of giving "vails" to servants by visitors sensibly increased the wages in houses where visitors were frequent, much as they do at the present time. Our Sussex squire, on one visit, paid 10s. 9d. (half a guinea) to the man ; 10s. to the chambermayde; 10s. to the cook ; to the coachman, 5s. ; to the butler, 5s.; to the chief gardener, 5s.; to the undercook, 2s. 6d.; to the boy, 2s. 6d. ; to the undergardener, 2s. 6d. ; and to the nurse, 2s. 6d.

We may conclude this chapter with some further entries in the Squire's carefully-kept journal, although they are of a rather later date.

On November 7, 1703, he writes : "After receiving the Sacrement, determined to live a better course of life," and adds, remorsefully, on November 9th, "Rather too irritable with servants." These are both in Latin, a language which he employs for his more confidential notes. There is another Latin note no less human and scarcely less pathetic, in which he explains that he has had a quarrel with his sister, who had been insolent to him ; probably she had been interfering with his household or his motherless little girl. At all events he complains that it has seriously upset his stomach, and he takes "Tipping's mixture and one or two doses of *Hiera picra*," a sovereign remedy when in trouble. We have heard of a nurse who poulticed a lady for temper, but here is the Squire's prescription, to be recommended with discretion to all irritable housewives.

"Take an ounce of *hiera picra*, prepared with aloes, saffron, cloves, ginger, mace, half a quarter of an ounce of each ; put them into a pint of the best rum or brandy, with a pint of white wine. Take four spoonfuls going to bed, with some warm wine, or three or four spoonfuls of ale." And, as Lady Brilliana would no doubt have added, " May the Lord bless all means to you !"

CHAPTER IX

THE LONDON HOUSEWIFE—THE COMMON-WEALTH—THE RESTORATION

WHILE the moderate people of both parties stayed quietly in the country, it was in London that the opposing and contrasting habits of Puritan and Loyalist households were most in evidence.

It might be expected during the Commonwealth that the Puritan fashions would be set by Mrs. Elizabeth Cromwell, the wife of the Protector, during her brief reign at Whitehall. This lady, however, seems to have had very little influence, even in her husband's party, outside her own four walls.

A curious tract exists entitled, "The Court and Kitchen of Elizabeth, commonly called Joan Cromwell, the Wife of the late Usurper." It is a Restoration tract published in 1664, and would naturally not be flattering to its subject; but no other testimony exists to the lady's virtues or more amiable characteristics. From this tract we learn that when Mrs. Cromwell came to Whitehall "much adoe she had at first to raise her mind and deportment to this Sovereign grandeur, and very difficult it was for her to lay aside those impertinent meannesses of her private fortune." She was, in fact, of humble origin, accustomed to live in a small way on small means, and no doubt was regarded in her own walk of life as a thrifty and careful housewife. But there was no place for thrift at Whitehall, and her care could certainly not have commended itself to the household. She employed a surveyor to make her "some convenient accommodation and little labrynthes and trap stairs, by which she might at all times unseen passe to and fro and come unawares upon her servants and keep them vigilant in their places and honest in the discharge thereof." Madame Spye-fault indeed! The poor lady was also much embarrassed by her "roomy and vast dwelling," and would never under any circumstances consent to be left alone in it.

Occasionally her excessive thriftiness appears to have overreached itself. We are told of a peasant woman from the outskirts of London who, hearing of Madame Cromwell's love of green peas, brought a dish from a small early crop in her own garden to Whitehall. On the way she had been offered an angel for them, which was a gold piece, but to her extreme disappointment the protector's wife accepted the peas with becoming enthusiasm and—sent her down a crown! The good woman, however, had the strength of mind to demand her peas back, and refused to stir until she received them.

It is to Joan Cromwell, so nicknamed, apparently, from her lack of feminine grace, to whom we owed until recently the pastoral presence of two or three cows in St. James's park, which the tide of modern improvement has swept away. She had her dairy in Whitehall, run by a company of minister's daughters, who were also her serving-women—a distinct economy.

She would have liked also to have her own brewery, but a very small ale called "Morning Dew," and sold in barrels at 7s. 6d., came into fashion at this time, and found such favour with the Protector that this pleasing prospect had to be abandoned. In spite of her zeal for economy, however, either Madam Cromwell or her husband felt that there should be "something of the Prince about him," if only in appearances; so "about noon time a great clattering of plates and marching of servants" could be heard, but they seem to have brought very little to table. The food is described as "ordinary and vulgar," and no such dainties as *Quelquechoses* were ever suffered. Scotch collops of veal was an almost constant dish, varied by leg of mutton, a pig collared like brawn, or liver puddings. Mrs. Cromwell's usual drink was *Punnado*, which reads like a glorified edition of toast and water.

"Take one quart of running water, put it on the fire in a skillet, then cut a light roul of bread in slices about the bigness of a groat, and as thin as wafers; lay it on a dish on a few coals, then put it into the water with two handfuls of currants, pickt and washt, a little large mace; season it with sugar and rosewater when it is enough."

Under her portrait left at Whitehall some wit of the Restoration had inscribed the following verse:

> "From feigned glory and usurped Throne,
> And all the greatnesse to me falsely shown,
> And from the Arts of Government set free,
> See how the Protectress and a Drudge agree."

There have been parsimonious housewives in all grades of society from the beginning of time, and Madam

A Puritan Housewife.

Cromwell's drab qualities, such as they were, would of course receive scant justice from her enemies if only on account of her prominent position. Oliver Cromwell's mother, on the other hand, seems to have been much respected by the few who knew her as a quiet, homely woman, a thorough housewife, and a devoted mother. She had no love of splendour and no wish to ape it, but went her own way in the apartments at Whitehall which her son allowed her, suffering much in her love for him, but without apparently exciting the taunts of the enemy. Here she died at an advanced age in 1654, and would not have been at all gratified by the costly funeral Cromwell ordered for her, and which gave dire offence to the Puritan party.

Madam Elizabeth Cromwell, as we have said, attempted to be no leader of fashion; and indeed the fashion mainly followed by the fanatical Puritans of the middle-classes was to wear exactly what the despised "other people" were not wearing. While ruffs were worn they would only be seen in wide falling bands of plain linen, and when falling collars of delicate lace came into fashion the Puritans must wear narrow ones. Their shoes were pointed when the rest of the world wore them wide, and their stockings were black when coloured stockings were the mode, and coloured when the Cavaliers affected black ones. They did not approve of delicate or starched linen, and they were accused of wearing linen which was not spotlessly clean. According to Jasper Mayne, however, who wrote the "City Match" in 1639, one Puritan housewife had her own ideas of beauty and embroidered texts upon her husband's shirts and upon her own petticoats.

"She is a Puritan at her needle too
She works religious petticoats : for flowers
She'll make Church histories ; besides
My smock-sleeves have such holy embroideries,
And are so learned, that I fear in time
All my apparel will be quoted by
Some pure instructor."

But it must not be supposed that the eccentricities of
a certain number of ill-educated fanatics were adopted
by the majority of the Puritan party. With the lower
classes Puritanism inevitably degenerated, like other
political and religious questions, into one of mere
class hatred. So bitter was the democratic spirit,
Mrs. Alice Thornton tells us in her autobiography, that
during the Commonwealth "the citizens and common
people could not abide the sight of a gentleman
walking in the streets of London."

To the serious and educated Puritans of the upper
class, however, both men and women, their convic-
tions represented a political creed as well as a form
of Church defence against the attempt of the Stuart
Kings, as they understood it, to thwart the religious
sentiment of the nation. Plain living and plain
dressing, often unassumingly practised, were merely
the outward expressions of their protest against the
extravagance of the age.

Meantime the merchant's wife under the Commonwealth, in her close hood and heavy stuff gown with
its stiff-pointed bodice and full panniers, must have
looked out upon a rather dreary world. The May-
poles, she heard tell, had already been pulled down in
the country, and here in London plays and bear-
baiting and all fashionable amusements were forbidden,
and even from the fairs the gaiety had been sternly

banished. Her husband, good man, conscious of full money-bags, could smoke his pipe and drink his mug of home-brewed ale with a sober-apparelled boon companion, and make merry over the misfortunes of that elegant gentleman and his friends over the water. But for the housewife, when she had scrubbed her house and done her marketing, a dull affair nowadays, and cooked the food for her lord and master, there was small chance of recreation. When in 1654 Christmas Day fell on a Wednesday, an appointed fast, and not only were mince-pies swept from her board as idolatrous, but she was permitted to cook no festive dinner nor take any notice of the occasion whatever, she should have felt her cup was full indeed. A woman must needs have had a distorted instinct as well as a rigid Puritanical training to submit tamely to such an outrage on all respectable traditions.

We may, and indeed we must, deplore that wave of joylessness which swept the country, crushing all love of beauty, all spontaneous joy in living, qualities none too common in this country at the best of times, and condemned as wanton wickedness alike all innocent pleasure-seeking and every effort at cultivation and refinement. And yet we must still admit that England owes a debt to the Puritans. The essential elements of the English character, strenuousness and endurance, received a fresh impetus which no doubt helped to preserve its reputation through a succeeding period of self-indulgence and the unsettled atmosphere which attends a change of dynasty. The Puritans have left us a legacy of gloom, but they have also left us a stoutness of heart and a rigidity of conscience which may make a strain of Puritan blood in the veins, when

kept in proper subjection, an asset not to be despised.
Had their influence been paramount for longer the
devastation that they wrought who

"Waged war not against Rome alone,
    But against storied past and sculptured stone,"

might have been very much more serious both to the
country and to the national character.

As it was, under the Commonwealth, the labour
market being relieved by the immense enlistment into
the armies during the civil war, wages rose a little,
and temporarily the working-classes were rather better
off. Whether those of them who did not "raise
conscience to her sole and awful throne" felt com-
pensated by this improvement in their wages for
longer hours of work, for the absence of feast days and
holidays, and for the prohibition to roast their bit of
meat on Sunday is, however, doubtful.

But the tide was soon to turn. A cramped and
chastened country stretched itself in the sun of the
Restoration, which naturally shone with peculiar
brightness in London in the near neighbourhood of
that Sovereign whom Mr. Evelyn describes with
cautious affection as "a Prince of many virtues, and
many greate imperfections," and whom he admits
"had a particular talent in telling a story."

As we have seen, the great ladies early in the century
had preferred to stay in the country, and there was
little to attract them to London during the Commonwealth, when the dame who considered herself fashionable took her pleasures rather coarsely. Consequently
the virtues of housewifery and hospitality had alike
languished sadly in the capital.

A writer of the first half of the century complains that while in the country "Fat capon or plenty of beef and mutton largely bestowed" upon a guest was the invariable custom, in London "a cup of wine or beer, with a napkin to wipe the lips, and an 'you are heartily welcome' are thought to be a great entertainment." He adds that the London ladies "are well dressed, fond of taking it easy, and leave household matters or drudging to their servants. They sit at their doors dressed in fine clothes. Great honour is shown them at banquets and feasts. They walk, ride, play cards, amuse themselves at churchings, christenings, and funerals." London, he considered, was a Paradise for married women, many of whom, neglecting to follow Queen Henrietta Maria's example of industry, gave themselves up to "worldliness, bombastings, quiltings, perfumes and corked shoes."

And if this was the case before the storm of the Civil War burst upon her, how much more did the London lady set out to enjoy herself and to make up for lost time when the clouds at length had rolled away. The return of the Merry Monarch, bringing with him all sorts of new French customs and fashions, and restoring all the amusements of society to much more than their former brilliance, was naturally delightful.

Once more she was able to go to the theatre without hindrance, and carefully masked to drive in the Ring in Hyde Park in the evening, a walled enclosure, very select, where 6d. was charged for the entry, and cakes and syllabub could be procured at the lodge. She could attend horse-racing and even sometimes cock-fighting, and make her own bets. Gambling was the chief resource of the day. Indulgent husbands and fathers had to allow money for this purpose in addition to pin money. Spanish ombre, basset, gleek, and whist, and occasionally hazard, were played from morning till night. Times were changing for the young unmarried woman, who now when she had found her way to London seems to have shared in all her married sister's diversions, and when money was procurable to have gambled it away with entire lightheartedness. No wonder that in such an extravagant age husbands were hard to find unless the bride were well dowered, which was not usual, since the Royalist families had suffered heavily from the expenses of the Wars, the sequestration of their properties, and the exaction of the Commonwealth designed to impoverish landowners. After all, it was the swing of the pendulum, and many of the amusements of the day, if not altogether harmless, were certainly childish.

Dear, garrulous Mr. Pepys, the social historian of the Restoration, describes dining with some of the Maids of Honour, and the manner in which they spent the evening. "Drink most excellent and great variety and plenty of wines." The dinner was at the Treasurer's house at Deptford, and they went up and found "the Duke of York and the Duchesse with all the great ladies sitting upon a carpet on the ground, there being no chairs, playing at 'I love my love with an A because of this and that.'" Some of the ladies, especially the Duchess and Lady Castlemaine, he appears to have found very witty— we might also have found them very coarse !

If we compare the portraits by Lely of the Court favourites of the Restoration with Van Dyck's ladies, we cannot fail to notice a certain deterioration and lack of refinement in the former, which is not entirely a matter of costume. It must be conceded that if Henrietta Maria did nothing else for her adopted country she, as a French-woman, at least taught the English ladies of her day how to dress. The costumes of the Royalist ladies are familiar to us all in Van Dyck's beautiful portraits, nor is it within the scope of the present volume to describe them in detail. But the accounts for the housewife's dress are so perpetually made out upon the same piece of paper as her bills for beef and mutton and household posses-sions, that it is impossible to ignore them if we would. Nor would there be any sense in doing so, since in every age dress is a sure index of a woman's mind, and the competent housewife who would have all things fair about her and live up to the high standard demanded of her in an earlier age, would certainly have been too well balanced to neglect the graces of her own person.

The preposterous farthingale, beloved of Anne of Denmark, had been speedily banished, and it was not long before the saffron starched ruff, odious since its inventor, Mrs. Turner, had been hanged in it, also dis-appeared. Instead we note the falling lace collar, the string of fine pearls, the favourite Stuart ornament, the rich fabrics of velvet, silk, or satin, hanging in graceful and undisturbed folds. The quiet taste of the French Queen in colours, aided by the encroaching austerity of Puritanism, had introduced what were known as the "sadd" colours, such as purple, orange, tawny, deer-colour, and graine colour. The Queen herself, as we may see from her portraits, was much attached to shades of orange and amber, which she would skilfully relieve with that touch of black or dull red of which she so fully realised the subtle value.

The lady of this reign may in London have neglected her household duties, and have occupied herself more nearly with the silver trimming for her pearl satin gown, but it is seldom indeed that we do not find in her portrait that little touch of personal dignity and self-restraint that is somehow absent from the redundant charms of the beauties of the later Stuart period. The latter, with their prominent eyes, which had suddenly and mysteriously become the fashion, with their puffs and false curls set out on wires, which had replaced the close clustering little ringlets on the brows of their predecessors, seem to be for ever in an attitude of assumed modesty, clutching at a fragment of drapery which, if it existed, would certainly be insufficient.

The ladies of the seventeenth century had a great number of materials to choose from. James I. had tried the experiment of breeding silkworms in England, and though it had not succeeded, owing to the comparative scarcity of mulberry leaves, he had started silk factories, and imported foreign throwsters, dyers, and broad weavers. An innumerable variety of silk fabrics were to be had; gold or silver tissues, taffetas, plushes, velvets, damask, satins, plain and figured, silk mohair, and every sort of ribbon. It was probably after a visit to London at this period of licence and pleasure-seeking that Mr. Evelyn, in the peaceful security of Wotton, wrote his lament for the good days that were past. "Men courted and chose their wives," he said, "for their modesty, frugality, keeping at home, good housewifery, and other economical virtues. . . . 'Twas then ancient hospitality was kept up in town and country. . . . The virgins and young ladies of that golden age *quaesiverent lanam et linum* put their hands to the spindle, nor dis-

dained they the needle, were obsequious and helpful to
their parents, instructed in the managing of the family,
and gave presages of making excellent wives."

With more humour, perhaps, because he was collabo-
rating with his daughter Mary, who died shortly afterwards, he published a few years later the tract " Mundus
Muliebris," a satire on the ladies of fashion. In this he,
or more probably Mary, describes the trousseau required
by a young bride, and the fittings for her bedroom.

> " Twice twelve day smocks of Holland fine,
>   With cambric sleeves, rich point to join,
>   . . . Twelve more for night all Flanders lac'd,
>   Or else she'll think herself disgraced.
>   The same her nightgown must adorn,
>   With two wastcoats for the morn
>   Of pocket mouchous nose to drain,
>   A dozen lac'd, a dozen plain."

The bride of the twentieth century would consider
this a modest list. The "nightgown" was a garment
equivalent to the tea-gown or matinée of the present day,
and had little connection with her night attire. Her
bedroom was to be sumptuous.

> "With Morelack tapestry, damask bed,
>   A velvet richly embroidered :
>   Branches, brassers, cassolets,
>   A cofre-pot and cabinets,
>   Vases of silver, porcelain, store
>   To set and range about the floor :
>   The chimney furniture of plate
>   (For iron's now quite out of date),
>   Tea tables, screens, trunks or stand,
>   Large looking-glass richly japanned,
>   An hanging shelf to which belongs
>   Romances, plays and amorous songs.

> Repeating clock the hour to show,
> When to the play 'tis time to go,
> In pompous coach, or else sedan'd,
> With equipage along the Strand."

Poor Mr. Evelyn, no doubt, rubbed his eyes, and was sure that his Mary, with her playful fancy, must be overstating the case, while the impecunious bachelor felt a little shy of embarking upon matrimony if this were the kind of establishment he was expected to provide.

To us the poem is mainly interesting as showing the furniture and fittings in use in luxurious houses at the latter end of the century. The bride would probably have further insisted upon a silver toilet service, not far behind those of to-day, the earthenware unguent pots of her mother being wholly insufficient.

The fashionable residential quarter in London at this time seems to have been north of the Strand, between Chancery Lane and Holborn. We hear of a great house in Chancery Lane over against Lincoln's Inne, "nigh to the Pumpe," having a very handsome garden, with a washhouse in it, rent £55 a year.

Earlier in the century Covent Garden seems to have been the chosen neighbourhood, which is curious, considering the close proximity of the market, with its undesirable and noisy vendors, not to speak of the filthy heaps of decaying cabbage stalks and rotten apples, which were probably seldom cleared away.

By the Navigation Act of 1561 the carrying trade, which had formerly been exclusively monopolised by the Dutch, had passed more into the hands of the English, so that there were ever fresh luxuries obtainable for the kitchen and the table ; but the innumerable taxes levied by Charles II. must have pressed heavily upon the housewife of moderate means. The price of coal rose to £5 10s. per chaldron. Meat remained fairly cheap, but wheat continued to rise in price owing to the bounties offered for the export of corn, which for nearly a century made England a corn exporting country. Coffee had been introduced in the middle of the century, and the first coffee-house, which was speedily followed by others, was opened in 1652. These coffee-houses were a resort for the men after dinner, but do not seem to have made any appreciable difference in the amount of strong liquor consumed. Water was scarcely ever drunk, even the children being given small beer.

Tea was slowly becoming a fashionable beverage, but owing to the customs duty of 5s. a pound on the imported leaf it was exceedingly dear, and was only to be found in the houses of the rich. In 1660 Mr. Pepys writes : " I did send for a cup of tea (a China drink) of which I had never drank before." And again, two years later : " Home, and there find my wife making of tea, a drink which the Pothicary tells her is good for her cold." Tea being then about £5 a pound, it is not probable that Mrs. Pepys was often permitted to indulge in the luxury. The same historian tells us that at the opening of Parliament in November, 1664, he went first, to warm himself, " to a coffee-house to drink Jocolatte—very good ! " The West India drink called chocolate was beginning to be much resorted to, and was to be a great comfort presently to the fine lady before she began her toilet.

Meantime hospitality of a sort flourished once more in London. A dinner party would begin about one o'clock, and the guests would stay drinking or playing cards until 7 or 8 p.m. Mr. Pepys describes a dinner at Sir John Robinson's at the Tower, "where was great

12

good cheer. High Company. After dinner to drink all the afternoon. Towards night the Duchess and ladies went away. Then we set to it again till it was very late." How much satisfaction may we not read into this entry and how bad a headache next morning !

The king and many another gentleman who had been in exile had, like Sir Ralph Verney, developed a taste for French cooking, so the menus in exalted circles became a little lighter, or rather, there were more courses and fewer dishes in each.

Giles Rose, the king's chef, who had studied under the cooks at the court of Louis XIV., preferred to have six courses, only three dishes to each course.

A dinner for the summer season of six services was heralded "at the entry" with fresh fruit of different kinds, bread, good wine, and little pasties of venison or such a dainty as the brain of a capon minced and baked like a cheesecake.

Then followed three sorts of pottages thickened with poultry, venison, and vegetables.

Five of the six services of three dishes each were composed of venison, game, and poultry, roast with a cordial sauce for the most part or in pies.

In the third service, however, was included "soust or pickled meat," and the sixth service consisted of pig, followed by pears and peaches and finally a sturgeon. At the "Issue of the Table," as it was called, "three things baked upon a dish" were served as well as jelly and apples.

We must observe from the bill of fare that the invariable brawn and mustard with which every feast had formerly opened had now again given place to pottage, thick, rich, and greasy, but none the less the remote forerunner of modern soup.

It is interesting to note that the French cooks of the seventeenth century had already discovered the value of beginning the meal with some slight dishes which could be trifled with by the hungry guests while the more serious part of the menu was in course of preparation. Thus the cooking of the more delicate dishes need not be begun until the guests were actually seated at table, and the dinner need not be spoilt for the whole company by the unpunctuality of one. We know that while we nibble our radishes and spread our caviare on hot toast in a Paris restaurant, our fish and our *poulet* are occupying the whole attention of the chef in the kitchen, and the secret of the original superiority of French cooking may perhaps be found in the creation of the *hors-d'œuvre* and its forerunner the "entry."

The Plague and the Fire swept through London, raising rents and prices and causing horrible suffering and loss and discomfort to all classes. Mr. Pepys remarks that so high are the rents after the Fire that "Mr. Pierce hath let his wife's closet and a little blind bed chamber, and a garret to a silk man for £50 fine and £30 per annum," while he himself with his usual astuteness is looking out for timber in Scotland in the hopes of getting a good price during the re-building of the city. While the fire is still in progress he is given a dinner at a friend's house "in an earthen platter, a fried breast of mutton—as good a meal though as ugly a one as ever I had in my life. An "earthern platter" was evidently by now most ungenteel. With his own dinners, over which he takes at least as much trouble as his wife, he is usually well satisfied, though on one unlucky occasion he is vexed because a guest "could not endure onyons in sauce to lamb, but was overcome with the sight of

it, and so was forced to make his dinner of an egg
or two !"

Neither the Plague nor the Fire seem to have made
much difference to the dissipations of the town, nor were
these confined to the rich who could give smart banquets
and join in the new dances introduced from Paris by
the King at the Court balls.

The housewife of modest means, living perhaps with
one servant in the then unfashionable neighbourhood of
Piccadilly could have her own circle, play cards all the
afternoon, and go and see Mr. Wycherley's plays in the
evening and be quite as frivolous as she pleased in her
own more modest fashion. The King had thrown St.
James's Park open to the public, so if nothing else offered
itself as a distraction, she might take fashionable exercise
and watch His Majesty and the Duke of York feeding the
wildfowl; or if she wished to order a new gown she
might, like Mrs. Pepys, walk in Gray's Inn Gardens to
see the fashions.

Mr. Pepys, with his modest household, of his wife's
gentlewoman and a maid and a boy and his salary raised
to the magnificent sum of £350, kept a good balance and
yet never found it necessary to deny himself any pleasures.
It is true that he found his pleasures awaiting him everywhere and even on the most innocent occasions. He
could scarcely walk the streets without seeing something
to amuse him. A dinner, a wedding, a christening, a
childish entertainment of fireworks, even a sermon or a
funeral seldom failed to entertain or at least interest him.
Such was his happy nature, and if he spent more money
upon his own clothes than upon his wife's, he was well
pleased when she looked "extraordinary fine" in her
flowered Tabby suit or her "French gown called a sac,

COMMONWEALTH & RESTORATION 165

which becomes her very well." There is no contradicting the well-established fact that the Restoration was a vicious age. But it was also an age which sought and loved its pleasures, even the innocent ones, and as has been justly remarked, loved them equally well when at the expense of comfort.

This twentieth century is also an age of pleasure, but it is essentially an age of comfort. The two must be elaborately combined to give us satisfaction. Yet what hard-worked man or woman of the present day might not envy Mr. Pepys' light-hearted capacity for catching his pleasures as they passed, wholly regardless of personal convenience, and, we may add, for never forgetting to be grateful !

CHAPTER X

SHOPPING UNDER THE STUARTS

I**T is to be feared that the pleasant fragrant vision
called up by the poet Gay did not adhere too strictly
to the facts of the London streets as he knew
them.

> "Successive cries the Seasons' change declare
> And mark the monthly progress of the year.
> Hark! how the streets with treble voices ring
> To sell the bounteous product of the Spring."

But history no less than life would be a dull business
were it not for the occasional relief of poetic licence, and
Gay's poem and Wheatley's charming prints of London
cries have alike helped to arouse in us an interest in the
picturesque if discordant customs of a bygone day.

The street vendors who were so great a feature of
London two centuries ago have gradually disappeared.
Even within the last twenty years quite a number have
vanished. In back streets we still occasionally come
upon a knife grinder or, more rarely, an old gentleman
seated on the edge of the pavement mending a seedy
umbrella. Three times a week the raucous cry of "Chairs,
baskets to mend; cane chairs to mend!" resounds
through the quiet streets and squares of Westminster.
The muffin man is ever more rarely heard on Sundays,
and the town crier who, twenty odd years ago, was the joy

of every child on its seaside holiday, only survives in very unsophisticated places.

True, the butcher of the slums still invites his clients to "Buy, buy, buy" various miscellaneous portions of the sheep or pig with a vigour almost worthy of his fore-fathers, while the barrows of ripe strawberries and bananas are enthusiastically proclaimed in unintelligible cockney. The coal cart has taken the place of the "small coal" man who found a sack of small coal on his back, used for the lighting of fires, a sufficient means of liveli-hood. The flower girls with their tousled heads and fine feathers and their overflowing baskets of blossom have displaced the herb sellers for whom we have no use in these hygienic days, when we use herbs only for cooking and buy them at the greengrocer's. The coster-monger with his smart donkey is a genuine survival of the old "custard monger" who hawked his apples, called "custards," or pears, noisily through the cobbled streets, getting himself and his successors a bad name for all futurity by his quarrelsome habits.

Small chance has the human voice now, bawl it ever so loudly above the hoot and whirr of the taxicab and the perpetual scrambling clatter of the motor bus. It is only those who penetrate into the back streets of London on a Saturday night within earshot of the poor man's market, and that certainly need not be very near, who can get any idea of the music of old London. These open-air markets with their barrows of provisions and miscellaneous objects, their bawling vendors, their flaring naphtha lights, the strange crowd of humble housewives doing their week's marketing, the little children waiting in long rows for discarded fragments from the butchers and fishmongers, or playing hide-and-seek under the

barrows, have a charm of their own for some of us, but
it is a charm which, it must be at once admitted, is not
universally appreciated.

In the seventeenth, and to a rather less extent, in the
eighteenth century, practically everything that was required for use and for the maintenance of daily life
was carried and cried through the streets, which in the
morning hours must have been a veritable Babel. As
early as the reign of James I. " Potatoes, ripe potatoes ! "
were hawked about the city, though potatoes were still
something of a novelty. It was from these itinerant
vendors that the housewife could supply nearly all her
needs without going further afield to seek them. Fish
of every available kind and probably none too fresh
would pass her door.

> " Here's fine herrings, eight a groat,
>   Hot codlins, pies and tarts,
>   New mackerel I have to sell,
>   Come buy my Wellfleet oysters, ho !
>   Come buy my whitings fine and new."

Vegetables and fruit of all descriptions from the Lambeth
gardens, from "cherry ripe" and "pippins fine" to
"white-hearted cabbages" and artichokes were cried in
female voices of varying tones and ages. The old clothes-
man was a rooted institution, as well as the old hag, the
terror of the thrifty housewife, who tempted the kitchen
wench to part with her " stuff."

"Lily-white vinegar," brooms, poultry, calf's foot and
tripe and such miscellaneous objects as singing birds in
cages, garters, writing-ink and pens, feather-beds, foot-
stools, bow-pots and glasses from Venice, were hawked
through the streets before and even after fashion per-

mitted the housewife to do real shopping at the New Exchange.

The water-carrier with his iron-hooped buckets slung from a yoke on his shoulder and his cry of " Any fresh and fair spring water here," was not among the least important of these cries. He continued to be patronised by old-fashioned people, even when, by the end of the seventeenth century, the city was supplied with water from the New River, bought in small wooden pipes and stored in those decorative leaden cisterns attached to the better houses in Queen Anne's reign, which are now so eagerly sought after for less utilitarian purposes.

In the second act of " Bartholomew Fair," Ben Jonson gives us a very living picture of Smithfield at " Barthol'me-tide." This play, originally acted at the Hope Theatre in 1614, was a great favourite with the people, chiefly for the ridicule with which it covered the Puritans. For this reason it was suppressed during the Commonwealth, but was revived with redoubled enthusiasm at the Restoration. From one point of view its interest lies in the crowd of street sellers, gathered together with their booths and baskets. There is Lanthorn Leatherhead, the hobby-horse seller, Nightingale, the ballad-singer, and Joan Trash, the gingerbread woman. There are also a costard-monger crying his pears, a tinder-box man who cries " Buy a mouse-trap, a mouse-trap, or a tormentor for a flea," and a corn-cutter who publishes his trade in loud and unvarnished terms. Leatherhead and Joan Trash carry on a wordy warfare :—

" *Leatherhead* : Do you hear, sister Trash, lady of the basket ? sit farther with your gingerbread progeny there, and hinder not the prospect of my shop, or I'll have it proclaimed in the fair what stuff they are made on.

"*Trash :* Why, what stuff are they made on, brother Leatherhead ? nothing but what's wholesome I assure you.

"*Leatherhead :* Yes, stale bread, rotten eggs, musty ginger and dead honey, you know—I shall mar your market, old Joan.

"*Trash :* Mar my market, thou too proud pedlar ! Do thy worst. I defy thee, I, and thy stable of hobby-horses. I pay for my ground as well as thou dost "—

and so on, until the customers begin to arrive and the disputants join in the general clamour. "What do you lack ?" shouts Leatherhead. "What is't you buy ? What do you lack ? rattles, drums, halberts, horses, babies of the best, fiddles of the finest ?" Old Joan tries to yell him down in her harsh croak, "Buy any ginger-bread, gilt gingerbread ?" and so the chorus of ballad-singers, corn-cutters, and all the rest of them is started, each trying to produce more noise than his neighbour and no one cry in the general pandemonium is distinguishable from another. These were the same people congregated at the fairs who were ordinarily patrolling the streets, the peripatetic stores and markets of the London housewife.

Early in the eighteenth century Addison contributed a paper on "Street Cries" to the *Spectator*, in which he remarks that "we appear a distracted city to foreigners, who do not comprehend the meaning of such enormities."

We, in the twentieth century, whose ears are outraged by the cockney boy crying the "Evening Special" and shudder at the sound of the approaching milkman when he ventures to give tongue, can well believe it !

The old cries of London were apparently instrumental as well as vocal, for in this same paper Addison says that "a freeman of London has the privilege of disturbing a whole street for an hour together with the twankling of a brass kettle or a frying-pan," and he further complains of what, to this day, is the idiosyncrasy of such few criers as remain of "that idle accomplishment which they all of them aim at, of crying so as not to be understood, . . . people know the wares they deal in rather by their tunes than by their words, insomuch that I have sometimes seen a country boy run out to buy apples of a bellows-mender !" Asses' milk was much in request, being a favourite recommendation of the doctors, and could be procured at 3s. 6d. a quart, the milch asses daily parading the streets much as the goats do to-day in many continental cities. "Any milk here ?" or " Milk-maids below," accompanied by the rattle of the milk-pails, was naturally the most punctual and regular of cries and the one that survived the longest, being indeed hardly yet silent.

But the milk cried by the pretty country girls of the seventeenth and early eighteenth centuries, came from cows that were pastured in the fields round about St. Martin's Church or in the meadows of Finsbury and Clerkenwell. Gradually, as time passed, and bricks and mortar covered the pastures, the cows retired further and further into the country. The milk-maids were trans-formed into unattractive old women, and later into the accustomed and by no means poetical milk-man ; while the carriage of milk is associated in our minds with clattering cans rolled about the platform with the sole purpose, as it may appear to a jaded traveller, of a young porter working off his superfluous spirits or an old one his ill-temper. But in the days when ladies of quality read Mr. Addison's comments upon their minds and manners in the *Spectator* as they sipped their morning chocolate, the pretty milk-maids were people of importance and held their own street festival once a year on May day.

This little festival is described by Misson, who published an account of his travels in England during Queen Anne's reign in 1719. He says, "On the first of May, and the five or six days following, all the pretty young country girls that serve the town with milk, dress themselves up very neatly, and borrow abundance of silverplate, whereof they make a pyramid, which they adorn with ribbons and flowers, and carry upon their heads, instead of their common milk-pails. In this equipage, accompanied with some of their fellow milk-maids, and a bagpipe or fiddle, they go from door to door, dancing before the houses of their customers, in the midst of boys and girls that follow them in troops, and everybody gives them something." The silver-plate was borrowed from clients who appear to have associated themselves very willingly with a custom which lent romance to the milk supply, a romance which in these hygienic days of sealed cans and several daily deliveries is entirely absent.

With most of the necessities of life brought to her door, or obtainable in the nearest market, meat from Smithfield and fish from Billingsgate, shopping, as we understand it, did not take a great deal of the housewife's time. As an amusement for the fashionable lady we first hear of it in the latter half of the seventeenth century. Lady Russell, in a letter to her husband, describes going with his two sisters, Lady Alington and Lady Margaret Russell, to a Dutchwoman's in Paternoster Row, probably what was called an India-house, that is a warehouse where tea, china, and other Indian goods could be purchased, all wares from the East being

MILK-MAIDS BELOW!

at this time called Indian. This, however, was evidently regarded as a mild adventure. Still more exciting was it for the ladies under a proper escort to visit the Indian merchant ships when they came into dock bringing Eastern goods, and especially dress materials, damasks, muslins, and Oriental silks, which they could cheapen at their leisure on board.

But while the tailors had been in the habit of booking their orders in the nave of St. Paul's Cathedral, which was also a sanctuary for debtors, and Paul's Walk was a fashionable promenade, the new Exchange had by the Restoration become the chosen place for shops and shoppers.

Mr. Pepys we know loved shopping on the New Exchange. Here, on one occasion, the pretty woman who served him induced him to buy for himself a pair of gloves trimmed with yellow ribbon, and a petticoat for his wife which cost him 20s., petticoats being at that date a very important article of dress; "but she is so pretty," he piously exclaims, referring, of course, to the shopwoman, "that God forgive me! I could not think it too much."

The ladies who remained in the country were in the habit of ordering their goods to come down by the carrier, and it was generally the duty of the husband, son, or other male relation to attend personally to their requirements when in London. Lady Dorothy Osborne, who will not trouble to distil her own water, or perhaps has not the knowledge, begs Sir William Temple when next he goes to the Exchange to call at the great shop above the "Flower-Pott," and enquire for a quart of orange water which she had ordered, and which had failed to appear.

The irrepressible Lady Sussex expects Sir Ralph
Verney to do a great deal of domestic shopping for
her, her elderly husband of the moment being apparently unable to face the exertion of a visit to London.
He is to choose satin for her curtains and the backs
of her chairs, and her carpet, for which she gives most
minute directions, so that it may not be too dull to
suit her hangings, also some calico—a rather recent
importation from the East, "spotide with golde" to
line her bed. She further requires a "hansom mofe,
a fasyonable mofe," and the material for a sweet bag.
She decides however that Ralph's wife had better
choose the ribbon to make the strings for this latter
article, "some shadoede sattine ribbinge and some littill
eginge lase as slite as may be to ege the strings, and
but little silver to it." Another request is for some
wine glasses, but little ones and not such as my lord
uses to drink in ! Her confidence in Ralph's taste and
patience was evidently infinite, and no doubt justified,
since she was not by any means the only lady in his
large circle who entrusted him with the choice of her
clothes, and other vanities. She never, however, forgot
to thank him, and on all occasions she was the best and
kindest of friends and neighbours.

Some years later, on the meeting of the Long Parliament, she writes to Ralph: "I will send you some
bisket to put in your pokete and ghelly to comfort you
up as soon as my woman is in time to make it."
Such a kind thought would certainly be welcome, for
the hours of the Parliament were long indeed, from
7 a.m. to dusk with small opportunity for obtaining
food during the sitting. She adds, "You must remember let them be tosted !" Oysters which were sold

in great quantities in the streets of London, the choicest of Colchester oysters "fat and green," at 3s. a barrel, were a favourite present to send into the country in exchange for those home-made pies and jellies, the pride of the country housewife, which were considered a great delicacy.

The carriers were indeed most important people, since upon them depended most of the carrying of letters and parcels between London and the country. They stayed in different inns in town and they all had their own days. Thus "the carriers of Oxford do lodge at the Saracen's Head without Newgate, near Saint Sepulchre's Church, they are there on Wednesdays or almost any days." During the Civil War these same carriers must have had a heavy time trying to carry communications from their friends outside to the Royalists in Oxford. The Bedford carriers, who were responsible for the voluminous correspondence between Dorothy Osborne and Sir William Temple, lodged at the Three Horse Shoes in Aldersgate Street. They left London on Thursdays, and at so early an hour that it is to be feared that more than once Sir William failed to catch them. Dorothy frequently laments that he should have to rise betimes to write to her when he has a cold !

By 1657, however, a considerable advance had been made in the postal arrangements. Within a radius of eighty miles from London a letter could be sent for 2d., outside it for 3d., to Scotland for 4d., and to Ireland for 6d. A penny post was dreamed of, and by the reign of Queen Anne it had actually arrived in the city, while for a country letter a penny must be paid at each end. Times were getting fast indeed, with hackney coaches and sedan chairs plying for hire, and a weekly and presently a daily newspaper! There were also by now what were called "flying coaches" which at what we should consider a very sober pace, conveyed people who could not afford their own carriage backwards and forwards into the country.

Meantime by the reign of Queen Anne the fine ladies crowded to the New Exchange to buy their own petticoats, or, according to the poet Prior, "To cheapen tea or buy a screen." Tea might well be cheapened, for by now it had become fashionable to drink a dish of tea after dinner, and it was still fetching a high price. Thomas Garway, tobacconist and coffee-man, had been the first to sell tea at his house in Exchange Alley in 1657, and he charged from 16s. to 50s. the pound. He had recommended it as a cure for all disorders, and it was no doubt from him, though he is referred to as an "apothecary" that Mrs. Pepys procured the cup of tea which was to vanquish her cold. By the beginning of the eighteenth century black tea was being sold at from 12s. to 30s. a pound, and green tea from 13s. 6d. to 26s. Bohea tea of the purest, sold only by R. Farey at the Bell in Gracechurch Street, a druggist, was 16s. a pound, and Bohea was apparently the right drink for the lady who respected her social position.

In 1704, owing to the French wars, the duties on tea, coffee and chocolate were all doubled, coffee even going up from 2s. 6d. to 6s. and 7s. a pound, while chocolate, which by this time was only drunk in the early mornings, was from 2s. 6d. to 3s. a pound.

It was largely due to the enterprise of the smugglers

that by the eighteenth century tea and tobacco came into such general use. Towards the close of the Stuart dynasty increasingly heavy duties were levied on all the commodities of life. Malt, salt, sugar, spices of all kinds were taxed. During the war with France the tax on French imports was prohibitive. Meantime the Huguenot immigration had given a great impetus to some branches of English trade, especially the silk industry. Here their superior taste and skill were of great value, and so much under their tuition did the English silk trade increase that by 1698 all importation of silk was forbidden. They tried also to do cloth-weaving, but this was an effort on their part by no means appreciated or required, for woollen manufactures had been for long the staple industry of the country. Throughout the seventeenth century the Yorkshire cloth had not attained the reputation which it acquired a little later, and has ever since sustained. At this time it was coarse and of inferior quality, and perpetual proclamations were issued against the bad work and the dishonesty employed in its preparation. The housewife procured her woollen goods chiefly from the West of England, and her serges from Exeter, her kersies from Ottery St. Mary, and her "pin-whites" from Totnes, while her bombazine and russets came from the East of England, and principally from Norwich. Her fine muslins were still brought her from the East. Escorted by her footmen the lady of quality however spent enjoyable hours at the New Exchange or elsewhere, turning over and cheapening a variety of goods which she had not very often the remotest intention of buying.

Mr. Steele, writing in the *Spectator* as Rebecca, *the*

13

distressed, "one of the top China women about town," describes a habit from which the ladies of all ages since the first pedlar brought his first pack to the castle gates, have not, it is to be feared, been exempt. Rebecca complains of a club of female rakes, "idle ladies of fashion, who, having nothing better to do, employ themselves in tumbling over my ware. One of these no-customers (for, by the way, they seldom or never buy anything), calls for a set of tea-dishes, another for a basin, a third for my best green tea, and even to the punch-bowl, there's scarce a piece in my shop but must be displaced, and the whole agreeable architecture disordered, so that I can compare them to nothing but to the night goblins that take a pleasure to overturn the disposition of plates and dishes in the kitchens of your housewifely maids. Well, after all this racket and clatter, this is too dear, that is their aversion, another thing is charming, but not wanted ; the ladies are cured of the spleen, but I am not a shilling the better for it."

The day was past when the great lady made her rare and stately pilgrimage to the shops to choose such goods as could not safely be trusted to her male kind, or if she preferred to remain in the country, contented herself with selecting a pattern among those brought down by the carrier. Far removed already seems the day some thirty years earlier, when the pious Lady Warwick meditated in the hour set apart daily for that purpose "upon choosing a pattern of fine stuff, but thinking it much finer when I viewed it in the shop, and in the whole piece, "and found in this a fitting symbol of the dangers of earthly delusions !" Her daughter and her granddaughter might have turned

over rich brocades at £7 7s. a yard, and satins,
flowered damasks and lustrings by the hour together,
the variety of silks and dress materials being, as we have
seen, infinite. For children a material called "Tammy,"
probably a mixture, was considered more suitable than
real silk. When according to a devoted nurse in the
country, "Mis wants a nupper coat," Tammy is the
material chosen by the kind aunt in London, and we
hear of another child's "nupper" coat of "Morelly striped
yellow and black" which sounds very smart, and
indeed the little girls' dresses in London do not seem
to have differed at this time greatly from those of their
mothers.

The shops in the narrow streets with the gabled
houses, and each with its large overhanging sign, an
object alike of astonishment and interest to the foreigner,
must have presented a very picturesque appearance.
As yet there was no plate glass to jealously guard the
wares which were often heaped up on a ledge outside
the window no less than on the counter within. Outside stood the apprentice or the shopman himself
crying, "What d'ye lack—what lack ye?" with all
the power of his lungs, doing his best one would
imagine to scatter any ideas on the subject of their
wants with which his customers might have started.
But apparently our ancestors had not learnt to
value quiet, and would probably find our noiseless
swing doors and obsequiously attentive shopwalkers
and assistants extremely unsympathetic and tire-
some.

Ward's poem in the "London Spye" gives a good idea
of how the ladies early in the eighteenth century
expected to be encouraged in their shopping.

" Madam, what is't you want,
    Rich fans of India paint?
    Fine Hoods or Scarfs, my Lady ?
    Silk stockings will you buy
    In Grain or other Dye ?
    Pray Madam, please your eye ;
    I've good as e'er was made ye."

It is hardly to be wondered at that madam did not
make up her mind very quickly !

CHAPTER XI

THE DUTCH INFLUENCE

IN her commerce, her industries and her horticulture, and as a consequence in many of the details of her domestic life, England already owed much to the Dutch influence, before ever, in November, 1688, William of Orange sailed into Torbay.

The confusion that had prevailed throughout the brief reign of James II. and the sense of instability which pervaded the country had left society so demoralised that a strong hand was sorely needed to restore the national life to a sound basis.

This, Dutch William was fully prepared to do. He came to save England, to save her from herself if necessary, and while this fact was recognised and welcomed by the more level-headed and patriotic, the Dutchman had not unfortunately the power nor the wish to make himself personally beloved in his adopted country. Mary, although a Stuart, was not much more successful, for she had inherited little of the Stuart charm and sociability. With their arrival, however, the careless irresponsibility and licence which had characterised society since the Restoration, gave place, at all events in Court circles, to a decided sobriety in tone, inspired by the new sovereigns and their followers. Judging by the pictures we have of London society in the

succeeding reign it is not the less improbable that this
sober influence spread very far, or was very lasting,
especially as owing to William's delicate health, the
Court was little at Whitehall, the King preferring to
spend most of his time at Hampton Court, where the flat
surrounding country reminded him of his beloved
Holland.

Too much common-sense does not always conduce to
popularity. William's expressed contempt for the old
custom of touching for the King's Evil, which he refused
to continue, as well as his ultra-Protestantism, which
caused him to suppress all church music, and to wear his
hat in chapel, naturally outraged the susceptibilities of a
people in whose solid character has always remained a
deep vein of superstition.

The Queen was severely criticised by Mr. Evelyn for the
apparently heartless manner in which she took possession
of her father's palace at Whitehall. But Mary had lived
many years in Holland, and while she had undoubtedly
become entirely Dutch in her sympathies, she had also
acquired from her husband a habit of severely controlling
her emotions. In any case, if her reserve and absorption
in William's more personal interests prevented her from
contributing much to the brilliance or distinction of
Court society, her example did a good deal to purge it of
its worst features. She detested gossip and scandal and
extravagance of every sort, and must have given dire
offence on her first arrival to those who strove to entertain her with the prattle of the town, by changing the
subject with an abruptness which permitted of no com-
promise.

Neither, it is to be feared, would her excellent
qualities as a housewife in a degenerate age have

greatly recommended her to the Court ladies. The
Duchess of Marlborough, in attendance on her first
arrival at Whitehall, relates that she ran about "looking
into every closet and conveniency, and turning up the
quilts upon the beds, as people do when they come into
an inn, and with no other sort of concern in her appearance but such as they express." Such carefulness was
almost as much out of place in a palace as Madam
Cromwell's thrift; but even a Queen may like to know
that her bed is aired and comfortable in an apartment
which has been unoccupied for some weeks, and it is the
ill-fortune of a Queen that such a want of tact should be
handed down to her prejudice through successive ages !

At Hampton Court, where the Court removed with as
little delay as possible, Mary found full scope for her
domestic energies. The place had been much neglected,
and in her opinion was wanting in many of the
conveniences of a modern palace. William being of the
same opinion, though he was delighted with the seclusion
of the palace and its situation, at once started upon
improving it. A great deal of the old Tudor palace with
its irregular roofs and twisted chimneys was pulled down,
and the new quadrangle known as Fountain Court and
the buildings at the east end with their classic lines and
fine proportions, so strangely out of harmony with what
is left of Wolseley's beautiful building, were begun. It is,
indeed, only due to William's comparatively early death,
and the amount of money expended on his French wars,
that so much of the old palace, described by a lady at the
close of the eighteenth century, as being in the "dull and
narrow style of Harry 8th.", remains to us.

Tastes and times change together, and while after the
lapse of two centuries Christopher Wren's apartments

have become mellowed and endeared to us by their
associations and historical interest, as well as by their own
architectural merits, we can feel nothing but gratitude to
the providence which stayed Williams hand and preserved for us the beautiful inequalities, the mullioned
windows and brick courts, and the unsurpassed charm of
what remains of Wolseley's palace. The King himself,
with the uncomfortable consciousness of which the
most strong-minded alien cannot wholly free himself,
had no reverence for the historic homes of his predecessors in England. When, through the carelessness
of a Dutch washerwoman, Whitehall was burnt to the
ground in 1698, he seems to have felt little emotion but
one of satisfaction, and the palaces at Greenwich and
Richmond he left wholly unvisited.

But meantime he busied himself greatly, in the
intervals of reforming his new kingdom and keeping the
French at bay, in superintending and interfering with
Wren's designs for the rebuilding of Hampton Court, the
laying out of the gardens, and the prolonging the canal,
of which he highly approved. Queen Mary also
interested herself in the planning of the new state apartments which she was destined never to occupy, as well as
of the gardens, which, except that the geometrical and
elaborate flower beds and some of the fountains have
disappeared, were by the time they were finished very
much the same as we see them to-day.

The fashion for box edgings and borders was brought
from Holland, and they were used in large quantities, but
were afterwards uprooted by Anne, who disliked the
smell. The Queen was a great collector of choice exotics,
some of which, together with the citron and orange-trees
brought from the gardens at Loo, have survived to the

present day. The little Dutch garden on the south side of the palace was also a result of Dutch influence in gardening, and in the long avenue of entwined wych elm, known as Queen Mary's Bower, she sat and sewed with her ladies through those summer afternoons which in the Thames Valley are apt to be so exceedingly oppressive.

During this time the Queen lived in the Water Gallery, which was destroyed on the completion of the palace. Here she occupied herself with her dairy and with all sorts of domestic matters, as well as in playing cards like all the other ladies of her day. She spent many hours in working with her needle, finding in this rather soothing and mechanical occupation a relief from the cares, regrets, and anxieties with which, as a wife of the strenuous, unpopular Dutch sovereign and the daughter of his exiled predecessor, she must have been continually beset. Burnet says, that "in all those hours that were not given to better employment, she wrought with her own hands and sometimes with so constant a diligence, as if she had been to earn her bread by it." Bed-hangings, chair and stool covers and screens were covered with the work of her hands in preparation for the new rooms which she did not live to inhabit. These were mostly in what was called "shadow" work, a form of needlework which was revived a few years ago; but the Queen was indeed an expert at every sort of embroidery and useful work with her needle.

But there is another debt besides the example in house-wifely diligence, which it is to be feared made no great impression, which English women owe to Queen Mary II. It was she who first set the fashion of collecting china for decorative purposes, and not merely for use. From

Holland she brought a number of blue and white Delft jars and vases of quaint shape and design, and she also made a most valuable collection of Oriental china imported from the East. Specimens of the Famille Rose and the Famille Verte first came to England at this time to set a fashion in design and colour—copied at a very long distance by the English porcelain makers of the eighteenth century, who, however, could never discover that wonderful secret of paste and glaze. The Queen was very fond of tea, and drank it regularly after her two o'clock dinner, and of such superfine quality that it is said she paid £3 3s. a pound for it. As a consequence, she bought a number of Oriental tea services with tiny teapots and handleless cups, and these with the Oriental vases were ranged on graduated shelves above the fireplace or in cabinets especially constructed for the purpose. She filled both Kensington Palace and Hampton Court with her treasures, and in the latter palace may still be seen some curious specimens of blue and white Dutch and Oriental jars—pathetic reminders of the Queen for whom these rooms were so carefully prepared and beautified and which she was never to see completed. There are some tall vases made in stories, tapering towards the top, with holes at the sides, in which her Dutch bulbs were evidently planted. In the gardens are still some handsome large vases, also of her choice.

In 1693, a year before Mary's death from smallpox, when the state apartments at Hampton Court only awaited their interior fittings and decorations, Mr. Evelyn writes: " I saw the Queen's rare cabinets and collection of china, which was wonderfully rich and plentifull, but especially a large cabinet, looking-glasse, frame and stands, all of amber, much of it white, with historical bas reliefs and statues, with medals carved in them, esteemed worth £4,000 . . . divers other china and Indian cabinets, screens and hangings." From this time it became the fashion for all parlours of any pretensions to be furnished with a china cabinet, a fashion which not only added greatly to the charm of the housewife's living-room and appointments, but has proved a source of unfailing joy and interest to the modern collector who can fill her shelves and cabinets with such treasures of the past.

The brothers Elers, to whom we have referred in a previous chapter, who had followed William to England, are supposed to have first introduced salt glazing into Staffordshire about the year 1698, thereby inaugurating a revolution in English pottery which was to find further development under the Wedgwoods and their later successors and imitators in Staffordshire. Whether they really discovered the salt-glaze secret or not, they made a sort of fine red ware, or china as it was then called, in imitation of the Oriental, from the fine ferruginous clay, which they could obtain near their factory at Burslem. Presently they opened a shop in London in the Poultry, where they sold teapots in prices ranging from twelve to twenty-five shillings each.

It was now becoming necessary for every housewife to possess elegant teapots, teacups, and indeed whole tea sets in which to serve the fashionable drink, as well as the larger and more substantial chocolate pots. The Elers, nevertheless, do not appear to have made too much profit on their goods, probably because at the very time that they used the process of salt-glazing a heavy tax was levied upon salt—one of the hardest taxes which had yet been enforced and one which was not finally repealed until 1823.

William's taxes, which he levied in order to maintain the large standing army he felt to be essential to the safety of both England and Holland in face of Louis XIV.'s schemes of aggrandisement, did not increase his popularity. The people had suffered heavily from the war, and the cry was for peace where there was no peace. The consent of the merchants had been won to these taxes on home goods by the institution of protective rates against foreign competitors, and there is no doubt that in spite of the wars there was considerable industrial progress in the reign of William and Mary.

The Bank of England was founded in 1794, and some of the country gentlemen at all events were in a position to build themselves new houses in imitation of their sovereign. True, there was not the same fever for building, and certainly not the same rampant prosperity among the country squires which had characterised the Elizabethan and early Jacobean period. But in a small way architecture became a fashionable amusement. The English style had gradually become entirely Italianised and everything Gothic was held in abhorrence. Houses began to be built upon the severe lines of the new apartments at Hampton Court, of red brick with stone cornices and facings, with large sash windows. The heavy hospitable porch of the Stuart age was replaced by the more graceful hood or pediment, often fashioned internally in the similitude of a huge shell. William granted a quantity of land to his Dutch favourites, and nowhere did the Dutch influence show itself more decidedly than in the domestic architecture and fittings and furniture of the houses of this and the succeeding period.

It was about this time in 1688 that Sir Roger Hill, the son of that Baron Hill, whose accounts we have already

glanced at, and who himself owed his knighthood to
Charles II., moved from the house in Somersetshire
which he had inherited, and built himself a house in the
new style in Buckinghamshire.   No name of the architect
has been preserved, but as a gentleman's house of
moderate dimensions, it is probably a singularly perfect
specimen of the domestic architecture inaugurated in this
reign.

Denham Place is a substantial red brick building of
bold unornamented lines with white stone facings and
many large windows, the kind of house which suggests
roominess and comfort.   It is characteristically set to the
north-west, the kitchen and all the offices being to the
south, an aspect which was apparently still shunned as
undesirable.   But it is the interior of the house which is
the most unique and interesting and which gives a very
real impression of the domestic life of the time.

In the billiard-room is a coloured plaster cornice
representing a village and landscape, much of which is so
obviously from Holland that it seems incredible it should
have been the work of English artists ; yet in the
accounts of the building and decoration of the house,
carefully preserved by Sir Roger Hill's descendants, not
a foreign name appears, only those of Mr. Parker,
plasterer, and Maurice Gardner, painter.   There is no
mention of a designer, so it must be supposed that these
plasterers and painters had either learnt their trade and
subjects from the Dutch workmen imported by William,
or as is quite probable, had themselves made an expedition
to Holland.   At any rate, in the cornice in the billiard-
room, against a decidedly un-Dutch background of
billowing clouds and waves and rocky mountains and
magnificent trees, there are churches and windmills and

canals and bridges which could have had their counterpart nowhere but in Holland. There are also, however,
little thatched whitewashed English cottages, one of
which has an extremely crooked chimney, and red brick
houses exactly like those which stand to-day in Denham
Village. They are all decidedly realistic, the tavern being
recognisable by the great hanging sign. There is no
repetition of the pattern, and oddly enough except for
one man in a boat and the driver of a dray, who is
presumably asleep inside, there is no sign of human life.
It is easy to imagine the delight it must have been to
succeeding generations of the children who have lived
here to choose their own particular little red and white
house with its green shutters, in the fascinating village
which their ancestor or his architect designed, as they
must suppose, for their especial entertainment. The only
drawback to this pleasure is that the room is so lofty that
it requires a very bright day to see the cornice at all in
detail. Beneath the cornice hangs some magnificent
Flemish tapestry, brought by Sir Roger Hill from his old
place in Somersetshire.

In the drawing-room, adjoining, the ceiling is painted
brown, decorated with all sorts of musical instruments in
white plaster; and here again is a raised plaster cornice,
this time unpainted, representing the English sports.
It is wonderful with what vitality the plasterers have
managed to invest both the creatures and their pursuers.
Here is a hunt in full cry, there are men fishing with rods
and lines, others hawking—every form of English country
pursuit, and again no repetition of the pattern, if such it
can be called. In this same drawing-room are two very
beautiful ebony cabinets inlaid with red tortoiseshell, of
the kind which were brought by the rich and the travelled

from Italy in the sixteenth and seventeenth centuries. Here also we see a notable change in the manner of treating the interior of the walls, which was now though as yet rarely adopted.

With the increase of coal fires and the improvement in grates it appears that the desire for warmth which had found its expression in inner courtyards, in wainscoted and heavily tapestried walls, had begun to decrease. At Denham the drawing-room walls and several others are painted, and in one room upstairs we find what is probably one of the earliest wall papers introduced into England. This is of course Oriental, and the pattern is of large trees and birds on a buff-coloured ground, each panel entirely different from the others, with a fascinating variety of detail. From his "old house," as he calls it, in Somersetshire, Sir Roger brought much of his Jacobean panelling, with which the chapel is furnished, and one or two of the rooms have the larger panelling of the eighteenth century ; but it is interesting to notice that neither this nor the beautiful Flemish tapestry which was also brought from Somersetshire were any longer the only alternatives for wall covering.

In the panelled rooms pictures are let into the panelling over the fireplace, a fashion which became very prevalent in Queen Anne's reign, and in the plaster work of the ceilings armorial bearings are still employed as decorations. There is a sense of space and dignity in this house ; nothing is cramped, and neither taste nor labour nor the best material seem to have been spared. The back stairs are of the same handsome dimensions as the front, with great lanterns hanging on chains from the roof, of the same period. A good deal of the furniture, including some severe Cromwellian chairs, must also have made the journey from Somerset, and everything in the house has been carefully treasured by successive descendants and occupiers since the days when Sir Roger built it.

From the housewife's point of view, there is nothing of greater interest than the little linen-room opening out of one of the largest and handsomest bedrooms. This is entirely lined with cupboards in very finely carved panelling, holding endless shelves for those wonderful supplies of fine linen which continued to be the pride of our grandmothers and which was still largely spun at home early in the eighteenth century. From the linen-room a little winding stair leads straight down to the servants' offices, thus giving the gentlewoman, and later no doubt the housekeeper, access to it without disturbing the lady of the house in her adjoining apartments, under whose superintendence, however, it most conveniently remained.

Building was apparently cheap in those days. Sir Roger's accounts, kept in great particularity with every little sum paid to every workman, have been most carefully preserved in his neat, clear handwriting. The house was in course of building from 1688 to 1701, most of the years of William's reign, and at the end he notes: "Money laid out on building my new house £5,591 16s. 9d." It does not seem a large sum to have expended upon a house which, without any pretentions to being more than that of a country gentleman, is yet so spacious and admirable in its design and proportions, and so unique as to its interior decorations. The village of Denham appears to be all of the same date, and has been mercifully preserved from the attentions of the jerrybuilder.

In the furnishing of the home at the end of the seventeenth century the Dutch influence is even more noticeable and direct than in the architecture which, after all, merely followed the accepted classic lines which were the prevailing fashion. But from about the middle of the reign of Charles II. Dutch furniture was being very much imitated.

The heavy oak of the Stuarts had, as we have seen, begun to give place to walnut, and now marquetry as a decoration began to supersede carving. The lavish garlands of Grinling Gibbons still adorned the walls of those who could afford them, acting as frames to the pictures and mirrors, and decorating the overmantels and doorways as in the new rooms at Hampton Court ; but these were a luxury for the rich, and for furniture the ordinary carving was certainly going out of fashion. Instead we find the ornate Dutch marquetry increasingly in use ; the china cabinets were handsomely inlaid, as were the chests of drawers, which were now raised on twisted legs, the tall clock cases, the chairs and tables. The first English marquetry copied from the Dutch was very heavy and rich, a number of coloured woods and ivory being used, but in the next reign a simpler style was introduced to suit the English taste.

It is very much the habit to ascribe all that is quaint and charming in furniture, china and house decoration in the eighteenth century to the reign of Queen Anne. A pleasant but confused vision rises before the imagination of pannelled rooms, straight-backed chairs, spindle-legged tables, probably of mahogany which was not yet introduced at all, glass-fronted cabinets, and with more truth those delightful bureaus filled with innumerable little drawers and hiding-places. The jerry-builder meantime thrusts upon our notice red brick gabled villas of very mixed design, if design it can be called, of distorted lines and angles which he assures us are Queen Anne houses.

Queen Anne, however, was responsible for none of these things, and it has even been said that the so-called Queen Anne style "never had any existence at all except in the brains of modern aesthetics and china maniacs." Certainly judging by the decorations of the Queen's own rooms at Hampton Court her taste was remarkably florid, and there is no evidence to show that she shared her sister and her brother-in-law's interest in furniture and household appointments.

But this by no means prove that a new era in furniture inaugurated by the Dutch influence was not very much developed during her reign. It is not after all in royal palaces that we look for the most characteristic taste of the period but rather in the houses of the well-to-do upper and middle classes. The room now in the Victoria and Albert Museum, brought with all its furnishings from Clifford's Inn, gives us naturally a better impression of the manner of living in the reign of William and Mary than Wren's state apartments at Hampton Court, however laboriously we may reconstruct their fittings. In the same way the simple and elegant and essentially useful furniture which has been preserved for us from the succeeding reign certainly never saw the inside of a palace, but probably came from the rich merchant's houses in the fashionable neighbourhood of Covent Garden and Leicester Square. The age of Queen Anne has been justly called an age of assimilation, and in nothing is this truer than in the case of house furnishing. While in architecture the comfort and convenience of houses were already being made to give way to the due proportion of the exterior, formality and stateliness being the first consideration, the same can hardly be said of the furniture.

If we glance into the home of a lady of this period we shall find much to envy and little except in the absence of modern conveniences to lament.   To begin with, her drawing-rooms would not be overcrowded either with furniture or ornaments. Superfluities in the decoration of furniture itself had been cast out in favour of the greater simplicity of English taste.   The marquetry imitated from the Dutch was now lighter and more graceful in style, and the wood was more often simply veneered oak or pinewood veneered with walnut, or again we find highly polished walnut feathered or plain.

A table in the centre and some spoon-backed walnut chairs round the wall, a magnificent bureau with a flap to let down and endless drawers and hiding-places in which the master of the house might keep his ledgers and business papers or the lady her love-letters, her diaries, her treasured recipes, her jewels, and her money. It is impossible to look at one of these old bureaus, the pattern of which, with their double sets of drawers above and below the writing-desk, unhappily disappeared from England with the Dutch influence, without scenting romance. It is a pattern which seems to have been designed expressly to preserve confidences. The china cabinet of our imagination would be there but the china would be entirely Oriental, for the Bow and Chelsea china which filled the cupboards of the Georgian period had not yet been invented. There were tall grandfather clocks and bracket clocks, and there were occasional tables for tea on turned legs and more elegant card tables.

But in nothing was there a greater revolution than in the chairs. These, though still for the most part high and straight in the back, began to accommodate themselves more decidedly to the exigencies if not of the human figure at least to those of costume. The immense perriwigs of the gentlemen and the elaborate headdresses of the ladies which prevailed in the early years of Queen Anne's reign were of a weight which required a high-backed chair or settee to support them.

This head-dress, which was called a *commode*, was built of many tiers of muslin and lace tapering to the top, its only advantage apparently being that it obviated the necessity for a bonnet when the lady took her walks abroad. Presently this was cast aside and the hair rolled and brushed on the top, hanging in curls behind under the modest shelter of a lace scarf, but the high-backed chair was still desirable for the upright posture of a figure tightly laced into outside stays worn over a stomacher.

The wide seat of these chairs, which those of us who possess them, occasionally find a trifle inconvenient at the modern dinner table, were equally necessary for the hooped petticoat to which Swift in a letter to Stella took such exception on their introduction in 1710. Addison wrote in the *Spectator* with equal severity: "Their petticoats which began to heave and swell before you left us are now blown up into a most enormous concave, and rise every day more and more. . . . You praised them a little too soon for the modesty of their head-dresses, for as the humour of a sick person is often driven out of one limb into another, their superfluity of ornaments, instead of being entirely banished, seems only fallen from their heads upon their lower parts. What they

have lost in height they make up in breadth, and contrary
to all rules of architecture, widen the foundations at the
same time that they shorten the superstructure."

But in spite of these male animadversions the hooped
petticoats went merrily on their way with a considerable
interval until they ripened into the crinoline of the
Victorian era. Those charming chairs of Queen Anne and
the succeeding Georges, with their wide seats, their conveniently set backs, and no arms at all, to give more room
for the hoops, have remained as treasured possessions to
the descendants of these wrong-headed ladies who thus
persisted in disfiguring "their lower parts."   But the
pride of the housewife's heart at this period would
probably have been lacquer, which was highly fashionable.
The Dutch taste had in its turn been greatly influenced
by the Oriental, and "Japanned" furniture was speedily
introduced into England. Certainly the Oriental china of
which there was such a quantity in the rooms of the ladies
of quality, looked its best in those glass-fronted lacquer
cabinets.

An imaginary gentleman complains in the *Spectator* of
how his fashionable wife "next set herself to reform every
room in my house, having glazed all my chimney pieces
with looking glasses, and planted every corner with such
heaps of china, that I am obliged to move about my own
house with the greatest caution and circumspection for
fear of hurting some of our brittle furniture."   It was
probably not only the china which this unfortunate
gentleman had to complain of, but the lacquer-work
tables and card tables, chairs and clock cases, and he
would have retired with relief to his own solid walnut
bureau and dependable chair; to which a few knocks
more or less would outrage nobody's feelings.

So much was Japanning the fashion that the little girls learnt it at school, and it was considered a good and virtuous occupation, an essential accomplishment for a young lady.   History does not reveal what were the results of an art that could be learnt for a "guiney entrance and some 40s more to buy material to work upon," but they probably had slight connection with the charming old English lacquer-work which has survived the centuries and is now so much sought after.   Occasionally an English-made cabinet was sent out to Japan to be lacquered, but considering the length of time such a journey would have taken in those days, the housewife who so confided her possession to the vagaries of wind and weather must have had both faith and patience. More usually, except where real Oriental lacquer furniture could be procured, the English furniture was lacquered at home—black, green, blue, buff and red, which latter colour is considered nowadays particularly valuable. The pagodas, mountain landscapes, and the cheerful little figures wrought in gold on the surface were regarded at the time as remarkable reproductions of the original patterns, but it is doubtful whether the Japanese visitor would always have recognised his native surroundings.

The lady's bedroom of this time is well worth a visit, and indeed elegance was desirable since she had borrowed the French custom of receiving her gentlemen friends while she was still in bed after her early cup of chocolate, though she perhaps indulged herself less in this habit than the ladies of the early Georgian period who came after. Swift in his journal to Stella describes dining with a lady of his acquaintance who was sick in bed, upon three herrings and a chicken. "The dinner," he adds, "was of my bespeaking." The Dean had a passion for herrings which it is to be hoped was shared by his hostess. The tall four-post bed is upholstered with curtains and hangings of velvet, brocade, or needlework with two stools at the foot to match. There is also a high-backed settee covered in "shadowed" needlework, or *petit point*, and perhaps a Granny upholstered chair for the further accommodation of her friends. For her clothes she would have more room than her grandmother. The old chest has grown into the chest of drawers, and that again has further developed into the tall boy, while there is a roomy wardrobe borrowed from the Dutch, progenitor of our own and probably a great deal larger and handsomer. Her minute washing stand is certainly out of all proportion to the rest of the furniture and the little jug and basin look as if they could never have served any more serious purpose than a rinsing of the hands. Let us hope a tub or bath of some kind, or as we find sometimes in these old houses, a marble basin let into the wall, was occasionally requisitioned.

In the adjoining dressing-room would be a walnut or lacquer dressing table with many drawers, such as we use in these days for a writing table. There were no lack of drawers in Queen Anne's day, and the old toilet glasses on boxes also provided receptacles for the paint and patches which were essential to a lady's toilet. Sometimes the dressing table would be dispensed with, and the glass mounted on a tiny miniature bureau with drawers and pigeon holes all complete and generally decorated with marquetry, would be merely placed upon a stand.

We, who in our time have had occasion to wrestle with the inferior furniture of the Victorian era may appreciate the admirable workmanship of the eighteenth century. Every drawer lined with oak ran with smoothness in its proper groove, and these ladies should certainly have had nothing to ruffle or discompose them in the course of their morning toilet, unless it were a difference of opinion with their beaux.

The bedroom, like the parlour, would probably be panelled. An Oriental paper such as we have seen at Denham could be procured but was still rare. At the Blue Paper warehouse were sold figured paper hangings, some resembling tapestry or needlework, others marble or real wainscoting, but it was reserved for a later and less fastidious age to find much pleasure in such atrocious imitations. On the panelled walls the lady would have one or two of the pretty mirrors of the period in a frame of marquetry or gesso, or she might have one of Venetian fashion from the Duke of Buckingham's factory at Lambeth with the bevelled edge and the blue glass rosettes.

If we envy the eighteenth-century housewife in nothing else, and there is little reason why we should, we may at least try to emulate the simplicity, usefulness, and elegance of her bedroom decoration and appointments.

CHAPTER XII

THE LADY OF QUALITY

FROM a superficial standpoint it must always seem curious that a good but admittedly stupid woman such as Queen Anne should have lent her name to so brilliant a period of English history and English literature.

Anne, the last of the Stuarts, had inherited neither the charm nor the ill-regulated vivacity of her forbears. She had neither the genius of Queen Elizabeth nor the personality and intelligence of Queen Victoria, and could have lent no spark of inspiration either to the great soldier who fought for her, nor to the writers and poets who have set her reign in some opinions on the same level as the Augustan era in Rome or the Age of Pericles in Greece.

It was an accident of circumstance that she should have ascended the throne at a time when England, after a period of internal upheaval destructive to all development, had begun under the Constitutional government of William III. to find herself once more and to recover her self-assurance. But William was after all a foreigner, and it was known that his heart was rather in Holland than in England, while Anne was essentially an English princess. To this fact and to her strong Protestantism she owed such mild popularity as she could boast, and this was no doubt enhanced by the sense of protective chivalry which a civilised country naturally accords to a woman sovereign. It was an accepted fact, moreover, after the death of the little Duke of Gloucester that another foreigner would succeed her, and one as it proved who had much less claim to respect than Dutch William.

Meantime the country had re-awakened to the sense of her own greatness. While the Duke of Marlborough won her glorious victories in the field, while a galaxy of famous writers—Pope, Swift, Addison, Steele, and others —made her age famous in the annals of literature, and while commerce prospered exceedingly, Queen Anne sat on the throne, inert, fat, commonplace, ruled by the Duchess of Marlborough, and later by Mrs. Masham, no more personally associated with the universal greatness and activity about her than she was with the admirable domestic furniture which we still call by her name.

But she was an undeniably virtuous woman. Both she and Queen Mary must have inherited from their mother Anne Hyde and her progenitors a true British middle-class respectability; they certainly did not owe their indifference and dislike to the accepted diversions of the time to their Stuart ancestry. But Mary died young, and there is nothing to show that either she or her younger sister had any far-reaching or inspiring influence upon society in general.

While Anne kept her court free from scandal, all the literature of the time, the plays, memoirs, and newspapers give a picture of fashionable society which is certainly not elevating. The coffee-houses, of which there were now an enormous number, were largely responsible for an increase in that deterioration in manners which had

already characterised the Restoration. The men acquired
the habit of retiring to the coffee-houses and taverns to
drink and gamble, to talk politics and read the newspapers, which could be seen there for 1d. The merchants
met one another at Garraway's, the clergy at Child's in
St. Paul's Churchyard, while the more fashionable
repaired to the "Cocoa Tree" in Pall Mall, or still more
select, to White's Chocolate House in St. James's Street,
where the entrance was raised to 6d. For the generality
of men of all social grades and professions there were
hundreds of others.

Meantime the ladies sat at home or visited their female
friends, drank a dish of tea and gambled as furiously as
their husbands. Money for gambling now meant a
heavy item, and the lady was constantly in debt and
difficulties. She could also if she liked attend one of the
four theatres then opened at Dorset Gardens, Lincoln's
Inn Fields, Drury Lane, or the Queen's Theatre, and
regale herself with the coarse and witty plays of Congreve
or Wycherley, or other dramatists of the period. But the
separation of the sexes in society naturally tended to
greater coarseness in the men, and an increasing indulgence in gossip and tittle-tattle in the women.

Feminine intelligence had sunk to a low ebb since old
Markham set up his standard for the moral and mental
equipment of an English housewife. In the *Spectator*
Mr. Addison publishes an imaginary journal of a Lady of
Quality, which, though a satire may give us a not wholly
fancy picture of the manner in which the Clorindas of
those days spent their time.

"*Wednesday.* From eight till ten. Drank two dishes of chocolate
in bed, and fell asleep after them.

" From ten to eleven. Eat a slice of bread and butter, drank a dish of bohea and read the *Spectator*.

" From eleven to one. At my toilette ; tried a new hood. Gave orders for Verry to be combed and washed. Mem. I look best in blue.

" From one till half an hour after two. Drove to the 'Change. Cheapened a couple of fans.

" Till four. At dinner. Mem. Mr. Froth passed by in his new liveries.

" From four to six. Dressed ; paid a visit to old Lady Blithe and her sister, having before heard they were gone out of town that day.

" From six to eleven. At basset. Mem. Never set again upon the ace of diamonds."

Here is a glimpse into a life " filled with a fashionable kind of gaiety and laziness," which without being vicious is entirely empty either of duty or intelligent occupation, and gives an impression of quite remarkable dullness.

Well might Clorinda have envied the ladies who sat on the carpet with Mr. Pepys and played, " I love my love with an A," in an age which if one of no greater refinement at least had the merit of more variety and enjoyment ! Lord Chesterfield, in a later and still more corrupt age, refers regretfully to the " decent days of Queen Anne," when " the shamelessness of public dissipation was impossible." " Every woman of fashion kept what was called 'a Day,' which was a formal circle of her acquaintances of both sexes, unbroken by any card-tables, tea-tables, or other amusements. There the fine women and fine men met perhaps for an hour," before the latter repaired to the coffee-houses and the ladies began their cards. This may have been decent, but it was as dull as demoralising, and the ladies, taking as a rule little interest in politics, which were then a burning question, the conversation between the sexes

appears to have languished. Sunday calling was also
fashionable, and on other days when the ladies did not
attend on one another personally they sent a footman
to ask a "How do ye?" or as it was commonly called, a
"Howdie."

No wonder that in this rather uneventful round of
occupations for the fair sex the ambition of a young lady
of quality was to be a toast of the season. Lady Mary
Wortley Montague attained this distinction at the Kit-
Kat Club at the age of seven. Could the gallant gentlemen, her father's friends, who chose her to this honour
and cut her name with a diamond upon the glass goblet,
have foreseen the boon she was much later to discover
in the East, and to introduce into Europe against over-
whelming opposition, the weapon which was to combat
the all-pervading terror of small-pox, it is doubtful
whether they would have been nearly so interested as
they were by the pert prattle of a precocious and pretty
child!

The origin of the toast was a roasted pippin dropped
into a hot drink, a tankard of spiced ale or sack. There
are wild and not too reputable legends of how in the
days of the "Merrie Monarch" the toast became a lady!
Charles II. is said to have issued a proclamation against
so much toast drinking, but was naturally himself the
first to ignore it. The toast drinking and the drinking
of healths began when the cloth had been removed, and
in Queen Anne's reign punch was first introduced for
the purpose.

> "A Cordial that supports the troubled Heart,
>   And dost infuse new life in ev'ry part,
>   Thou clear'st our Reason, and inform'st our Soul
>   And mak'st us Demy Gods when o'er a Bowl."

This at least was Edward Ward's opinion of the new drink, and the author of the " London Spye " had an exhaustive knowledge of most of the things of his day.

Here is a contemporary recipe for this potent drink which was now served out liberally on every festive occasion, including christenings and weddings, and even funerals may almost be placed in this category—"Two quarts of Water to a Quart of Brandy with 6 or 8 Lisbon Lemmons, and half a Pound of fine Loaf Sugar. Then you will find it to have a curious fine scent and flavour and drink and taste as clean as Burgundy wine." Burgundy wine, and indeed, all other French wine were rather at a discount owing to the heavy tax put upon them during the war. Port, however, and all wines from Portugal were comparatively cheap, and England began in consequence to be a port-drinking country, with increasingly bad effect upon the manners and morals of succeeding generations in the Hanoverian period. It is a rather curious reflection that but for the wars with France, at the close of the seventeenth and the beginning of the eighteenth century, our forefathers need not have learnt to eat so many sour (Spanish) grapes, and we ourselves might not have been such a gouty generation ! The lower classes drank a pernicious drink called Brunswick Mum, which after a very little made the consumer speechlessly drunk. All sorts of hot ale were also favoured including gill-ale, which consisted of ground ivy mixed in strong ale with a touch of horseradish, and should have been a sufficiently stimulating mixture to the most hardened interior !

Early marriage was another form of escape from prevailing feminine boredom, or another sign of precocious masculine activity, from whichever point of view we may

like to look at it. Marriages continued to be arranged,
and arranged with much care among the better class of
people. But if it was exciting for a young lady to be the
cause of a duel fought in Lincoln's-inn-Fields between
her admirers, how much more exciting was it (seeing that
marriage was the end and aim of female education), for
a little girl less well brought up to slip away and marry a
boy of fourteen, so that they might both as they thought
be free from the inconvenient and inconsiderate tutelage
of parents and guardians. Unfortunately these marriages
sometimes proved the worst of inconveniences, for if
they did not, as too frequently happened, turn out a
success, it was no easy matter to dissolve them. A secret
marriage in a private house with only a couple of friends
present was constantly resorted to to avoid expense, the
banns being dispensed with and a license obtained for
the modest sum of £1 1s. Such a practice, however,
was put a stop to by the Marriage Act of 1712, but the
rates on births, marriages, and funerals, were all very
heavy, while a yearly tax of £1 had actually been levied
on bachelors over twenty-five years of age !

All the ladies were not such lie-a-beds as Clorinda.
The Morning service at St. Paul's, Covent Garden,
became quite fashionable, since it was pleasant to take
an early walk in the market and smell the herbs. The
Mall was still a favourite exercise ground, but here as a
security for good behaviour, the ladies were no longer
allowed to go masked.

The fashionable life of London at this period was
lived round the neighbourhood of Covent Garden, Soho
Square, Leicester Square, and the streets south of
Piccadilly, while the charming houses of Queen Anne's
Gate, in the City of Westminster, were now building. Swift

writes that he pays 8s. a week for two rooms in Bury Street, on the first floor. "Plaguey deep," he considers it, but he spends nothing on eating! When he removed to Chelsea, which was still practically in the country, he is not unreasonably disgusted to find that he is expected to pay "6s. a week for one silly room with confounded coarse sheets." House rent, however, was not dear. A "lightsome," fashionable house in some genteel part of the town could apparently be had for £30, £40, or £50 a year.

Hackney coaches and sedan chairs plied the streets in great numbers, the coaches being hired for 1s. for a mile and a half, the fare of a chair being 1s. a mile. Neither the coaches nor chairs were as yet protected by glass, and the ladies did not always have a very pleasant time of it in their expeditions for shopping or visiting, since there was no proper police force, and the city watch were quite unable to deal with the street ruffians who in those days were recruited from the young bloods and rakes of London society, and who found considerable amusement in tormenting the peaceable citizens. Naturally the "Lady of Quality" usually went abroad in her own magnificent coach and four, which found some difficulty in making its way through the jostling crowds in the streets, at night lighted only by small oil lamps, or in her own chair attended by numerous running footmen.

Another fashionable means of locomotion in Queen Anne's reign, and one which must, under privileged circumstances, have been far pleasanter, was by barge on the river. People of quality kept their own barges—dressed their watermen in livery, and time being a matter of less importance in those days, an agreeable airing could be enjoyed from Chelsea to Westminster or to the

city. The less favoured individual who had to find his
way by the public barges, had, however, much to endure
from the roughness and rudeness of the watermen, and
certainly a lady would have been safer in a hackney
coach. The penny steamer, which we have found too
slow for ordinary purposes, would have seemed a
dangerously rapid form of navigation to Queen Anne's
folk, who glided gently in their gaily caparisoned barges
between the green fields and market gardens about
Lambeth Palace, with little to detract from the harmony
or dignity of London's finer buildings, of the towers and
spires of Westminster and the city.

It was the age of the South Sea Bubble—an age of
speculation and gambling in cards and lotteries and
insurance. A lottery ticket throughout the eighteenth
century was a very common form of present to a lady,
and considering the dulness of her life, it cannot be
wondered at if she thankfully accepted such a diversion.
During the French war even dress, her most congenial
pre-occupation, had become a difficulty. A prohibitive
tariff was put on French goods, so naturally the English
woman's dress had deteriorated. Much wearing of the
slovenly "mob" called forth well-deserved comments in
the *Spectator*, as did the "immodest" assumption of the
riding-dress copied as far as possible from that of the
opposite sex, with which were worn a hat and feather,
and the hair was tied up in imitation of a perriwig.

There is an amusing letter in the *Spectator* of January,
1711–12, describing the sufferings of a lady during the
war who had laboured under the insupportable inven-
tions of English tire-women. At last, one Sunday morning in church, she overhears one lady whisper to another
that at the "Seven Stars," in King Street, Covent Garden,

15

there was a *Mademoiselle*, completely dressed, just come
from Paris. With great difficulty she restrained herself
until the service was over, and then regardless of the fact
that it was Sunday, hastened to the milliner's, only to
find that *Mademoiselle* (a wax doll), had already been lent
to a Lady of Quality in Pall Mall. When at length she
did get a sight of the " dear Moppet," she was shocked to
find how ridiculously she and English ladies in general
had been "trussed up" during the war, and, what she
already knew, how infinitely superior was the French
dress. Forthwith she sent herself for a French baby (or
doll) for the year 1712, and had her dressed by the most
celebrated tire-women and mantua-makers in Paris. To
no one was the conclusion of the war, brought about
by Marlborough's enemies and involving his downfall,
more welcome than to the fashionable lady, even it is
to be feared in some cases though her husband were a
whig !

Meantime we have not heard much of housewifery.
We have seen in the education of girls towards the close
of the seventeenth century that the domestic arts of
housekeeping, cookery, and needlework were being
greatly superseded by more showy accomplishments. In
the reign of Queen Anne at the famous educational establishments at Bethnal Green and Highgate, a fresh effort
was made to initiate the young ladies into these neglected
virtues. It is doubtful, however, whether the daughters
of the more fashionable mammas were encouraged to
trouble themselves much with such matters. They learnt
the needle (but did not practise it), dancing, French, a
little music on the harpsichord or spinet, to read, write,
and cast accounts in a small way. A great point was, of
course, made of the dancing, and some of the dances

ntroduced gave considerable uneasiness to the more old-
ashioned parent. "Just as my daughter was going to be
made a whirligig," exclaims one old gentleman, "I ran
n, seized on the child and carried her home!" A
radesman's daughter who was sent to school to be made
a complete gentlewoman, that is to say, a pert Miss who
would flutter her fan and sip her tea as if to the manner
born, describes her education in the female *Spectator*.
She was taught to dance, to sing, to play on the bass
viol, virginal, spinet, and guitar. She also learnt to make
wax work, to japan, and to paint upon glass, to raise
paste, make sweetmeats, sauces, and "everything that
was genteel and fashionable," but it is noticeable that the
sweetmeats and sauces were included under the category
of accomplishments.

Though they learnt the "needle," embroidery went
curiously out of fashion with the young ladies of this
period. This was of course partly due to the amount
of time spent on cards, and while they sat and sipped
their tea and gossiped, it was presumably not convenient
to have a large piece of embroidery on hand. Perhaps
also, they no longer felt called upon to work chair-covers
and bed-hangings as their mothers and grandmothers had
done before them, now that the charming chintzes and
calicoes had been introduced to help in their furnishing.
Calico-printing was a new industry and the calico and
cotton goods imported originally from the East became
extremely popular with the housewife, both for her own
adornment and that of her rooms. Its cost was a great
deal less than that of wool, and as it began to be
prejudicial to the woollen trade, a heavy tax was
presently imposed upon it. The wool industry was
indeed so rapidly declining, that a fine of £5 was

exacted where linen was used instead of wool for
purposes of burial. Neither was it to be worn during
life, for not many years after the death of Queen Anne,
the poor ladies, victims alike of politics and commerce,
were prohibited from wearing " painted calicoes " at all.

There is no doubt that the London lady was beginning
to have serious trouble with her servants. " Like mistress, like maid," is an old saying, and one which in
common with many platitudes has a surprising amount
of truth in it. The pleasure-loving dissipated days of
the Restoration had set the servants an example of
pleasure-seeking also, which they were naturally not
slow to follow. In Queen Anne's reign the wages in
London, at all events, began to go up. The country girl
who came up to town in a waggon and engaged herself
for a situation at forty or fifty shillings a year, very soon
got the herb woman or the chandler woman, recognised
agents for this purpose, to find her something better,
while the housewife of small means who had trained her
carefully in her duties was left lamenting. A not uncommon situation however for the housewife of small
means of all ages ! Wages rose to £6, £7, and £8 a
year, and the lady's maid aped her mistress's clothes,
took snuff, and drank tea when she could get it,
pouring fresh boiling water no doubt on the leaves
already used in the parlour.

An innumerable number of men-servants were necessary to run a house of any consideration in London,
and these were always a difficulty. There was the valet,
the butler, the hall-porter, the steward, and many footmen, a particularly insolent race, who had somehow
acquired all sorts of privileges. These men, who had
to escort their masters and mistresses everywhere and

wait for them, were allowed the use of the upper gallery
at the theatres, and often adopting their master's titles,
held their own parliaments in the ante-chamber of the
House of Lords.

Naturally the worst characteristics of the domestic
servants of this time have lived after them in the
pamphlets, newspapers, and memoirs, their virtues
which must surely have existed—and they had much
to put up with—were, we imagine, "interred with their
bones." Swift, who as chaplain in a nobleman's house
had suffered many indignities, such as being obliged to
leave the table before the sweets were served, and greatly
from the impertinence of the lacqueys, throws a very
lurid light upon their habits in his "Advice to Servants,"
and also tells us a good deal about their duties and perquisites. The former, for the indoor servants were
beginning to approach much more nearly to our own,
except that more men and fewer women servants were
kept. The perquisites were many, including, after an
evening of play, the old packs of cards and wax candles
for the butler. Bottles were an important perquisite
then as now, and clear crystal glass having come in to
general use on the table, the glass man gave the butler
quite a large percentage in the pound for all broken
glasses which he was called upon to renew.

Vails again were a very important item to the servant
and a heavy one for the visitor, who if he were only
dining in the house, had to run the gauntlet of all the
men-servants in the hall on leaving. If he "had lain
a night," he was expected to remember not only
the · cook and the housemaid in addition, but also
the scullion who then took the place of a kitchenmaid, the gardener, and the stablemen, as we have

seen from the journal of the Sussex squire at this period.

Some of us find it a dread ordeal to leave a modern hotel with the ever doubtful decision between the number who expect a tip and the number who have earned one, but this is a comparatively light matter to the exodus from a country house in the old days.

The little foot-page was a small but important member of the household of a gentleman of quality. His livery was very handsome, and it was his business to accompany his master when he went abroad. In this manner he received his training and became a real page, and ultimately a valet, but meantime, when he was in the servants' quarters, at the mercy of his superiors, he was probably the recipient of a good many knocks to remind him of his proper place. No doubt he was as troublesome as the " buttons " of the modern household, and deserved it all, and grew in his turn to be as insolent as the rest of them.

But the little " Black-guard " boy upon whom, in the absence of master and mistress so much work was thrust by his betters, always has a certain pathos. Much more was this the case when they were really little black boys, slaves brought home from the Indies, whom it was for a time the fashion to keep. These poor children wore silver collars round their necks, engraved with their owner's name, and were more especially the property of the lady. While they were little, they would be her pet and plaything, fed with sugar-plums, and at the mercy of her caprices, but on the whole kindly treated. Sometimes a lady had her portrait painted with the little nigger-boy at her knee, on much the same footing as her King Charles spaniel, her parrot, and her monkey.

Readers will remember the charming passage in
Esmond, where Beatrix is flouting her cousin and
enumerating her claims to a good husband : "I cannot toil, neither can I spin, but I can play twenty-three
games on the cards. I can dance the last dance, I can
hunt the stag, and I think I could shoot flying. I can
talk as wicked as any woman of my years, and know
enough stories to amuse a sulky husband for at least
one thousand and one nights. I have a pretty taste
for dress, diamonds, gambling, and old china. I love
sugar-plums, Malines lace (that you brought me, cousin,
is very pretty), the opera, and every thing that is useless
and costly. I have got a monkey and a little black boy—
' Pompey, sir, go and give a dish of chocolate to Colonel
Graveairs '—and a parrot and a spaniel, and I must
have a husband. 'Cupid, you hear ?' 'Iss, Missis !'
says Pompey, a little grinning negro Lord Peterborough
gave her, with a bird of Paradise in his turbant, and a
collar with his mistress' name on it. 'Iss, Missis !' says
Beatrix, imitating the child. 'And if husband not come,
Pompey must go fetch one.' And Pompey went away
grinning with his chocolate tray."

But unfortunately, the little Pompeys grew big and
awkward, their mistresses tired of them, and the situation was altogether less pleasant. Not infrequently
they ran away, and were advertised for in the papers,
but their chance of escape with the silver dog-collar
about their necks was lamentably small.

When the seventeenth-century housewife wished for
an airing, as with her comparatively modest views she
usually did about once a year, she betook herself to
Epsom or to Tunbridge Wells, which latter place, with
its iron water and fine air and country, provided a

suitable resort for the fashionable folk who wished to carry their society with them. Writing some years after the death of Queen Anne, Defoe speaks of Tunbridge Wells as the most respectable of the spas, where a lady need not lose her reputation "without some apparent folly of her own, since the company who frequent Tunbridge Wells seem to be a degree or two above the society that use some other places, and therefore are not so very apt, either to meddle with other People's Affairs, or to censure rudely and causelessly if they do."

As a place of amusement, Bath was beginning to be a serious rival to Tunbridge, though the latter with its charming Pantiles continued to be much frequented until comparatively recent times. At Bath, throughout the eighteenth century, quality, fashion, and folly could in the Pump-room find plenty of food for gossip and scandal. According to Defoe, it was now "a resort of the sound as well as of the sick, and a place that helps the indolent and the gay to commit that worst of murders—that is to say, the killing of time. In the morning the young lady is fetched in a close chair, dressed in her bathing clothes that is, stript to the shift, to the Cross-Bath. Then the music plays her into the bath, and the women who tend her present her with a little floating wooden dish, like a basin, in which the lady puts a handkerchief and a nosegay, and of late the snuff-box is added. She then traverses the bath, if a novice with a guide, if otherwise by herself, and having amused herself an hour or two, calls for her chair, and returns to her lodging!" Bath holds a unique place in the social history of the eighteenth century, and is still steeped in its most "rakish" atmosphere.

It was at Bath that George II. and his Queen, before ever they came to the throne, held for a great part of the year their rival Court. At Bath Beau Nash at a late period ruled as absolutely and with a greater tyranny of detail than any prince could have done, and it is to Bath that we owe some of the most sprightly scenes of Jane Austen's novels.

CHAPTER XIII

THE PUDDING AGE

"WHAT an excellent thing is a English pudding!" exclaims Misson, the French traveller who visited England in the reign of George I. and carefully noted his impressions.

He finds a pudding rather difficult to describe, however, and can only explain that flour, milk, eggs, butter, sugar, suet, marrow, raisins, etc., are the chief ingredients : that it is baked in an oven, boiled with meat, and that there are fifty different ways of making it. "*Blessed be he that invented Pudding,*" he adds, though whether with genuine admiration, or with something of a sneer at the solidity and want of imagination of English cooking, is not clear.

Puddings had been popular in English kitchens ever since there was an oven to bake them in, but apparently up to the eighteenth century they had been principally made of meat. Blood puddings we have heard of constantly, on the tables of the common folk, and puddings in the bill of fare of their betters usually meant some baked concoction of marrow or suet and the meat of internals of an animal. The sweet pudding of more innocent ingredients only begins to appear at the close of the Stuart dynasty, when, and henceforward, however, it is heard of quite incessantly.

Queen Anne was a stout lady with a large appetite. She thought she required, and she certainly enjoyed, plenty of nourishment, and she no doubt influenced the cooking of her period a great deal more directly than she did any of those brilliant achievements for which her reign has become famous.

> "Queen Anne, Queen Anne, she sits in the sun,
>   As white as a lily, as brown as a bun,"

are the words of an old rhyme which served as the accompaniment to a nursery game many years ago, and may even do so now. At all events they helped to impress upon the childish mind a vision of a stout, comfortable lady who sat still and enjoyed a good dinner, and childish impressions are hard to uproot.

Queen Anne was even, perhaps, a little greedy : she sipped chocolate incessantly, and a chocolate-pot was her favourite present. It is said that she wept when her brother-in-law, William, did not offer her the green peas, and she once ate too many cherries. Her palate was not, however, very delicate, and she liked her food to be solid and plentiful.

When everything French was at a discount, when to be called a "French Dog" was the worst and most forcible insult that could be hurled at a well dressed gentleman in the street, the French cooking favoured by Charles II. also suffered something like eclipse, and the early Hanoverians certainly preferred quantity to quality. A few noblemen still had French cooks, however, and added the more elegant French dishes to the roast meats and puddings of their English table.

It is generally wholesome, and always interesting, to

see ourselves as other people see us, and the foreigners
who from time to time have visited our shores have,
as regards the details of our habits which impressed
them, proved valuable social historians. Misson, oddly
enough, thought the English beef over-rated, and the
mutton bad, but found the poultry more excellent and
tender than that of France, and he was probably the
only individual who ever held such a strangely inverted
opinion.

De Saussure, a Swiss who visited England at about
the same time, considered the meat more succulent and
delicate than in his own country, where, then as now,
apparently it was boiled or roasted to rags. They both
agree that the English of that day were large eaters,
and that a great deal of meat was eaten in comparison
to bread. They "nibble a few crumbs," says Misson,
" while they chew the meat by whole mouthfuls."

The dinner hour was by this time moved on to four
in fashionable circles, and was at two or three o'clock
among ordinary people. The fine folk could hardly
have been ready for it much sooner, since the lady had
her chocolate in bed, followed by a dish of tea and
something in the nature of breakfast quite late in the
morning. Supper was still a negligible quantity, but
the dish of tea again which followed the dinner, and
was a very sociable occasion, as much as five o'clock
tea is at the present day, almost amounted to a meal
in itself.

Those less exalted people who were not in a position
to keep French cooks contented themselves with many
fewer courses and dishes than their grandfathers before
them. One substantial dish of meat, a joint, roast or
boiled (stewing had gone temporarily out of fashion),

would be accompanied by the inevitable pudding, made of rice, flour, or breadcrumbs, which according to De Saussure, all foreigners greatly appreciated. Sometimes there would be fish, of which at this time there was a great quantity in London, and De Saussure complains that an English cook's only idea of preparing fish or vegetables is with butter. He laments, as he might lament almost as justifiably now, that vegetables are only served with the meat, though in his day they were apparently put in one dish under the roast or boiled joint. The dessert consisted of cheese and butter, fruit only appearing at the tables of " The Great."

" Among middling people," says Misson, " they have ten or twelve sorts of common meats, which infallibly take their turn at their tables, and two Dishes are their dinner, a Pudding for instance and a piece of roast Beef. Another time they will have a piece of Boiled Beef, and then they salt it some days beforehand, besiege it with five or six Heaps of Cabbage, Carrots, Turnips, or some other Herbs or Roots, well peppered and salted and swimming in Butter." Mutton was served in the same way, also fowls, pigs, ox-tripes and tongues, rabbits, pigeons, etc., all well moistened with butter without larding. "Two of these dishes," he adds, "always served up one after the other, make the usual dinner of a substantial gentleman or wealthy Citizen." Occasionally a guest might fancy the broth of boiled meat, which was thickened with a little oatmeal and flavoured with herbs, and served up in a porringer with bread crumbled in it.

It is gratifying to know that Monsieur de Saussure was much impressed by the cleanliness of the English table, the whiteness of the linen, and the brightness of the plate which in gentlemen's houses was kept with great care. He is particularly surprised at the perpetual changing of the knives and forks, "every time a plate is removed," which seems to him a great extravagance! English table manners may have been still very bad, and the Hanoverian Court was not at this period likely to improve them, but the little niceties and appointments of the table were, notwithstanding, it appears, in advance of other nations.

When the Sussex Squire entertained his humbler friends and neighbours, as was his custom, to a dinner on January 1st, he gave them the following bill of fare:—

Plumm Pottage
Calves Head and Bacon
Goose
Pig
Plumm Pottage
Roast Beef—Sirloin
Veal—a loin
Goose
Plumm Pottage
Boiled Beef

———

Two Baked Puddings
Three dishes of minced Pies

———

Two Capons
Two dishes of Tarts
Two Pullets.

The rather curious arrangement with the repetition of the same dish, suggest not that there were three courses, but that all the dishes were placed, according to an earlier custom, on the table at once, and that the table was a long one. The fact that the puddings were cooling while the Plum Pottage and the Sirloin were occupying the attention of the guests was an obvious fact which never seems to have claimed attention.

His receipt for Plumm Porridge is extremely suggestive of the plum pudding which was later to take its place and rank with mince pies in popularity at Christmas : "Take of Beef soup made of the legs of Beef 12 quarts ; if you wish it to be particularly good, add a couple of tongues to be boiled therein. Put fine bread, sliced, soaked and crumbled ; raisins of the sun, currants and pruants, two pounds of each ; lemons, nutmegs, mace and cloves are to be boiled with it in a muslin bag ; add a quart of red wine, and let this be followed, after half an hour's boiling, by a pint of sack. Put it into a cool place, and it will keep through Christmas."

Meat was undoubtedly cheap in those days when two tongues could be lightly added to a dish of pottage. The red wine and the sack were the inferior and exceedingly nasty substitute for brandy, the superiority of which as a preservative and for flavouring, was only discovered when it became more accessible. At Mid-Lent, on what was called "Refreshment Sunday," when the Gospel of the Loaves and Fishes was read, it was the custom to have a dish called Firmity, which still survives in the West of England. This was made of "cones" of wheat deprived of their skins and gently boiled, to which were added the yokes of eggs, sugar and flour, currants and raisins, and grated cinnamon.

The following recipes taken from an old MSS. recipe book, dated 1719, give us a good idea of the substantial dishes in favour two hundred years ago :—

A Pasty of Beef or Mutton.—A small rump or loin or shoulder of mutton boned ; beat it very well. Rub 10 lb. of meat with 4 oz. of sugar, let it stand 24 hours. Wipe it very clean or wash it with a glass of claret. Season high with pepper, nutmeg and salt. Lay in crust and cover so much meat with 2 lb. butter. Make a strong gravy of the bones, and add to the pasty.

All-a-brace Chickens or Pigeons.—Take your pigeons and beat them flat. Put butter in your stewpan, brown it very well and put the pigeons in and fry them very brown. Take as much gravy as will cover them, then put a fagett of sweet herbs and onion stuft (stuck ?) with cloves. Then cutt the livers and gizards each in two pieces and stew them with the pigeons. Then put in a few mushrooms, some lemon peel and anchovies, a little pepper ; stew them together, and when you see they are enough then put in a piece of butter, a little white wine and a little flower to thicken it. Lett it boyle over the fire till it is thick, then squeeze in the juice of a lemon, put it into your dish. Garnish with lemon.

To make an Apple Pudding.—Take as much pulp of boiled apples as you think will make your pudding and six eggs well beat, leave out half the whites. Two large spoonfuls of Naple biskett finely grated, sugar to your palate. Take the rind of a lemon or orange boiled tender and beaten in a mortar with a quarter pound of butter, and putt it in your dish with a fine paste att topp and bottom. Let it not be baked too much. You may add a spoonful of cream if you please.

The author of the "Compleat Housewife," which in several successive editions covers the first thirty years of the eighteenth century, regrets in his preface that " since we have to our disgrace so fondly admired the French Tongue, French Modes, and also French Messes," he is " obliged to include some Receipts of French Cookery as may not be disagreeable to English Palates."

There is a distinct difference in this book from the more elaborate dishes and bills of fare recommended in similar works in the preceding century. In turning its pages we seem to come on the foundations of that old-fashioned English cooking which, with the richer ingredients gradually weeded out, survived far into the nineteenth century, and is still to be occasionally met with in old-fashioned country inns of the better sort. Here there are over fifty recipes for puddings, and forty for cakes such as we might have on our tables to-day.

It must be remembered that materials used for such things were cheaper and more plentiful than they are now, and the housewife of those days could afford to be lavish with her cream, eggs, and butter, while the members of her household were immune from diet lists, and bilious attacks were accepted as periodically necessary evils !

For a good seed cake, two pounds of fresh butter, ten eggs with five whites, three spoonfuls of cream, four spoonfuls of good yeast, and a pound of carraway-comfits were all to be used. Here is the recipe for a characteristic baked pudding of the period, one of those which aroused the interest and admiration of foreigners :—

"Blanch half a pound of Almonds, and beat them fine with sweet Water, Ambergrease, dissolved in Orange-flower Water, or in some Cream ; then warm a pint of thick Cream, and melt in it half a pound of Butter ; then mix it with your beaten Almonds, a little Salt, a grated Nutmeg, and Sugar, and the yolks of six Eggs, beat it up together, and put it in a dish with Puff-paste, the Oven not too hot : scrape Sugar on it just before it goes into the Oven."

Even a "fine rice pudding" could not be made without half-a-pound of fresh butter, a quarter of a pound of sugar, six eggs, with a spoonful or two of sack ! In this worn little volume remain the actual markers of its original possessor, one Mary Wycke, to whom it was presented by Sir George Beaumont "in ye year 1734." This copy of the fifth edition was published in 1732, and had previously belonged to Jane Beaumont, who was perhaps Mrs. Wycke's mother, and her death or the

marriage of the daughter may have been the reason of
its changing hands.   The markers, strips of flannel or
fragments of a page of accounts, we may presume to be
Mary Wycke's.   One slip, black with age, remains em-
bedded between the pages on which are many recipes
for puddings, little hasty-puddings and the baked
pudding above mentioned being obviously first favourites.
One or two very special recipes are marked with a pin,
a pin obviously of the period, with a thick body, and a
quaint little brass head.

One of these recipes so marked is for baked herrings,
and we wonder if it was from such a dish that Dean
Swift had supped when his hostess was sick in bed.
Here, however, there are thirty herrings (all recipes are
for immense quantities), and they are laid in rows in a
venison pot and seasoned with onions, cloves, mace and
ginger.   To these is added a quart of claret, and they are
baked with household bread.   Another pin marks calf's-
foot jelly, which was then starting on its long and
dishonourable career as a sustaining food for invalids.
There are few households which do not possess some of
the minute glasses in which it was served to the patient,
and one of which within the memory of the last
generation was considered a sufficiently sustaining meal
to satisfy the insatiable pangs of a convalescent child's
hunger.

In old books we constantly read of the syllabubs which
were an invariable feature of hospitality in the country.
The following was the manner in which Mrs. Wycke
was ordered to prepare hers :—

" Take a quart of cream, not too thick, and a pint of
sack, and the juice of two lemons, sweeten it to your
palate, and put it into a broad earthen pan, and with a

whisk whip it, and as the froth rises, take it off with a spoon, and lay it in your syllabub-glasses, but first you must sweeten some claret or sack or white wine, and strain it and put seven or eight spoonfuls of the wine into eight glasses, and then gently lay in your froth. Set 'em by. Do not make them long before you use them."

There was another syllabub "from the cow," one which was a good deal simpler in its ingredients, but was probably considered in the country a greater luxury. This was made of wine or cider previously sweetened and flavoured with grated nutmeg, and the cow was milked straight into the mug, while half-a-pint or a pint of cream was poured on to the top. If the cow was not procurable, new milk warmed and poured from a height out of the spout of a teapot was considered equivalent !

To the many caudles of Mrs. Wycke's day, which were by no means restricted to the entertaining of " the Lady in the Straw" and her friends, was now added a *Tea Caudle*. "Make a quart of strong green tea, and pour it out into a skillet, and set it over the fire, then beat the yolks of four eggs, and mix with them a pint of white wine, a grated nutmeg, sugar to your taste, and put all together, stir it over the fire till 'tis very hot, then drink it in china dishes as caudle."

A great point is made throughout this little book of *China* dishes. The Pope's posset must be served in a china dish, although a basin is considered a more suitable receptacle for King William's posset, which is chiefly a mixture of cream and ale without the blanched almonds which were the principal ingredients of the former, and raised it to the dignity of a sweet.

Candied orange flowers, again, must most particularly

be put into a silver or china basin, pewter or common earthenware not being considered suitable. These so-called "china" dishes must, if English, have been made of Lambeth delft or the finer kind of Fulham ware, for in the first half of the eighteenth century there was as yet no actual porcelain manufactured in England at all. There are, however, as we have said in a previous chapter, plenty of those charming old delft posset and caudle pots and chocolate dishes still in existence which may pass for a very good imitation of china.

Mrs. Wycke was further assisted in the "Compleat Housewife" by "a scheme engraven on copper plate" for the best manner of arranging her dishes on the table. These "schemes" are to be found, sometimes much elaborated, in all the later cookery books, but this seems to have been one of the earliest to introduce them.

From this scheme we see that the dinner was not quite so limited to joint and pudding as the foreign critics would have us believe. There were still two courses, at all events for a dinner of ceremony, each consisting of five dishes. It is here also that we find the first mention of a "remove," which was an invariable feature of all subsequent dinners, while the dishes stood on the table. The "gravy soup" in the first course of a winter menu was to be removed with chicken and bacon. In the middle is a giblet pie, on either side Scotch collops and a fine boiled pudding, and at the end roast beef with horse-radish and pickles round. The second course consists, in the middle of the table, of a tansy garnished with orange, flanked by woodcocks on toast and a hare with a savoury pudding; at either end is a "turkey roasted" and a "buttered apple pie hot."

The elegant trifles of the Restoration table—the *quelque*

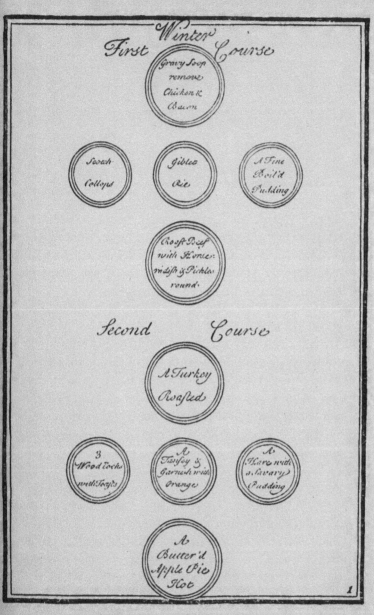

THE "COMPLEAT HOUSEWIFE'S" DINNER-TABLE.

chose and *devised paste,* the *warners* and *subtleties*—are all
conspicuous by their absence.   Here is good substantial
food, and plenty of it, suited to the healthy appetite of
an honest Briton with no superfluous follies and ele-
gancies, and nothing to encourage the dainty or
fastidious !

French cooking was indeed sadly in disgrace.   In the
preface to Mrs. Glasse's cookery book some twenty years
later, which was the most famous of those of the eighteenth century, it is remarked that, "So much is the
blind Folly of this Age, that they would rather be imposed on by a French Booby, than give encouragement
to a good English Cook !"   From this we may infer that
in the greater houses, and among those who aped their
betters, a chef with his superior skill was still held in
some esteem, and took advantage of English ignorance
to rob his master on every occasion.

A tansy was a favourite dish in the eighteenth century,
and was as inseparable from a bill of fare for Easter as a
roast goose at Michaelmas or a gooseberry tart at Whitsun-
tide.   Tansy juice was the forerunner of mint sauce as a
suitable flavouring for lamb.   There were tansy puddings
and tansy cakes, and these seem to some extent to have
taken the place of the grand sallets of an earlier period.

The baked tansy which Mrs. Wycke and her contemporaries were recommended to place in the middle of the
table for the second course, was to be made in most
extravagant fashion with twenty eggs, with eight whites
which were to be beaten and strained into a quart of
thick cream, one nutmeg, and three "Naples-biskets"
were to be grated into this compound, with "as much
juice of spinage, with a sprig or two of tansy, as will
make it as green as grass."   Then it must be sweetened

to taste, placed in not too hot an oven, and when done turned out on to a pie-plate, with "scraped sugar" and squeezed orange upon it, and the dish must be garnished with orange and lemon.

Apple and gooseberry tansy made a pleasant variety, and there was also a water tansy, which was not, however, so economical as it sounds, since it required sixteen eggs, half a pound of butter, sack, orange-flower water, sugar and salt, in addition to the other ingredients mentioned above !

Our ancestors, both in the seventeenth and eighteenth centuries, dearly loved sugar and all sweet flavouring, and the tax on sugar seems to have had little or no deterrent effect upon their lavish use of it. The "Compleat Housewife," however, adds several remedies for the "Panes of the Gout," which was by now a well-established malady, though little thought of prevention had as yet occurred. A milk diet is urgently recommended, or, for external use, " Mix Barbadoes Tar and Palm Oil an equal quantity, just melt them together, and gently anoint the Part affected."

The remedies recommended in these eighteenth-century books are as confiding in their faith as the earlier ones. "For the Biting of a Mad Dog," primrose roots stamped in white wine and strained are recommended. " Let the Patient drink a good draught of it " is the simple advice which two hundred years ago was considered apparently as efficacious as the whole Pasteur Institute. We can only hope that the dogs were not really mad, but merely out of temper.

The so-called " Mrs. Glasse" gives only three medical recipes in her cookery book, two of which are certain cures for the bite of a mad dog ; but these are a great

deal more elaborate. In one of them, "the Patient must
be blooded at the Arm, and a mixture of ground Liverwort and black pepper must be taken every morning
fasting for four mornings, in half a pint of cow's milk
warm. The patient must then go into the cold Bath
fasting for a month. He must be dipt all over, but not
stay in (with his head above water) longer than Half a
minute, if the Water be very cold. After this he must go
in three times a Week for a Fortnight longer."

This is indeed a drastic measure when we consider
that a bath at this period was still a comparatively rare
event, and a cold one would have been interpreted by
the majority as certain death. If the simple morning
tub and an unpleasant mixture of pepper and some
harmless herb were considered a certain cure or preventive against the terrors of hydrophobia, we may safely
conclude that some of the dogs of those days suffered
merely from a severe form of nervous irritation.

Yet medicine had made a great advance under the
reign of Queen Anne. Hospitals were opened, and the
idea of dispensing had been founded as long ago as
1687. Science, however, made its way but slowly against
the credulity of ages, and the housewife who cherished
her grandmother's favourite recipes and did her own
distilling was infinitely shocked at the possibility of their
being superseded by impertinent new-fangled notions.

The English people suffered heavily then, as now,
from colds. "When a cold grows inveterate in England," says Misson, "you maye reckon it the beginning
of a mortal Distemper, especially to strangers. You must
beware therefore how you neglect a cold." Dr. Ratcliff's
recipe for a cold, then quite recent, is included in the
"Compleat Housewife." "Make some sack-whey with rose-

mary boil'd in it, mix a little of it in a spoon with twenty Grains of Gascoin Powder, then drink half a pint of your sack-whey, with twelve drops of Spirit of Harts-horn in it, go to Bed and keep warm, do this two or three nights together."

Misson's description of lighting a coal fire at this period is so quaint as to be worth quoting. The small coal man was still going his rounds with his sack on his back, and he must have found it a profitable business, since in London no coal fire could be lit without his assistance. "To make a coal fire they put into the chimney certain Iron Stoves about half a foot high with a plate of Iron behind and beneath, before and on each side are bars placed, and fastened like the wires of a cage, all of Iron. This they fill with coal, small or great as they run, and in the middle they put an handful of small coal, which they set fire to with a bit of Linnen or Paper. As soon as this small coal begins to burn, they make use of the Bellows, and in less than two minutes the other coal takes fire—you must blow a little longer after this, till the fire is a little spread round about, and then you hang up the Bellows."

The lighting of a fire was indeed a serious business until it occurred to some ingenious mind to use wood. There was no convenient box of matches to be produced from the housemaid's pocket, or pilfered from the nearest bedroom, with an unfailing supply to be drawn upon until an obstinate fire was coaxed into life. A hundred years hence, a box of matches will be as interesting a relic of the past to be preserved in museums as a tinder-box is to-day, and our descendants will commiserate us for such a clumsy and dangerous device.

It should always be a consoling reflection that each age

in turn may have so much food for self-congratulation and feel so immeasurably superior to the one that preceded it. Meantime the match, whether of the old Lucifer description, wax, or safety, has been a "very present help," as Mrs. Wycke might have said had she been fortunate enough to possess any !

The "Compleat Housewife" would have been in no sense "compleat" had it not contained instructions for other matters besides cooking and medicine. There is a recipe for "destroying Buggs"—very necessary in those days of wainscoted rooms, and streets in which the scavengers only came round at stated intervals. There is "An excelment way of washing, to save soap and whiten cloaths," and there is a recipe "To Boil Plate," which to modern notions is positively alarming.

"Take twelve gallons of water, or a quantity according to your Plate in Largeness or Quantity. There must be water enough to cover it. Put the water in a Copper or large Kettle, and when it boils put in half a pound of red Argil, a pound of common Salt, an ounce of Rock-Alum ; first put your Plate into a charcoal fire, and cover it till it is red-hot, then throw it into your Copper, and let it boil half an hour, then take it out and wash it in cold fair water, and set it before the charcoal fire till 'tis very dry."

That the charming plate of the Queen Anne and early Georgian period survived this drastic treatment is all that can be said in its favour, and indeed it is not unimaginable that such of Mrs. Wycke's silver as remains is suffering more acutely from pernicious acids and plate powders in the modern pantry than ever it did from a good "charcoal fire."

Another instruction of some interest is for the "Wainscot Colour for Rooms," from which we learn that "'Tis

now the universal fashion to paint all Rooms of a plain
Wainscot Colour, and if it should alter, it is by mixing
any other colour with the White Lead instead of Yellow
Oaker. There must be bought six pots of earth and six
brushes and keep them to what they belong to." The
painting of walls referred to at Denham Place had
evidently gained ground, but why, we wonder, did our
ancestors bequeath us the horrible heritage of "yellow
Oaker" which, highly vanished, became rampant by the
Victorian era, and still survives in imitation of grained
wood, on the walls of the more depressing lodging-
houses !

According to Misson's point of view, there was not
much informal hospitality among the Londoners of his
day. There were banquets on set occasions, but a dish
of tea among friends seems to have been usually considered sufficient. This was no doubt due to the men
preferring to find their social distractions at the clubs
and coffee-houses and taverns, where they were free from
even the very slight restraint imposed by the presence of
ladies upon the coarseness of conversation and table
manners under the early Georges. Lord Chesterfield's
famous letters to his godson, while they made little effort
to improve the moral tone of society, laid tremendous
stress upon the value of external manners and good
breeding, and perhaps did not fall on wholly barren
ground judging by the slight improvement in these
matters, and in the high value set upon superficial gentility
as the century progressed.

The famous Mrs. Glasse's cookery book, "The Art of
Cookery made Plain and Easy," which seems to meet
every need of the housewife, not only in the number of
the recipes but also in the careful directions for

marketing, was in its authorship one of the cleverest
frauds of the eighteenth century. " Mrs. Glasse " never
existed at all, nor was the famous book written "by a
Lady," as is set forth on the title page of the first editions.
The real author was a very ingenious person called Hill,
a Jack-of-all-trades, whose pretentions were the scorn and
the laughing stock of his contemporaries.

None the less he throve upon them, and with a facile
pen and inventive mind he made a considerable amount
of money in Grub Street, while pursuing the combined
trades of apothecary, naturalist, and quack in St. Martin's
Lane.

In his leisure moments it occurred to this versatile
gentleman to make a collection of old recipes, and,
while altering the language and adding a little fresh
material culled from his own or his neighbour's
experience, to produce a new and most inclusive volume,
which was pronounced by his two inimical critics, Dr.
Johnson and Edward Dilly, the book-seller, to be the
best of their time. It was not here, however, that his
ingenuity showed itself.

" Dr." Hill, as he chose to be called, decided that a
cookery book would have a greater chance of popularity
with the housewife if written by one of her own sex, and
if it could be bought at a place where she also procured
her household necessities. Consequently, in the two first
editions it was announced, as we have seen, " By a
Lady," and in the later ones " by Mrs. Glasse" with so
much success, that to this day it is known and spoken of
with a certain modicum of respect as " Mrs. Glasse's
Cookery Book." By a special remunerative arrangement
it was sold at Mrs. Ashburn's china shop at the corner of
Fleet Ditch, where it was brought before the lady's notice

while she chose her teacups and caudle pots, and seems to have received so warm a reception that the sale presently spread to other shops in the City.

Dr. Hill and Mrs. Ashburn both had every cause to be satisfied, the former by a financial success which did not, owing to his anonymity, interfere with what he chose to regard as his literary prestige, and the latter with her handsome percentage. The book certainly deserved its reputation for its innumerable number of recipes for roasting, boiling, made dishes, sauces, puddings, ways of dressing fish, distilling, etc., but there is much less of the miscellaneous entertaining information that is usually to be found in old books of this description. In this particular the author at the same time betrays his sex, and gives a more business-like appearance to his volume !

It is interesting to note that, though in this book occurs the recipe for a " Boiled Plumb Pudding," this is not the Plum Pudding of our Christmas table, which succeeded Plum Pottage. This plum pudding had, as yet, assumed no especial significance, Mince Pies continuing to be of supreme and solitary importance.

Supper dishes begin now to have their own appointed chapter, and as the century moved on supper became an established meal, and suitable little dishes increasingly occupied the housewife's attentions. We all know the china supper dishes of a rather later date, the bowl in the middle, the semi-circular dishes which surrounded it. In the reign of George II. there were various small delicacies for supper : " Hog's ears forced, pickled Pig's feet and ears, ox-Palates, and other such delicacies."

Cocks-combs for this purpose were forced in the following manner :—" Parboil your Cocks-Combs, then open them with a point of a knife at the great end.   Take the white of a Fowl, as much Bacon and Beef Marrow, cut these small, and beat them fine in a Marble Mortar, season them with salt, pepper and grated Nutmeg, and mix it with an egg, fill the Cocks-Combs, and stew them in a little strong gravy softly for half an hour, then slice in some fresh Mushrooms, and a few pickled ones ; then beat up the yolk of an egg in a little gravy, stirring it. Season with salt. When they are enough, dish them up in little dishes or plates."

This last meal, following soon after a prolonged and substantial dinner, and in the case of the men much drinking of port and other heavy wines, must be designed to tempt a jaded appetite, and to be a light and inspiriting conclusion or, more probably, accompaniment to an evening of high play. Such dishes as we have mentioned, little pasties, a salamongundy, that is to say, veal or poultry minced small with pickles and salad or forced cucumber, served in small quantities, might well prove alluring !

Among home-made drinks, *Cock-Ale* was a repulsive but popular drink of the period. The recipe is not attractive, but it was no doubt considered to have some special value, just as " Cock-Water," still more unpleasant in preparation, was considered an admirable cure for consumption. " To make Cock-Ale, take ten gallons of ale and a large Cock, the older the better, parboil the Cock, flea him and stamp him in a stone Mortar till his bones are broken (you must craw and gut him when you flea him), then put the Cock into two quarts of sack, and put to it three pounds of Raisins of the sun stoned, some blades of Mace, and a few cloves : put all these into a canvas bag, and a little before you find the Ale has done working, put the Ale and Bag together into a vessel. In a week or nine days' time bottle it up, fill the bottles to just above the neck, and give it the same time to ripen as other ale."

The illustration in the frontispiece taken from an old cookery book of the latter half of the eighteenth century gives us a good idea of the kitchen of the period and its appointments. We see the immensely wide open fire so extravagant of coal and the comparatively small ovens. The pot hangs on a smoke-jack controlled by a chain and over the fireplace are the usual kitchen utensils in pewter, and the long poles used for stirring the malt. Hams are hanging up to smoke on one side of the hearth, and on the other a large pudding is being placed in the brick oven reserved for baking. Here we may notice that men scullions are still employed. The cook is receiving a copy of the comprehensive manual which contains the picture from her mistress, and the " cook-maid" is basting the meat in a manner too seldom seen in these days, but one deserving of all praise.

In the foreground the butler is teaching a young footman to carve, and we have articles of cookery, confectionery and brewing displayed, all emblematic of the information contained in the same work.

A good deal of stress is still laid upon the art of brewing for which the directions are long and elaborate, and there are also supplementary exhaustive chapters in the proper management of the poultry farm, the dairy and the kitchen garden. Much water had flowed under the bridge since Markham published his "County Contentments," but he would have been gratified to find that a hundred years after his time the precepts with regard to the kitchen garden, the gathering and drying and distilling of herbs, though simplified had not been greatly departed from.

Cordial waters were still held in great esteem as well as home-made wines, cherry wine, turnip wine, an unattractive form of cider, balm wine and the old mead, in which however there are very few ingredients, only hops and sack or brandy, as compared with the much more elaborate recipe of Sir Kenelm Digby's of the previous century.

In what we have called the "Pudding Age" the English housewife, had through long and painful experience arrived at something akin to simplicity, but we must admit it was a simplicity which was far removed at this period from elegance. "An exquisite *bit* of roast pork" was considered a really dainty dish to set before a duchess !

CHAPTER XIV

WHAT MONEY COULD BUY

IN considering the question of the value of money at different periods of history, it is obvious that this can only be estimated by comparing people's wants with what their money can buy, and not by the intrinsic value of the coin. When we say that in the seventeenth and eighteenth century money was worth about five times what it is at present, and that the average income of a squire estimated at £450 would in these days be equivalent to between three and four thousand pounds, we must remember that the same rule applied to the price of the necessities with which he had to provide himself.

So in studying the housekeeping and other accounts which have been left us of the eighteenth century, we need not for ordinary purposes think of the value of the money itself as compared to that of to-day, but how far the income of an individual could meet his requirements.

Servants' wages may appear to us to have been very low until the nineteenth century, but an enormous number of servants had to be maintained in the most moderate establishments, the clothing and feeding of whom was no small item. Rents were low, but the tenants seem as a rule to have been entirely responsible for repairs, including the glazing of the windows and mending the roof. Travelling by post-chaise and even by coach was very dear, but on the other hand nobody wanted to travel so much as they do now. Clothes were dear, though certainly not dearer than at present, and as fashions did not change so rapidly they could be worn a great deal longer. Food on the whole was cheap, especially meat, but the taxes levied during the French wars, as we have seen, sent up the prices of a good many ordinary articles of consumption.

In the Sussex squire's journal which we have constantly alluded to, with its quaint English and Latin entries, and its spirited illustrations, we get a good notion of the expenses of a country gentleman in the opening years of the eighteenth century. We have already noticed his servants' wages in a previous chapter.

For a spinning wheel he gave 2s. 6d., and for spinning 6 lbs. of hemp, which was done in the neighbouring cottages, he paid 4s., and for carding 13 lbs. of wool he paid 3s. 4d. The prices for spinning and carding had risen to just twice the amount that had been paid by a country parson, also in Sussex, thirty years earlier, and the day-labourer's wage had risen to 1s. Our squire was very indignant, and with justice, at the taxes imposed upon him. The payment of his first Window Tax is illustrated in his journal by a small diamond-paned casement, and is made to convey every indication of annoyance. Presently he has to pay a Poll Tax for himself and his daughter amounting to 8s. 3d., and 6s. for his stock which is worth £50. For his land he pays a tax of four shillings in the pound which amounts to £4 4s., and another tax of £26 was levied upon him for the amount of his yearly income of £2,086. We can imagine that the old squire's expressions of opinion on this matter would be no less picturesque than those of his successor to-day, but if the

French war was expensive and not perhaps in his eyes altogether desirable, he had on the whole less to complain of than his descendants.

At Christmas he paid 10s. 3d. for tithes, 6d. to the fiddlers, 1s. to the "Howlers," that is to the boys who went round on New Year's Eve to wassail the orchards. He was a kindly charitable gentleman, and there are many little entries of his gifts to the poor. He constantly gave small sums to the poor widows in the parish, and occasionally there is an entry of 2s. 6d. to get someone he thought had been unfairly treated out of gaol. The insane who wandered about the country, "Mad Parson Perkins" and "Mad Maynard" are also frequent objects of his benevolence. Meantime the Poor Tax was perpetually rising, and at Easter he had to pay a Church Tax of 1s. 10d. in addition to his offering of 10s.

We may imagine him in his best long coat with the silver buttons, his flowered waistcoat, his breeches and his high top boots, his red weather-beaten face surmounted by the heavy wig, trying to keep awake in his square high pew through the lengthy discourse of the rector, in order to set a good example to his little motherless girl, and frequently relapsing into sound and unmusical slumbers. His loyalty to his Sovereign was only equalled by his horror of papistry, and while he paid 1s. 6d. towards the village bonfires to celebrate King William's return from the war, he had also subscribed yearly to the Protestant Briefe, a fund which had been raised in England for the support of the French Protestant Refugees.

It was still the custom in the country at Christmas for friends and neighbours, both rich and poor, to send one another presents of food or in kind, which was a great help to housekeeping expenses. Thus the squire receives from one neighbour two quarts of mead and two green geese, from another a dozen and a half of Lobsters, and from one of his farmer tenants the no less useful gift of two day's work with his team. Among his other presents are two dozen of china oranges, a haunch of venison, a "pott of cocks" (woodcock), "hammes, plumms and sweet meats," and one of his sisters always sends him half a buck and six bottles of brandy. Chocolate had become a regular item in the lists of his yearly presents, but tea in the country was still a rarity. He himself on one occasion gives his Aunt Salter £5, and in the same entry mentions that he had paid 1s. 9d. for fifty herrings. Let us hope that as he lived within appreciable distance of the sea they were not more than two days old !

With regard to the prices of his food, he is as a rule not very explicit, although we know him to have been a careful housekeeper. On one occasion after paying his butcher £5 12s. 6d. he mentions regretfully that " I returned a brest of mutton, but query if he ever crossed it." He complains a good deal of the tax upon salt which was at this time 5s. a bushel, and was to rise as high as 15s. No wonder that on one occasion he was "rather too impatient with my servant for having put too much salt in my broth !" "Cakes for my girl," begin to be a frequent item, and at seven years old " my girl began to learn to dance at a guinea entrance and a guinea a quarter." In this year among his presents was "a silver Te pot and porridge spoon for my girle," and later a "Tunbridge egg salver," for by the time Anne came to the throne, Tunbridge ware, with its minute intricate pattern of inlaid woods, was a fashionable present from ladies who went to drink the waters. Presently he buys a pair of fine scarlet stockings for his girl, price 3s., and a little later from a Scotchman a pair of " pink scarlet" stockings with garters, for coloured stockings were very fashionable.   When she is twelve years old he gives her to buy pins, 10s. for a mantle, pettycote, silk scarlet stockings, bought in London by my sister Goring £16 6.; for 4 ells of holland for shifts £2. 6. 6 yards of printed calico for a wrapper gown 17s., 21 yards of Norwich black and white crape at 2s. 6d. a yard £2. 2. 6. Six yards of Durance scarlet lining 9s., and 3s. for a pair of Spanish leather shoes." Her total expenses on this occasion, not including the waste of four pairs of shoes, which did not suit the young lady, amounted to £40. 16. 6., which seems a good deal for a little girl of twelve years old.

After such fond and reckless extravagance on her father's part she must have found it difficult to manage on the allowance of £80 a year, which he gave her when she was nineteen, probably on the occasion of her marriage. The old squire, however, would no doubt have seen to it that this was generously supplemented. It is sad to think that this only and beloved child should have made a not very happy marriage. She died at the end of two years leaving another little girl, and to his grand-daughter the squire transferred his care and devotion as far as he could. He was growing an old man, however, and did not long survive his " girle's " death, nor the trial of living with an uncongenial son-in-law, who did not allow him to do the housekeeping. He died on December 26, 1717, at the age of seventy-five.

He has left us a record of the expenses of his sister's funeral, that same sister who had so seriously upset his temper; but his own burial, as squire of the parish, must have been a much more costly affair.

For his sister he paid "for a crape and worsted shroud (linen being prohibited for burying), £1. 6, for making it 8s. For making and nayling the Coffin £2. 2 ; for bays to line it 11s. and cloth to cover it £1. 6. For black crape hat bands and gloves 6s. ; for our knots and use of pall £15. 1s. To Mr. Middleton for his sermon £2. 3. To the clerk and sexton for the passing bell and grave 2s. 6d. To Mr. Daw for his bill for charges for commission and probate of the will £2. 9. The total expenses being £30. 9. 6. This was a rather modest sum in a day when, and indeed for long after, people measured grief by the weight and costliness of the trappings of woe; but the squire's sister was a spinster, and only shared to a very small extent in his reflected glory, having none whatever of her own.

Meantime the ladies were learning to keep their accounts as well as their inventories. A very notable example was set to the English ladies early in the eighteenth century by Lady Grisell Baillie whose wonderful household books, with their minute accounts of all expenditure, have rather recently been published for the Scottish History Society. Her accounts when in London are of more immediate concern to us than those in Scotland, and we may see what a comparatively high price she had to pay for some necessities. Lady Grisell paid

	£	s.	d.
For a pound of white pepper	0.	3.	6
For 8 lb. Barlie at 3d. p. lb.	0.	2.	0
For a litle botle of Hungary Water (a famous cure of rheumatism	0.	1.	3
For a lb. Bohea Tea	0.	16.	0
For a lb. Beco Tea	1.	4.	0
For ¼ lb. fine green Tea	0.	8.	0

A tax on soap and candles had been imposed and bitterly resented in 1709, so that Lady Grisell had to pay 5s. for two lbs. of wax candles, and

For a firriken of sope brock up this day   ... £1. 8. 0

"Sope" for two weeks cost her 5s., and soap and sand to scour the house 3s. "Lisbon" sugar was 7d. lb., while finest sugar was 12d., and coarser sugar 9½d., or as she expresses it, 9–6/12d. The coarsest loaf sugar was 8d. lb. Lisbon sugar would probably be cheaper owing to the Treaty between England and Portugal of 1703, which had also so greatly cheapened the Portuguese wines. For salt she paid 6d. a peck in Scotland, but there is no mention of its cost in London. Defoe mentions it a few years later as very high, and that ships from Bideford go up the Mersey and bring back rock salt from Cheshire. The rivalry between this rock salt, and the brine salt originally obtained at Shields by boiling down sea water, had been incessant for nearly a century, and both had demanded Government protection.

Lady Grisell paid 4½d. oz. for coffee powder, 4s. lb. for snuff, and 2s. for tobacco ; very important items were these last to the fashionable lady. Beef in London was 3d. lb., and mutton 3½d., and pork 4d., the latter for salting. Good housewife though she was, Lady Grisell did not do all her own baking in London. She mentions that she spent £5 6s. on bread for her large household from April 1 to July 14, 1717. There had been great diffi-culties about bread in London at an earlier date, and it had been found necessary to pass an Act in 1710 to regulate the price and Assize of Bread sold in the city. "That the Assize of all White, Wheaten, or Household Bread to be made of wheat for sale within this City and

Liberties thereof, shall for the future be Penny, two Penny, Six Penny, Twelve Penny, and Eighteen Penny Loaves and no other and that on every loaf be fairly imprinted or Marked several letters for knowing the Price or Sort thereof. On every Penny Loaf I.F. (Finest or White), I.W. (Wheat), I.H. (Household)." The weight of the loaves was also fixed according to the quality of the flour, and such a regulation was no doubt of great benefit, especially to the poorer people who had been sadly cheated over the weight and quality of their bread.

Wine was naturally a very heavy and rather disproportionate item at this period in the housewife's accounts. For a hogshead of claret in 1716 Lady Grisell pays £18 and £7 3s. 6d. for French duty, while the customs-house dues came to 9s. 6d. Champagne was apparently about 4s. 6d. a bottle, Burgundy 4s., Hermitage 4s., and Arrack about 5s. 6d. In Scotland champagne was not drunk, but there is a note for seven pints of mum, that most intoxicating drink of the people, which came to 11s. 8d., while white wine was 4s. a pint, Brandy 4s. 10d. a pint, and Burgundy 7s. a flask, which probably meant one of the large flat glass bottles greatly in use in England in the seventeenth century and in the early part of the eighteenth.

The housekeeping in Scotland was, of course, upon a very different scale. Cattle and sheep were bought alive instead of beef and mutton, and much more of the work of supplying a household with necessities was done on the premises. When the family moved to London the expenses were a great deal more than doubled ; but when we consider the greater number of smart clothes which were required, the price of entertainment, such as

" Opera tickets £2. 3," "for Ticket to a Music Meeting £1. 1. 6," "to the bairns for operas 16s.," etc., this is not surprising.

There were also, perhaps, heavier losses at cards than at Edinburgh or Mellerstaine, and this was a regular item in everybody's expenses. It is curious in this connection to find a sum of " £2. 2 paid for 3 duson mother of pearl fish 6s. per dus. and 6 duson counters 4s. dus." Some of us can remember, as children, playing the old game of "Commerce" with just such pearl fish and counters, which had been carefully handed down through many generations, and very beautiful we thought them.

Coal was another item which was an extra expense in London, being about 28s. 6d. a chaldron at this time. Then there was the hire of coaches and chairs, news-papers, and the penny post to encourage more letter writing, the "Scavengers' Tax," "Poors Tax," the water tax, drink-money to the watchman and the waterman. Indeed, living in London was altogether much dearer than living in the country, for not only were there more diversions to spend money upon, just as there are at present, but whereas in these days it is possible to get food cheaper, and so to make money go really farther, two hundred years ago it was not, nor was it permitted to ladies and gentlemen to live economically at all.

A pretty little entry, which occurs constantly in Lady Grisell's accounts, is "To my Dear's poket £2," "to my Dearest's Pocket £3," which refers to the money which she gave her husband, and of which no account is kept. So admirable a business woman was Lady Grisell and so excellent a housewife, that Mr. Baillie thankfully left the whole of his financial affairs in her hands, and never obviously had any cause to regret it. We have, as it were, only peeped inside this most fascinating volume, and for readers who are interested in the manner of living and expenses of our forefathers, both in England and in Scotland in the first half of the eighteenth century, it would be difficult to find anything yet published that is so inclusive and detailed.

From this we may turn to some unpublished accounts of the Osbaldeston and Bosville families in the reign of George II. and later. Lady Osbaldeston, the third wife of Sir Richard Osbaldeston, Kt., of Hummanby Hall, Yorks, was left a widow in 1728. In those unhurried days it was not expected of the Dowager to remove herself with any indecorous haste to the Dower House or wherever the new home might be. So it was not until 1730 that we find Lady Osbaldeston making elaborate lists of her household possessions, her glass, house linen, plate, jewellery, etc., paying all her bills and generally setting her house in order.

The list of house linen in those days was naturally a very long one. Stores of sheets, tablecloths, etc., were still handed down from mother to daughter as treasured possessions, although we hear a good deal less of the ladies spinning themselves than in the previous century. Mrs. Delaney and her mother were notable spinners both in flax and wool, but as a rule much of this was now done in the cottages.

In Lady Osbaldeston's list the sheets and pillow bears, as they were called, are marked and priced together, and each is checked with a red pencil. Thus we find dated Oct. 16, 1780, "one Pair of Holland Sheets and Pillow Bears £3. 0. 0," and other pairs also with pillow bears £2. 2. 0 each set. The Cleaveland sheets with pillow

bears are valued at £2. 5 and the linen sets at only
£1. 9 each. The "el wide" sheets with pillow bears
come to £2. 4. 6 and the sheets of French cloth to
£1. 10. The ten pairs of servants' sheets, in which there
is no mention of pillow bears, are uniformly 12s. a pair
and were possibly made of hemp cloth. Evidently the
so-called Holland sheets were considered the finest, and
indeed, at an earlier period they are the only ones which
we hear of, the flax having originally, no doubt, come
from Holland. The list of Lady Osbaldeston's table
linen was made the following day, Oct. 17th, and
comprises—

	£	s.	d.
3 Fine Diaper Table cloths	2.	15.	0
2 doz. Napkins ditto	2.	12.	0
4 Flowered Damask Tablecloths	2.	8.	0
20 Napkins do	2.	4.	0
1 Damask Table Cloth and 1 doz. Napkins	2.	0.	0
1 Large Damask Table Cloth	0.	15.	0
2 Lozenge Hugaback Table Cloths	1.	9.	0
27 Napkins	2.	5.	0
1 Side board ditto	0.	10.	0
2 Large Hugaback Ta. cl. small work	2.	2.	0
2 Doz. do. Napkins	3.	0.	0
2 Little Hugaback Table Cloths	0.	16.	0
3 Diaper Hamborough Ta. Cloths	1.	4.	0
3 Diaper Table Cloths	1.	1.	0
3 Diaper Tab. Cloths 3 breadths	1.	16.	6
4 Diaper Side Boardes	1.	0.	0
2 Fine Damask Towells	0.	7.	0
1 Doz. Diaper Towells	0.	18.	0
1 Doz. Hug. Towells	0.	15.	0

In addition there are seven "small worked diaper
Table Cl. at 7s. each," and "coarse Towells and Servants
Ta. cl. unsett down."

In the list of her plate she gives the weight as well as

the value of each article, and from this we note that the silver at this period was all valued at from 5s. 3d. to 5s. 6d. an ounce. The list is too long to give in its entirety, but it suggests a very handsome array of that fine old Georgian and Queen Anne silver, and probably some of an even earlier date, much of which must have since found its way into the market and be fetching sums which would have surprised Lady Osbaldeston. Among the most characteristic and interesting items are—

	£	s.	d.
A Tea Kettle, weight 37 oz. at 5s. 3d.	14.	19.	3
A Lamp and Frame, wt. 31 oz. : 12 at 5s. 3d.	08.	05.	9
A Large Waiter, wt. 38 : 00 at 5s. 6d.	10.	09.	0
1 Soup Dish, wt. 34 : 16 at 5s. 2d.	09.	00.	0
1 Coffee Pot, wt. 30 : 00 at 5s. 6d.	08.	05.	0
1 Tea Pot, wt. 16 : 00 at 5s. 3d.	04.	04.	0
1 Milk Pot, wt. 11 : 00 at 5s. 3d.	02.	17.	0
1 Decanter, wt. 26 : 18 at 5s. 3d.	07.	01.	3
1 Sett of Casters, wt. 38 : 02 at 5s. 6d.	10.	09.	6
A paire of snuffers and stand, wt. 11 : 18 at 5s. 3d.	03.	02.	6
2 hand Candlesticks, wt. 19 : 06 at 5s. 6d.	05.	06.	0
A Skillet, wt. 4 : 12 at 5s. 4d.	01.	04.	6

There is a great deal more, amounting in all to £140 15s. There are more decanters and coffee-pots and teapots and "Soop dishes" and ladles and snuffers and extinguishers, and there is a teaspoon dish valued at 16s., the exact use of which we should like to know and which would certainly have a fictitious value nowadays. When the ladies drank their dish of tea out of those little handleless bowls did they all lay their spoons upon one little tray intended for the purpose? We wonder! In the rather elementary fashion of an age which prided itself upon its gentility the lady was in the habit of tapping with her spoon upon her cup when she wished for more tea, to attract the attention of any gentleman present. When she did not wish for more she calmly turned her cup upside down in the saucer !

Lady Osbaldeston's jewellery is chiefly of interest as showing the different value set upon the gold pieces of different countries. The English coinage had greatly improved under Queen Anne, both the gold and silver coins showing very superior design and workmanship, but the intrinsic value of the coin itself had not apparently risen since the Restoration. As yet the current coin was of the value of £1 1s., the present sovereign not having been coined until about 1815.

	£	s.	d.
A gold watch and chain	13.	10.	0
A Diamond buckle for a girdle	14.	10.	0
1 Ruby ring with 6 brylions	4.	00.	0
1 Ring with 3 Rose Diamonds	7.	00.	0
1 Ring with a green stone and 6 Table Dimons... ...	2.	00.	0
a fine guine pees of gold of King William and Queen Mary	5.	05.	0
a fine guine pees King Charles the II.	5.	05.	0
a fine guine pees King George the I.	5.	05.	0
a portegall pees of Gold	3.	12.	0
a portegall pees of gold	3.	06.	0
a 2 guiney pees of gold	2.	02.	0
a pees of gold of the king of france	1.	13.	0
a Spanish pees of gold	1.	13.	0
a Spanish pees of gold	1.	15.	0
a Dutch pees of gold	1.	04.	6
a Spanish pees of gold	2.	00.	0
Queen Eliz. pees of gold	1.	10.	0
a half pees of the same coyne	0.	15.	0
etc. etc.			
a Ring with a Ruby and 6 Bryl^t. Diam^d.	3.	13.	6
a ring with an Emerald and Table Diamonds	1.	14.	0

The list of Lady Osbaldeston's pots and pans and glass

and china gives a very good idea of the manner in which the housewife's kitchen and table were supplied in the reign of George II. Glass apparently was also sometimes sold by the weight. The London ale glasses were probably of great size and solidity, such as we now use for flower glasses when we can get them and which are also, in common with all other old glass, very successfully imitated.

Oct. 14, 1729.—THE LADY OSBALDESTON, BT. OF THO. JAMES.

		£	s.	d.
One Dozen of wine Glasses		0.	3.	0
five large ale Glasses 5d. apiece		0.	2.	1
one dozen of water Glasses		0.	4.	0
one Baskett Salt		0.	1.	6
Eighteen fine china pattron plates		0.	10.	6
15 two dishes		0.	0.	7½
six browne porringers 4½d one Nott^m. pint cup 2d.		0.	0.	6½
16 half a peck of Oatmeal		0.	0.	8
one Quart and a pint handle bottle		0.	0.	6
two white spout porringers		0.	0.	5
21 two potts		0.	0.	4
one fullam stone Jug		0.	1.	8
two Gallie potts 3d. apeice		0.	0.	6
five pots 2d. apeice		0.	0.	10
two potts 2½d apeice		0.	0.	5
23 four blue and white Gallie potts 2d apeice		0.	0.	8
three browne potts 2½d apeice		0.	0.	7½
three browne potts 2d apeice		0.	0.	6
six white marmelettes 2d apeice		0.	1.	0
four large Browne Venison potts 3½d apeice ...		0.	1.	2
Six London ale Glasses weight 4 pounds and a half at 15d. a pound		0.	5.	7

It would be interesting to know the history of the eighteen "fine china pattron plates" which were so remarkably cheap!

At the same date she pays 5s. to a certain Henry

White for one doz. knives and forks (of what quality is not suggested) and a few days later she pays the same person

						£	s.	d.
for 3 large Saucepans	...	...	...	...	...	0.	13.	6
One stew pann	...	...	...	...	...	0.	10.	0

which must surely have been a very large one !

Her bills, as was the custom when paper was comparatively dear, were all made out on one sheet and eccipted by the various tradesmen in their different handwritings. Thus on the back of the bill for the stew pans we find several small bills and receipts :—

Nov^{ber} ye 18th. 1729
Rec^{ed} then of ye Lady Osbaldeston ye sum of four pounds for 8 wallnutt matt^d (rush ?) chairs and all comands.

By Mr Jno. Davis.

Again on a scrap of paper

Rec^d febear 10. 1729
Of the Lady Osbaldeston for a par (chest) of Drors £2. 5. 0 by me

George Gordon.

and R^{ed} there of ye Lady Osbaldeston one pound one shilling for a mahogany screen Table and all commands

By me Jno. Davis.

and lastly, the paper being so torn that the signature has disappeared

Rc^d 23rd Oct. 1729 of Lady Osbaldeston five shillings in full for a blew and white china tea pot and all amounts

We have seen the accounts of Captain Bosville, of Gunthwaite Hall in Yorkshire, in the seventeenth century. Now it may be instructive to look at those of his descendant Godfrey Bosville, of Gunthwaite and Thorpe, about a hundred years later. Lady Osbaldeston's brother, Thomas Hassell, in default of direct heirs, left Thorpe to Godfrey Bosville, a connection by marriage, in 1773.

Meantime Godfrey Bosville was brought up like his ancestor the "Worshipful Captain" at Gunthwaite, and the first of the bills which has been preserved is for his education from 4th May, 1732, to 4th Feb., 1733. The sum charged for teaching was £1. 11. 6; for entrance 10s. 6d., for a Cyphering Book 1s. 8d. and for pens and ink 1s. 6d., amounting to a modest total of £2. 5. 2 for nine months. "The physic bill for Master Bosville" as a little boy is in proportion a much heavier item. In six month in 1734 it came to no less than £1. 11. 6. The chemist John Payne seems, however, to have supplied him with more reasonable remedies than those recommended in the books of the period ; probably his mother had been educated beyond superstition. At any rate we find nothing more alarming than—

					s.	d.
two cordial powders	...	...	...	...	1.	6
A Temperate Julep	...	...	...	...	1.	6
A Cardiac Draught	...	...	...	...	1.	4
The draught	...	...	...	...	1.	0
The gargle	...	...	...	...	2.	0
A chalybeate Tincture ...	...	...	...	...	2.	4
Milk Water	...	...	...	...		8
An estringent mixture ...	...	...	...	...	1.	6 etc.

We do not of course know the ingredients, but the prices are very much what they might be to-day at a country chemist's. By 1766 Godfrey Bosville has married Miss Diana Wentworth and has children of his own. There are twelve pages preserved of his neatly kept accounts for this year, which include sums of £10 or £10. 10s given to Mrs. Bosville at regular intervals. These sums were most probably intended for the housekeeping, and there are no items of food mentioned among all the others, so it may be supposed that Mrs. Bosville had to render a weekly account of this expenditure.

Comparing Godfrey Bosville's accounts with those of Lady Grisell Baillie some forty years earlier we do not find a great dissimilarity. The Bosvilles, like the Baillies, spent part of the year in London, where we may note that their expenses are £147. 0. 6 as against £52. 4. 6½ in Yorkshire. Servants' wages appear to have risen, one J. Chapman being paid £14 for the year, while Eliza Preston's wages were £7. 7 and the kitchenmaid was paid £6. Coals were about the same price, £18. 17. 4 being paid for 10½ chaldrons, while wax candles were nearly 3s. the pound. The following are some of the entries in Mr. Bosville's accounts in London :—

	£	s.	d.
James and Tommy to the Play		4.	0
Lobby Box door keeper		5.	0
A Bag wig	1.	8.	6
2 Livery hats and laces	2.	14.	0
(Losses at) Cards this winter	2.	9.	0
Dr. James' powders	14.	14.	0

(Godfrey Bosville evidently still had a large physic bill.)

	s.	d.
Tommy a pair of shoes	3.	0
Tommy Leather Breeches	6.	0
Do. Knee Buckles		5
Altering Tommy's clothes	2.	0

Tommy was evidently being advanced to garments more akin to man's estate with a view to school, for in the following January the items occur—

	£	s.	d.
Mr. Gilpin's Bill for Tommy	31.	5.	0
Usher and servants at Christmas	2.	2.	0

18

And at the same time—

					s.	d.
Tommy a hat	...	...	...	...	... 7.	6
Pair of shoes for Tommy	...	...	...	... 3.	6
Pair of gloves for Do.	...	...	...	... 1.	0

Tommy's education was rather more expensive than that of his father had been.

In January also occurs—

			£ s.	d.
The New River Water qʳˢ rent ...	...	... 1. 15.	0
Curate of St. Giles a year	...	... ... 5.	0

And in March—

				£ s.	d.
Lamplighter	...	...	... ...	17.	6
Lady Day Qr. Watch	...	...	... ...	2.	6
Lady Day year Window Tax	...	... ... 3.	2.	6
Lady Day year Scavenger	...	... ...	19.	4
Catkeeping the Summer ...	...	... ...	5.	0

The last is a curious item, and seems to mean that the Bosvilles had proper feelings of humanity, and did not leave their London cat to starve while they went down to the country for the summer.

There are three lottery tickets also entered for £37 1s. The journey up and down from York in a postchaise cost £9, but the move with servants and luggage, not to speak of children and horses, came to nearly £30.

One of Mr. Bosville's bills for wines in London was as follows :—

				£ s.	d.
Des Mages Madeira	...	...	... ...	3. 14.	0.
A Pipe Cask	...	...	... ...	7.	6.
Pardoc Pipe Port	...	...	... ... 38.	0.	0.
1 Doz. Canary ...	...	...	... ...	2. 0.	0.
Claret	...	...	... ...	5.	0.
Corks	...	...	... ...	12.	6.
Bottles	...	...	... ...	1. 6.	9.

Claret had by now dropped very far out of favour in comparison with the heavier wines. This 5s. probably represented only one bottle.

The next item in the Bosville accounts is for the trousseau of Lady Macdonald who was a daughter of Godfrey Bosville. She was married in 1768 and her wedding clothes were as follows :—

	£	s.	d.
17½ yds. silver ground silver and flowers £3. 3	55.	2.	6
22 yds. blue Brocaded Lustring ... ... 12s.	13.	4.	0
21 yds White with Sattin Spots ... ... 8s.	8.	12.	0
18¾ yds White and Gold Striped Gold Brocd. 22s. 6d.	20.	10.	0
Making a Silver Suit of Cloathes	1.	1.	0
Stomacher and Sleeve Knots made with silver net and flowers	2.	13.	0
Silver trimming for Robings Sleeves etc.	4.	9.	2
Making a Gold Sack	1.	1.	0
Stomacher Knots and Gold fringe to trim it ..	3.	3.	3
Green Bags to wrap them in	0.	5.	0
Making a white Sack petticoat and Wastcoat ...	1.	11.	6
3 yds of Cloth 5 doz and ¼ Trimming at 5s. 6d. p. doz.	1.	14.	3
Making a Flower'd Sack and petticoat	1.	1.	0
5 Doz. Trimmᵍ at 9s. per doz. and 1 yd of Persian	2.	7.	0
Long cane french Hoop and bag for suit of Cloathes	1.	13.	6
a silver girdle 6s. 6d. Gold for shoes		18.	7
a pink Sarsnet Quilted Coat	1.	16.	0
Silver shape for shoes and trimming		14.	3
Sattin Shoes 3 pair and making	1.	7.	6
A pair of stone Buckles	4.	4.	0
a pair of Silver		17.	6
Milliner's Bill for Lace etc.	49.	17.	6¼
a pair of Double Chain stitch Ruffles	1.	6.	0
a pair of Tribble Ditto	2.	2.	0
2 pair Jesuite Ruffles	1.	16.	6
2 fans one 18s. the other 10s. 6d.	1.	8.	6
Black silk Apron	0.	16.	0
Silk and thread stockings	3.	9.	0
a White Sarsnet Cloak and Hat full brimmᵈ with Blonde	3.	16.	0

	£	s.	d.
a Mignionette Handkerchief		15.	0
a fine Mignionette Handkerchief	1.	13.	0
12 Holland shifts 7d. per ell	7.	6.	11
Sleeves	9.	9.	0
2 ells of Lace for Little Ruffles		9.	0
6 Night Shifts	4.	1.	0
Cambrick 10s. per yd	1.	5.	7
peice of Cambrick for pocket Hand³.	3.	0.	0
15 yds and half of Corded Dimity for petticoats ...	1.	11.	0
3 pair of Dimothy Pockets		15.	0
2 Quilted Bedgowns	2.	8.	0
2 flannel petticoats		13.	0
Ticken Stay		19.	6
Making and Marking 18 Shifts	1.	9.	5
Combs and Brush		5.	6

As a whole the prices do not strike us as enormous, but
the price of material is not usually included in the bill.
The first rather mysterious item must have been something very magnificent, and was probably intended for
her wedding dress. Such a flowered sack and petticoat
as Lady Macdonald's may be seen to-day in the Victoria
and Albert Museum. What is chiefly noteworthy about
this and all the other female costumes of the period which
are exhibited is the extraordinarily small size of the ladies.
Compared with the buxom young persons of the present
day they seem to have been incredibly small and narrow
in their proportions, but no doubt our great-grandmothers
were paying the price for unnourishing nourishment
and insufficient air and exercise, not to speak of the
insanitary arrangements of their own, and to a greater
extent of preceding generations.

Lace was, of course, immensely dear, seeing that there
was at present no imitation lace, and the use of it was
plentiful. The fine "mignionette" handkerchief was
certainly extravagant, but the modest price of the

bridal brush and combs after so much splendour is
a little depressing !

The price of food did not alter greatly in the latter
half of the eighteenth century. We have it on the
authority of a very excellent housewife in George III.'s
reign that meat averaged 5d. a pound, bread was 4d. or
5d. a quartern loaf, eggs in spring were 16 or 18 for 4d.,
fowls in summer and autumn were 1s. 6d. a pair, and loaf
sugar was 7d. a lb. The sugar loaf continued to be sold
until well into the nineteenth century, and it was a cause
of complaint with the young lady of those days that being
trained in housewifely duties she had to spoil her pretty
hands in cutting it up ! No wonder that with fowls
and eggs at such a price several chicken could be put
into a pie and that the puddings were so exceedingly
rich. The price of tea in 1781 was 16s. or 18s. a lb.
owing to a new tax, and we find one lady apologising
to her husband for the bill and promising to use it
" with ceremony."

It is hardly within the scope of this book to deal in
detail with what was called the Industrial Revolution
in the eighteenth century, but the introduction of
machinery by its effect upon the price of materials, and
the expansion of trade owing to the improvement in the
means of communication, naturally made a difference
in supplying the needs of the housewife. If, however,
the lady in London had a good deal to gain, the women
in the country had something to lose. By the middle of
the eighteenth century the agricultural labourer was
enjoying a period of comparative prosperity. His wages
had risen, corn had gone down in price, and all other
food that he required was remarkably cheap. His cottage
was often rent free standing upon common ground.

These halcyon days were not, however, to last. The tendency of landowners to buy up small holders was exterminating the yeomanry class, and common rights were being curtailed. When the factory system took the place of home work, when weaving and spinning and carding were no longer done in the cottages, there was an inevitable tendency for the women to drift into the towns in search of employment in the factories or elsewhere. The small farmer and his vested right gradually ceased to exist, and his women must abandon the home life and earn their own living.

Some old verses, "The Farmer's Son," express the feeling of the country people with regard to these changes :—

"When my mother she was knitting, my sister she would spin,
And by their good industry they kept us neat and clean ;
I rose up in the morning, with my father went to plough.
How happily we lived then, to what we do now.

Then to market with the fleece, when the little herd were shorn,
And our neighbours we supplied with a quantity of corn,
For half a crown a bushel we would sell it then, I vow.
How happily we lived then, to what we do now.

How merry would the farmers then sing along the road,
When wheat was sold at market for five pounds a load ;
They'd drop into an ale-house, and drink " God-speed " the plough.
How happily we lived then, to what we do now."

The country housewife of the eighteenth century, with a diminished number of dependants, certainly had fewer claims upon her time and attention than her great grandmother, but she also was a less absolute monarch, and was probably a good deal less well served. No doubt, however, she had her compensations. She was certainly charmed with the new machine-made fabrics, and the lady who, both in the town and the country spent so much time in writing voluminous journals and letters, had no wish to devote too much of her attention to mere domesticities.

And as regards "what money could buy," it would seem that she found no greater difficulty in supplying her wants than we do at the present day. There is no reason to doubt that she kept, at least as handsome a margin in her income for personal pleasures, and if these were of a more restricted kind than our own they were not much less expensive.

CHAPTER XV

THE GEORGIAN HOME

THE great lady of the early Georgian period who had to live in one of the magnificent Palladian mansions which it was the fashion of the day to erect for the nobility, found herself obliged as a rule to sacrifice comfort to stateliness.

The English architecture of the first half of the eighteenth century was inspired by the Italian Andreas Palladio, and not only did trained architects follow and adapt his classical designs, but distinguished amateurs who could afford it, amused themselves by building fine Italian villas in ungenial English surroundings.

"Men of the first rank," according to Walpole, "contributed to embellish their country by buildings of their own design in the purest style of antique composition." Lord Burlington was busy in London, designing mansions in that part of London some of which still bears his name, and Blenheim remains a melancholy tribute to the success of the poet Sir John Vanbrugh, who was also an architect, to emulate the Italian style.

Stateliness and fine proportions these architects, amateur and otherwise, undeniably achieved, but some of the housewives of the time may have echoed

Pope's sentiments when Blenheim was described to him.

> " Tis very fine
> But where d'ye sleep, or where d'ye dine ?
> I see from all you have been telling
> That 'tis a house but not a dwelling."

In Kent's book " Designs of Inigo Jones," where, however, the master's original designs are certainly not strictly adhered to, their are many of these Palladian palaces and villas with their pillared porticos or colonnaded facades, and their lofty hall usurping most of the space and sometimes rising above the roof. The reception-rooms were magnificent, immensely high and well proportioned, but the bedrooms were comparatively few in number, and except for the principal ones were often small and poky.

The servants were generally lodged in the attic storey, where the rooms were large enough, but either they had no access at all to outside light or air, having to be satisfied with what came from the roof of the hall, or else these were obtained through windows let into the frieze of the entablature under the projection of the roof, of so minute a size as not to interfere with the elaborate carving of the design. No wonder that a much tried housewife was perpetually confronted by impertinence and discontent in her household.

The London houses built during the eighteenth century have a singular air of dignity and prosperity. Here where space was valuable there was less scope for extravagance in design. So we get the simple bold lines which suggest internal space and comfort. They are sombre, these Georgian houses, with the sombre-

ness of extreme self-respect and they make the best
efforts of the modern builder who has crept in among
them appear gay and garish to the verge of vulgarity.

In some of the great squares, the eighteenth-century
atmosphere continues to linger in spite of modern
innovations.   Leicester Square, once Leicester Fields,
where George II. as Prince of Wales and his wife held
their rival Court to St. James', is indeed hardly recognisable.   But Gray's Inn remains the peaceful abode
of antiquity and learning.   The lawyers have done
their best to preserve it.

In Berkeley Square or St. James's Square we may
yet in fancy see the lady of fashion returning in her
sedan from a rout or ridotto, accompanied by her
many footmen in the gorgeous Georgian liveries; the
grey light of a summer dawn creeping over the tall
houses, and the birds beginning to chirrup in the square
garden.   The   torch-bearers   thrust   their   yellowing
torches into the heavy iron extinguishers, and the
lady is solemnly helped to descend.   She may be
young and lovely or old and haggard, but the crude
morning light is not kind to the paint of her complexion,
her powdered head looks tired, and her brocaded petticoat is a little crushed and tumbled.   What matter!
She will disappear into the privacy of her spacious
bedroom where a weary waiting woman is in attendance
to disrobe her, and she will draw the curtains of her
carved mahogany four-post bed close about her until
such time as the sun is high in the heavens.   She will
certainly not consider the heavy sum of money she
has lost at cards until she has cleared her brain with
a dish of tea in the morning.

De Saussure on his visit to England was much

impressed by the houses which he watched in process
of building in Hanover and Cavendish Squares. The
area which was now first invented and which he
dignifies by the name of "moat" interested him exceedingly, and he observes that the "floor made in
the earth" containing the kitchens, offices, and servants'
rooms, is well lighted and has as much air as the
others have.

Mayfair, owing partly to the so-far merciful preservation of Shepherd's Market, remains essentially Georgian.
In one of the little old houses in Curzon Street with its
powdering closet, lived perhaps at a later age Becky Sharp,
and in Hertford Street "Capability" Brown sat and
designed the artificial park views and shrubberies which
were to adorn the Palladian villas.

One by one the little Georgian houses of London
with their singular individual charm are being torn
down to make room for pseudo Georgian palaces
and vast piles of expensive flats. Presently only the
solid classic mansions of the wealthy will remain
to remind us of the London of the eighteenth century. Even in memory the race in these days must be
to the rich! So the solid dignity of the Bloomsbury
houses with their charming Adams' decorations, for
ever associated with the prosperous merchants of
Thackeray's pages, have, we hope, a good chance of
escaping the destroyer.

In the country, the less exalted ladies of the eighteenth
century had far more comfortable houses to live in
than their wealthier sisters. We all know the mellow
brick Georgian houses with their stone facings and
their spreading cedar-trees about them, built, many of
them, not so many years later than Denham Place,

the direct descendants of the Dutch influence. The large square rooms could comfortably accommodate the hooped petticoat. Space was not economised in the bedrooms, and each bedroom almost invariably had a dressing-room opening through it of such generous dimensions as put to shame the inadequate dressing-room of modern times. Beyond was often a tiny powdering closet, and through the open door the lady could converse with a whole circle of friends in the larger room during her toilet.

On a smaller scale we constantly see these houses in the streets of country towns, and they seem to stand for all that is most representative and self-respecting in the British Constitution. The front door is always in the centre and is often surmounted by a graceful pediment. On either side are large sashed windows, the tiled roof slopes sharply up behind the parapet, and the chimneys are clustered at the four corners. We know that behind each of these houses is a large and charming garden, full of the sweet-scented, old-fashioned flowers for which Mr. Brown could find so little space among the shrubberies and plantations of the rich.

In the neighbourhood of London, and especially in the Thames Valley, quaint ginger-bricked, flat-roofed Georgian houses abound, many of them of quite a small size. At Kew and Richmond, Hampton Court and Windsor these were largely occupied by the Ladies-in-Waiting and members of the Royal households. There are charming specimens on Kew Green, and there is a rather pathetic row of them along the once quiet and dignified country road which leads from Hampton Court Palace to Kingston Bridge.

They stand back on the edge of Bushey Park in modest seclusion behind their brick garden walls or iron railings. One of them is covered by an ancient wistaria, which, with the artificial gentility of the day in which it was built, gave it the name of "Glycine." This little house has a singularly graceful, wrought-iron gate with an elegant but undecipherable monogram above it, and a flagged stone path leads up to the front door under its carved pediment. Old-fashioned moss-roses smile through the summer at their own reflections in the narrow miniature canal which flows through the kitchen garden and feeds Dutch William's fine piece of water in the palace gardens across the road. Against the mellowed uneven red wall which, much older than the house, is said to have stood there in the time of Wolsey, and in which so many little plants have struck their roots, is trained a vine which struggles each year to assert itself, and its memories of a more glorious past, but is entirely overshadowed by the flaunting sunflowers and red and white phloxes.

Alas! too many of these little old-world houses now stand empty. All along the road where the royal coaches used to lumber solemnly by under the shadowing elm-trees on their way to London—the same road along which Frederick, Prince of Wales, dragged his unfortunate wife at midnight in order that his first child should not be born at Hampton Court—the County Council tram now rattles past, disputing the road on high days and holidays with an increasing stream of motors. Sometimes, however, on a still summer morning the peace of a forgotten age seems to return. The cuckoo shouts her loudest in the Home Park, there has been no tram for twenty minutes, and the motors have not yet

arrived from London. On just such a scene might the
lady of those days have looked out as she prepared
herself to go across to pay her respects to George II.'s
Caroline.

Towards the close of the eighteenth century the ladies
also began to interest themselves in domestic architecture.
We have Mrs. Lybbe Powys's journal of her travels through
England, with detailed descriptions of the many country
seats which she visited. In the voluminous manuscript
diary of another lady, Mrs. Larpent, afterwards in her
own right Baroness de Hochepied, which has been carefully preserved by her descendants, we find that on visits
to friends and relations in the neighbouring counties, the
only entertainment in the daytime was for the guests to
be driven about the surrounding country to see whatever
great houses there may be, and many are this lady's
strictures upon the taste, or lack of it, of the architects and
inhabitants.

It was she who found fault with the "dull narrow
style" of the Tudor buildings at Hampton Court, and
she refers disdainfully to the great houses she is taken to
see which are built on the simple lines of the Queen
Anne or Georgian period as "plain and unpretentious."
Windsor suited her better, but Mrs. Larpent wrote quite
at the end of the century, when house design had reached
the uninteresting stage which has left nothing individual
to succeeding generations, but at the time was considered decidedly elegant.

Her observations on a little house in Kent have a
caustic humour which makes them worth quoting. The
lady to whom the house belonged had apparently been
her own architect. "A very neat square house in a dell.
She built it herself without an architect with country

workmen. She almost sat by it to see it done. It is furnished with needlework and drawings. The furniture is painted up by ye Misses H's with great taste and ingenuity. It is the mode of Oughts and Ends, yet really with effect as well as economy. The walls are coloured by themselves, etc., etc. They are clever, think it, speak it, look it, all day and every day, for they express nothing else but *self, self, self* and *clever self!*" Evidently the clever self had not appealed to Mrs. Larpent, who had no mean idea of her own superior intelligence.

About the same date in the old black and white gabled Tudor house of Brickwall at Northiam, in Sussex, lived another clever lady—Miss Frewen, a spinster, who was occupying herself in a very practical fashion with the care of the home of her forefathers. Actually with her own hands she laid down, brick by brick, a wide terrace path on the south side of the house commanding the lawns and fishponds, the cut yew hedges and formal gardens enclosed by the brick walls which gave the house its name. Her great nephews and nieces on a damp day may be grateful to their energetic ancestress who has made it possible for them to sit and enjoy such sun as there is and at the same time to keep their feet dry.

But after all it is the interior of the house which is usually the chief concern of the housewife, the furniture, the decoration, and the furnishings of her table. Here the Georgian lady had much upon which to congratulate herself, for she reaped the benefit of the English assimilation of the Dutch and other foreign influences which had, as we have seen, characterised the age of Queen Anne.

The early Hanoverians had the further immense advantage of the importation of mahogany, a wood which instantly became the fashion for furniture. The mahogany age in its opening years under the early Georges was very splendid in the strength and dignity of the designs, and well suited to furnish the vast rooms of the Palladian mansions.   The furniture of this period is familiar to us in Hogarth's pictures, and much of it has happily been preserved to the present time.

At first the designs of the chairs and tables of Queen Anne's days were not greatly altered, but presently it was felt that the heavier wood with its plain polished surface would be improved with piercing and carving, so the chairs become a little more ornate, and lower and wider in the seat, still to accommodate the hooped petticoat.   Both the chairs and tables were mostly made with cabriole legs and claw and ball or scroll feet, and the shoulders carved with the acanthus leaf or the scallop shell, which became as common a decoration as the cherub and the Tudor rose in the preceding century.

The panelled cupboard doors of the top part of the great secretaires were now transformed into bookcases with diaper glass doors, and this became and remained henceforth the usual pattern for the bureaus which retained the let-down flap and the set of drawers below. These were also made sometimes on a smaller scale for the housewife's special use.   Small, narrow, and elegant they are, so narrow indeed that those of us who use them, or more probably their modern imitations, find it difficult to write anything but what our great grandmothers would have called a "fiddle-fadle" note upon the flap.   A little dull gilt, a suggestion perhaps of Louis XV.'s influence, begins now to appear in the decoration, in the eagle which sometimes springs into the broken arch of a mirror, or again in the pinnacles of a grandfather's clock.

There is a solidity and strength about all this furniture which was desirable in a day when the gentlemen took their pleasures none too soberly. In Hogarth's pictures we see magnificent spoon-backed chairs hurled recklessly upon the floor. The wine courses freely over the polished surface of the table from the overturned glasses of English Venetian make, which must have been stronger than they look to have endured such usage. These polished mahogany tables were the pride and joy of the housewife for at least a century. Judging by the care which must be expended upon them at the present day, she must have had a hard task to keep them even presentable when her lord caroused half the night with his boon companions; when the cloth was invariably removed before the toasts were drunk, and wild revels and excesses of every sort and kind were indulged in. Nor was it unusual for several of these companions to spend the other half of the night under their host's hospitable board! In tavern circles, it was not even unheard of for the lady who was the toast to be set herself upon the centre of the table, but let us hope such customs did not often prevail in private houses.

Solid as this furniture had to be, however, there is an increasing elegance about it as the century moves on. The small tripod tables with their fluted pillar and carved legs, the banner screens and charming stools and stands would hardly have admitted of rough usage. We may conclude that these did not find their way into the "eating-room," as the dining-room was commonly called. The master's pedestal writing-table, at which in the sober daylight hours he would work at his political pamphlets, his business papers, or accounts or what not, was a splendid piece of furniture. Such

19

a specimen of tawny mahogany with its fretwork carving, and the carving on the panels of the cupboards all in dull gilt, was painted by Hogarth in the very room in which it stood.

By the middle of the century we get the graceful work of Chippendale and his contemporaries. Much of this was, as we know, in the Chinese manner, which was so much admired at this period. We hear of bedrooms being furnished and decorated entirely as in China, or at least as such a fashion would be understood by an English designer; of "exact Chinese houses" built in the grounds of a country house, where the ladies could go and drink their tea. It was a craze which had first come in with Queen Mary's china, had found expression in the passion for japanning, and was encouraged by the increase of commerce with the East.

But Chippendale was not affected to his own detriment by any foreign influence, either French or Chinese. Much of his mahogany furniture, his bureaus, his tallboys, card-tables, etc., remained on the simple dignified lines which were the essential characteristics of English taste in this century. His imposing library book-cases, their sets of shelves with diaper-paned doors, with three large cupboards beneath them delicately carved, are indeed worthy to share the library with Hogarth's pedestal table. In the great rooms there would also be marble consoles on heavily gilded stands, and the walls would be decorated with many gilt mirrors, gilt sconces, and sometimes hanging festooned garlands of carved wood and gilding.

The walls of the living-room were still constantly panelled in the wide simple panelling of this century, but hangings, except in great houses in the country, were

certainly going out of fashion. As early as 1743 Mrs.
Delaney was indignant at the suggestion that she should
have her room hung with mohair instead of paper. Why
indeed, she exclaims, should she, and she certainly shall
not, seeing that she wishes to cover her walls with pictures!

The English paper of this age was thick, with a small,
close pattern, usually in dark colours; the Oriental papers,
as a rule, were only to be found in great houses. The
desire to cover the walls with pictures predates a later
fashion, for one of the chief beauties of the early
Georgian ladies' square, spacious rooms, with their
polished floors, their shining handsome furniture in
which the silver candlesticks and wax candles made such
charming reflections, was the sparsity of pictures or
decorations except of the best kind, and the entire and
dignified absence of knick-knacks. These, however, with
the busy fingers of industrious ladies always at work, were
to come too soon. Already we begin to hear of cabinets
full of shells and fossils, and all those ingenious works of
such ladies as Mrs. Delaney must have gone far to crowd
rooms of modest dimensions. The style of " oughts and
ends " was, however, still some way off.

The last thirty years of the century brought what is
known as the classic revival. Adam, Heppelwhite, and
Sheraton gave their decorations and furniture successively
to the houses of the period. The discovery of Pompeii
had turned the minds of artists to the Roman classic
designs, which became exceedingly popular. The Adam
Brothers were architects who, however, when they had
built their rooms and added those light and graceful
decorations to the ceilings and the mantelpieces, which
happily are still to be found, felt a natural inclination
further to design the furniture.

This became, as we know, much more elaborate, which sounds like a paradox, since the designs of Adam, the wreaths and garlands owe their charm to their classic simplicity. But a number of lighter woods were introduced, satinwood, tulipwood, olive wood, feathered mahogany, and these were used to inlay the patterns rather after the manner of a former period, but lighter and more graceful. Heppelwhite provided the housewife with some more sober but extremely elegant furniture, especially for her bedroom. The posts of her bed became slim and tapering with a graceful canopy, a blessed change from the heavy roof of the earlier period. The shield-shaped toilet mirrors independent of a box were also his design, and some charming corner cupboards in feathered mahogany with glazed diaper doors and shell-shaped shelves. Sheraton followed with his greater originality but less restraint, which, influenced later by the Empire style, gradually deteriorated in his followers in the nineteenth century into the florid, meaningless and clumsy furniture which was accepted by the debased taste of the early Victorians.

Meantime the housewife who in the latter decades of the eighteenth century, could hang an Adam mirror of chaste design over the Adam mantelpiece in a drawing-room already furnished with settees and chairs and curved window seats of the same elegant workmanship, had little to complain of and no excuse for introducing too many of her own "ingenuities." She could furnish her dining-room with a Sheraton or Heppelwhite sideboard and chairs, and a brass-bound wine-bin, not to speak of the mahogany table inherited, perhaps, from her husband's father and grandfather, and which, while bearing the stains of convivial evenings, was by no

means beyond redemption.   But she had more than this.
Variety, all within classic limits, was the note of the age.
There was not only inlaid furniture and gilded furniture,
but there was furniture painted by Academicians for those
who could afford it, and for those who could not
there were all sorts and descriptions of pieces and all
beautifully made.   There were work-tables and screens
and card-tables and occasional tables and flower-stands,
and the pretty and useful long Sheraton sofa tables, with
the turn-down flaps at the ends, and those charming
circular writing-tables, with drawers in the frame.   She
had also the screen table mentioned in Lady Osbaldeston's list, probably a satinwood desk table with a screen
made to pull up behind.

A piece of characteristic Sheraton furniture designed
for a lady was what appears to be a small pedestal
writing-table, but while the middle is covered with
leather and intended for this purpose, the side covers lift
up and reveal charming receptacles in the shape of little
boxes for the accessories of the toilet on one side and for
work or writing materials on the other.   The cupboards
of the side pedestal contain little drawers and slides for
all feminine requirements.   Another curious piece of
furniture seldom seen in these days was to all appearances
a small and extremely elegant sideboard, but on a closer
inspection the top opened and inside was a little basin.
Here the best china, too sacred to trust to the tender
mercies of uninterested servants, was washed by the
careful housewife in her drawing-room.

To the same date belong the Sheraton double tea
caddies in satinwood, on a stand with tapering legs, or
separate, which were brought in with the tea equipage
and were always kept locked by the careful housewife,

since here she kept her tea and her sugar, both heavily taxed. There is, indeed, no end to the charming tea-caddie or teapoys of this period. We find them in silver, in porcelain, in Battersea enamel and in tortoiseshell, inevitable adjuncts to the tea-table, and all carefully designed and beautifully finished.

It was at about the end of the century that the convex mirror in a gilt frame was introduced, often surmounted by an eagle, a mirror which is calculated to turn the dullest room into the room of our dreams, and the outside world, if hung opposite a window as it should be, into the city of enchantment. How many of us and especially those of us who live in London, remember to offer our daily tribute of gratitude to the designer of the convex mirror, who, if we have the sense to hang it in the right place, and there be some trees outside, can thus convert our drab world into something like a fairyland ?

We have dwelt at some length over the architecture and furniture of the Georgian home, but there are other things which concern the lady of the house no less closely. In the first half of the eighteenth century English earthenware achieved its high-water mark. Whether or no the Brothers Eler really discovered the secret of salt glazing or whether, as some have said, they did not owe much of their success to the fact that they infringed Dwight's patents, they had many eminent successors in the Staffordshire potteries.

Foremost among these was Whieldon, the list of whose apprentices included such names as those of Josiah Wedgwood and Spode. Whieldon thought more of colour than of form, and his cauliflower teapots, his tortoiseshell and agate ware plates, and his toby jugs must have added some pleasing colour effects to the

kitchen dresser.   The salt-glazed ware was for a time
made in plain cream and white and wholly undecorated,
and the tea pots and teapoys or cannisters of the period
are among the most charming specimens of English
earthenware.   Presently, enamelling in colours began to be
used, and later transfer printing, invented at Liverpool in
1760, was regarded as a suitable decoration.   During the
period of enamelling in colours and of transfer we get
delightful punch-bowls and jugs in Staffordshire ware,
with portraits and inscriptions upon them.   A punch-
bowl with the portrait of the Young Pretender must have
figured at many secret Jacobite meetings after the rising
of 1745.

Josiah Wedgwood improved upon all the potters who
had gone before him.   Elers' red ware and Whieldon's
agate and tortoiseshell were further developed in his
factory, and the beautiful plain cream ware was hand-
painted for the table services of great houses.   The
cream ware dessert basket of Wedgwood design and the
dinner services known as Queen's ware, still made by
his descendants with Flaxman's designs upon the border,
are in great request by those who like to have an
essentially English table assisted by the reproductions
of eighteenth century glass.

Wedgwood's Jasper ware was probably his greatest
triumph.   In these days we perhaps feel less admiration
for his immense Jasper vases of different colours with
their frigid classic designs, and for those blue and lilac tea
services with their raised white cameos, medallions and
plaques, or the black basalt teapots which seem to lack
the comfortable homely qualities demanded of so
domestic an object.

It is impossible to enumerate all the different sorts of ware and designs which poured out from Wedgwood's works at Etruria, and indeed from all the other potteries in Staffordshire in the last years of the eighteenth century. Nothing is more characteristic, perhaps, than those old Staffordshire figures which were made for about a century and a half, and which, untouched by foreign influence, remained typical of the character, tastes, and habits of the humbler folk of England. At one time they adorned every farmhouse and cottage mantelpiece, but in these days when the genuine ones are so eagerly sought after, the descendants of the original possessors have been too easily induced to part with them, and have replaced them with modern penny fairings or more objectionable imitations of modern art. Not only the figures but the beer jugs and mugs with their transfer portraits and landscapes of a rather later date and their ingenuous inscriptions, generally of a seafaring or patriotic nature, have found themselves forced up the social ladder in the last fifty years.

On her marriage in 1783 Mrs. Papendiek remarks that " our tea and coffee set were of common India china, our dinner service of earthenware, to which, for our rank, there was nothing superior, Chelsea porcelain and fine India china being only for the wealthy. Pewter and delft ware could also be had, but were inferior." It is not quite clear what the " common India china" may have been (probably a coarse china clay which sometimes found its way to Lowestoft), but Mrs. Papendiek must have had a large choice of English earthenware to draw upon at this date. If the finer work of Wedgwood were beyond her means, there was the plain undecorated cream ware of Leeds, so beautiful in form as to compensate for the pierced or fluted edge with which this ware is most familiar to us, but which was probably expensive. Transfer printing had lately been introduced into Staffordshire if she preferred the interest of a pattern, and Spode was making his vast dinner services with the tower and bridge design, though it was not until a year after her marriage that, in imitation of the Oriental, he introduced the popular Willow Pattern, which was adopted by most of the other makers. Swansea was making those charming cream plates with the boarders of grape and vine leaves, and others enamelled with figures and smiling landscapes. After all, though she despised delft, which was of course thick and common in comparison to the newer makes, she had not so much to complain of.

Common kitchen pots and jugs of Fulham ware were, we gather from Lady Osbaldeston's lists, cheap enough.

The housewife of the period could also add to the beauty of her domestic utensils and ornaments with the gold, silver, or platinum lustre ware which some of the potters adopted with great effect. Wedgwood produced the gold lustre, with charming result in conjunction with the pearl ware shell dessert services. There were figures in silver lustre and mugs and jugs in copper lustre, decorated with landscapes, but these were of a rather later period.

Meantime, the Chelsea porcelain to which Mrs. Papendiek makes allusion as being only for the tables of the wealthy, must have been first manufactured somewhere about the middle of the century, and the four principal china factories in England came into existence at much the same time, that is, between 1745 and 1751. These were Chelsea, Bow, Derby, and Worcester, but at

first it was rather a glorified ware that they produced
than real china.

English porcelain, for all its charm in the first few
decades, can scarcely be described as original. The first
designs were naturally copied from the Oriental china
which, up to now, had filled the ladies' cabinets, or else
were largely influenced by the contemporary colouring
and patterns of Dresden and Sèvres. The best period for
the work which came from "the Great China Row,
Chelsea," was between 1759 and 1770. This was also the
time of Battersea enamel, and the lady of the day had
many charming objects to place behind the diaper panes
of her Heppelwhite and Sheraton cupboards—a great deal
more charming than the shells and fossils of her industrious fancy. There were lovely groups of Chelsea
figures and statuettes from Bow, which to the eye of the
amateur are only slightly and yet extraordinarily different,
perhaps because the glaze is whiter. There were exquisite
scent bottles, needle cases and snuff boxes well suited to
adorn the pretty occasional tables in her drawing-room,
while for her dressing-table there were trinket boxes and
patch boxes and rouge pots which would have put to the
blush the rough delft and Fulham ware unguent pots of
her great-great-grandmother, and with which her great-
grand-daughter, unless she happens to possess the same, can
scarcely compete. Her watch, her teapoy, and the taper
stands on her writing-table would be of Battersea enamel.
For her mantelpiece she would have wonderful vases
from Derby with biscuit handles, or with raised birds and
flowers from Bristol, or the plainer vases, Oriental in
form, painted with tropical birds and plants on a blue
salmon-scale ground from Worcester.

On her dinner-table she might rejoice in a whole

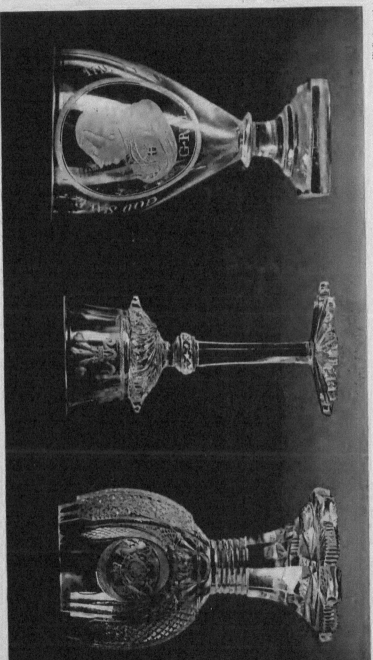

SOME GEORGIAN GLASSES IN THE LONDON MUSEUM.

dinner service adorned with the exotic birds and flowers of
Chelsea, and in delicate shell-shaped dessert dishes from
Bow. She could sip her tea from pretty Derby cups with
blue borders and the simple Chantilly sprig in gold or
colours, so infinitely more attractive than the blue and
red and gold pattern which was alone accepted as Crown
Derby by the Victorian generation. But, in fact, Derby
had also produced that wonderful apple-green border to
the plates which was copied by Coalport, garlands of roses
being added in the centre. The present writer was brought
up with a Coalport dessert service of this design, which
was banished to the schoolroom as unworthy to vie with
the handsome and showy red and blue Crown Derby of
the dining-room. Needless to say that the shell-shaped
dessert dishes and the many plates which have somehow
survived their unworthy vicissitudes now meet with an
appreciation which has not been extended to their more
gaudy rivals.

All the charm and beauty of English porcelain was
attained in the first thirty years of its existence. From
the last decade of the eighteenth century there was a very
definite deterioration. Sprawling naturalistic flowers
began to appear upon the surface of the dinner plates
and on vases of severe Greek form. Inferior landscapes
became an accepted decoration of tea services and dessert
dishes. It was that same desire for nature run wild
affecting the china which was originally responsible
for the debasement of all English taste. Is it too far-
fetched if, in the first place, we venture to lay the blame
of this also on the far-reaching influence of that amazing
Swiss, Jean Jacques?

It was about the year 1760 that Bristol and the other
china factories produced those little miniature dinner

services and tea-sets for children which are now the joy of collectors, and for which the dealers, owing to their scarcity, ask so prohibitive a price. There is one of these in Queen Victoria's doll's house at Kensington, which no doubt was the pride and delight of the little Princess between eighty and ninety years ago.   Mrs. Papendiek describes how as a little child she went out to tea with a small friend who had such a set, and how "dazzled," by the beauty of the little plates, she promptly stole one. We can hardly find it in our heart to blame her. Next day she and the plate were taken back together, and she relates how, in the agony of childish shame, she fell on her knees and repeated her usual prayers when she returned it !

CHAPTER XVI

THE AGE OF GENTILITY

"IT is the prerogative of this age to do everything in the *genteelest* manner. And though our ancestors were good, honest people, yet to be sure their notions were very *ungenteel*. Nothing now seems duller than their apothegms, and their reasoning is as unfashionable as the cut of their coats."

So, in 1756, writes the editor of a weekly paper called the "World," one of those which followed and imitated Mr. Spectator in his satirical comments on the manners and customs of fashionable society. According to this writer, the first principle of the "Genteel Mania" was "the imitating of every station above our own"—one of the least pleasing characteristics of society of all ages. It is easy to believe that the modish or would-be modish ladies who wished to shine socially under the early Hanoverians, found a veneer of so-called gentility a desirable adjunct where the standard of refinement was so remarkably low.

The society of every age has its own follies and vices, and those of the first half of the eighteenth century were no doubt particularly prominent. The pages of Richardson and Smollett give us a very living picture of a society which is by no means alluring. A lady's highly prized gentility, Pamela the servant-girl knew well, consisted in

her swooning or fainting when her feelings were outraged and when a little readiness and courage would
have been of greater service.

The average lady of fashion, as we have already seen,
had not in fact enough occupation, and gambling
remained her chief resource, with an occasional visit to
the theatre. She had neither warm clothes nor thick
shoes to protect her if she wished to take air and exercise
in cold or damp weather; she must visit her friends in
her sedan chair or cumbrous coach.

Parties, except of a large and formal description, were
few, and hospitality was no longer the chief virtue of the
housewife. We actually hear of a very admirable lady in
society who entertained her guests at a small musical
gathering from seven to eleven, and gave them nothing
more substantial than a fashionable and no doubt expensive dish of tea, and coffee, and at half-past nine had a
silver salver brought in with chocolate, mulled white
wine, and biscuits. After her guests had departed this
same lady sat down and devoured a chicken with her
brother! Surely the ghost of her great-grandmother
must have made her subsequent slumber uneasy! "Deepe
play and no entertainment but a cup of chocolate"
summed up, according to Swift, the liabilities of the
early Georgian hostess.

Social intercourse of a more sober kind where no
cards were played was limited to what was called the
"Circle." This was never a large gathering, and the
guests sat round the room in a semicircle, so that every
speaker had the whole company for an audience. The
Blue Stockings, Mrs. Montague and Mrs. Vesey, helped
to put an end to this stilted and intolerable form of
entertainment by breaking up their own circles into

groups, although we still continue to hear receptions referred to as "Circles" up to the close of the century.

Cards were not popular, even in this card-playing age, with every section of female society. We find Hannah More lamenting in 1742 that society

> "had been over-run
> By whist, that desolating Hun!"

De Saussure, when he visited England as early as 1725, greatly admired the women. He speaks of their modest demeanour, and says that they are gentle, frank, and artless, and not nearly so reserved as the men. He adds, however, that they are lazy and do very little needlework, and that they are fond of money and of all the luxury and ornaments which money could buy. He speaks of their pretty, well-kept hair, their neatly shod feet, their extreme cleanliness, and their pretty gowns of silk or cotton, according to the season. Legislation evidently failed to make woollen popular as a wearing fabric. De Saussure's estimate of the ladies was naturally superficial, and in the pages of such papers as the "World" and the "Mirror" we find only the foibles and follies of society recorded in order that they may be held up to ridicule.

But we have only to read some of the memoirs and biographies even of this dull period—dull, at least, for the women—to find that there were plenty of ladies who were awaking from the sloth into which they had been plunged for two generations, who exercised their intellects and their intelligence in all the business of life, and who did not even consider the care of housewifery as beneath the accepted standard of gentility.

One of the most notable of these was Lady Betty Germaine, the friend of Swift, who had been chaplain to

her father, the second Earl of Berkeley, and who had
found much consolation for real and fancied injuries in
the intelligent kindness and sympathy of this gracious
lady. She married Sir John Germaine, of Drayton, but
she spent much of her time at Knole with her friend the
Duchess of Dorset, to whose second son, Lord George
Sackville, she left everything that she could. Her
charming little suite of rooms at Knole may be seen
to-day, much as she left it. The books she read are
on the little mahogany table. The embroidered bed-
hangings and the chair backs are the work of her own
industrious needle, and her spinning-wheel still stands
in her dressing-room. The little casement windows
look out upon the garden which she loved.

The long gallery close by is still scented with her
famous *pot pourri*, which is made yearly from her own
recipe dated 1750 : "Gather dry Double Violets, Rose
leaves, Lavender, Myrtle flowers, Verbena, Bay leaves,
Rosemary, Balm, Musk, Geranium. Pick these from the
stalks and dry on paper in the sun for a day or two
before putting them in a jar. This should be a large
white one, one well glazed with a close-fitting cover,
also a piece of card the exact size of the jar, which you
must keep pressed down on the flowers. Keep a new
wooden spoon, and stir the salt and flowers from the
bottom, before you put in a fresh layer of bay salt, above
and below every layer of flowers. Have ready of spices,
plenty of cinnamon, mace, nutmeg, and pepper and
lemon peel pounded.

"*For a large Jar.*—½ lb. oris root, 1 oz. storax, 1 oz.
gum Benjamin, 2 oz. Calamino armatico, 2 grs. Musk,
and a small quantity of oil of Rhodium. The spices and
gums to be added when you have collected all the

flowers you intend to put in. Mix all well together, press it down well, and spread bay salt on the top to exclude the air until January or February following. Keep the jar in a cool place."

Country ladies still maintained their interest in all domestic matters, and one great lady who did not suffer from the prevailing disease of gentility describes herself as real a country Joan as ever frequented a hen-house or dairy, and concludes a letter by saying that she must go and see to her cheese chamber and apple loft.   In London the housewife had not these resources and her large staff of servants was still usually administered by the long-suffering gentlewoman.

The women often had much to put up with in their married lives, for marriages were still constantly arranged by interested friends and relations, and not infrequently rather with a view to financial advantages than with much regard to the happiness of the young couple. But we know that there were many women, and not only in the country, who, in spite of domestic unhappiness, could mix in society without losing their self-respect. Mrs. Delaney as a young girl was forced by an affectionate uncle, and with the consent of devoted parents, into a marriage with a man much older than herself and one wholly repugnant to her, for the sake of a Cornish property. She seems to have found consolation in working her tent-stitch, in spinning, and in all sorts of elaborate embroideries.

A foreigner's testimony to the contrary notwithstanding, we should have said that needlework became once more an increasingly popular occupation throughout the eighteenth century and a serious rival to the still fashionable pursuit of japanning. Mrs. Delaney was, of course,

20

to the end of her life, particularly clever at all these genteel employments. Later we hear of jonquil parroquets in the midst of purple asters on the back of a chenille chair, worked for her friend the Duchess of Portland, and she was constantly at work upon chair covers and bed-hangings. She cut out figures in paper, and was particularly famous for her chimney boards, which consisted of Etruscan figures and arabesques cut out in coloured paper and laid on a black ground and intended to cover what were thought to be ugly mantel-pieces. When we contemplate the graceful garlands and carved designs on those Queen Anne and early Georgian mantelpieces, we cannot but wonder whether in comparison these celebrated chimney boards were not rather quaint than beautiful ; it would be interesting to know exactly what Mrs. Delaney considered ugly. We gather that the buildings or furniture of previous generations made no appeal to these ladies. Mrs. Montague's remark when asked to sit at a gate-legged table of the Stuart period, " Why so many legs should be required to stand still whilst I can fidget on two I own surprises me," though more wittily expressed, is quite on a level with Mrs. Larpent's complaint of the "dull, narrow style of Harry 8th " at Hampton Court.

Dress was another great and absorbing occupation. A fellow-visitor in a country house, the uncomfortable third who spoilt a *tête-à-tête*, is described as a "sort of idle body," who dressed for the day when she got up in the morning, and consequently had no further call to leave the other ladies alone to gossip over their embroidery. The pretty dress of the first Georges may be seen, as well as the furniture and fittings of the houses, in Hogarth's pictures. The hooped petticoat was still and continued to be very much the mode, but the plain gown fell not ungracefully over it, and the handkerchief tucked into the low laced bodice, or stays as they were called, made a pretty finish.

A dress for the marriage of the Princess Royal in 1733 is made of brocaded lutestring, a white ground with great ramping flowers in shades of purples, reds, and greens. Some pink-coloured damask is described as particularly suitable for a night gown, and was 7s. a yard. A night gown at this period still did not mean what it does to-day, that article of attire being simply called a " shift," but was a loose garment of the same nature as a tea-gown, and generally made of rather magnificent material. In 1732 the pretty gipsy hats with cap and lappets beneath were worn in place of the tiny flat straw hat which De Saussure had found so vastly becoming. The dress ran to extravagance in design as well as in price.

Lady Huntingdon's dress at a Royal birthday in 1738 is described by more than one contemporary writer. It consisted of a black velvet petticoat, embroidered with chenille, the pattern, a *large stone vase* filled with *ramping flowers* that spread almost over a breadth of the petticoat from the bottom to the top ; between each vase of flowers was a pattern of gold shells and foliage, embossed and "most heavily rich." The gown was white satin embroidered also with chenille mixt with gold ornaments. No vases on the sleeve, but *two or three on the tail.* The dress is further and with justice described by Mrs. Delaney "as a most laboured piece of finery, the pattern much properer for a stucco staircase than the apparel of a lady."

Flowers in natural colours were at this time a good deal embroidered on paduasoy and other material for dresses, and gave an ingenious and industrious lady a further occupation for her needle. The famous Duchess of Queensberry's dress also constantly gave occasion for comment from her contemporaries. On one occasion she appeared in white satin embroidered "the bottom of the petticoat *brown hills*, covered with all sorts of weeds, and every breadth had an old stump of a tree that run up almost to the top of the petticoat, broken and ragged with brown chenille, round which twined nasturtians, ivy, honeysuckles, periwinkles, convolvalus, and all sorts of twining flowers, which spread and covered the petticoat, vines with leaves variegated as you have seen them by the sun, all rather smaller than nature, which made them look very light. The robings and facings were little green banks, with all sorts of weeds, and the sleeves and the rest of the gown loose twining branches of the same sort as those on her petticoat ; many of the leaves were finished with gold and part of the stumps of the trees looked like the gilding of the sun." Another time, when the long muslin apron affected by ladies in the reign of George I. had gone out of fashion, the Duchess appeared in one at a great reception and without a hoop to her petticoat. She also wore a close white hood, and there were no ruffles to her yellow mowhair gown, only little frills sewed to her shift. But we have it on the testimony of Mrs. Delaney, a critical lady, that "there was a grace in her that shone out in spite of her dress."

Amusements were increasing for the ladies. Ranelagh, near the old Chelsea hospital, was opened in 1742, and there were the gardens of Marylebone and Vauxhall ; but we know from the adventures of "Evelina" that a visit to these scenes of dissipation demanded a strong and careful chaperonage for the young ladies.

At Ranelagh they drank tea in the evening and paced solemnly round the Rotunda to the music of an orchestra until they met their friends, and it was not *polite* to enter the Rotunda until after eleven. Their hours were, indeed, as late as our own, for it was not genteel to appear at the Ridottos or, for that matter, at balls of any sort, until nearly midnight. The opera and the theatre also came to be more frequented by ladies as the century wore on, and before long they had Garrick and presently Kean to fire their imaginations.

Meantime, in 1760, George III. succeeded his grandfather, and chose for his wife the Princess Charlotte Sophia of Mecklenburgh-Strelitz, a lady who, as we all know, was a devoted wife and an admirable domestic character. She was not beautiful and she had none of the wit and readiness of George II.'s consort. But she had been brought up simply, had been carefully educated, and had plenty of intelligence, quite sufficient anyhow to do her duty, as she understood it, and often under the most trying circumstances in that exalted state of life to which she was suddenly and unexpectedly called. "Sensible, cheerful, and remarkably genteel," was the verdict of Horace Walpole, by which he meant that she was a lady.

The young couple instantly inaugurated a régime of simplicity and piety. Sunday drawing-rooms were done away with, and their large and ever-increasing family were brought up in something approaching frugality both in the little palace at Kew, which is nothing more than a small country house, and in the more regal residence at Windsor. The Queen's extreme domesticity and dislike of extravagance must have had a certain influence, though not perhaps a very wide-reaching one, on English society.

It is to be feared that her influence was much less evident than that of the Prince of Wales at Carlton House, when he came to man's estate.

From the interesting pages of Mrs. Papendiek's journal we learn a great deal of the home life of George III. and his consort. Still more interesting are they, however, for the picture they give of the manner in which people in those days on small means contrived to keep up a good appearance with no loss of self-respect. Nothing is sacrificed to false gentility, though at twenty-two and with most of her time given to her babies and her housekeeping, Mrs. Papendiek naturally enjoys her jaunts to London, being anxious to keep up and improve her acquired accomplishments and retain her " well-bred manner." Mr. Papendiek is of the same opinion, since as they can " derive no consequence from money," good manners and breeding are their only passport to good society, and nothing will induce him to allow himself or his wife to form connections or acquaintances in a lower walk of life ! We may smile when we read that Mrs. Papendiek felt that the taking in of two little boys and their tutor to eke out the rent of a house which was too large for her own family at Windsor lowered them in the opinion of their acquaintance, but we must remember that the reign of George III. was a patrician age, and that there were too many aspirants to gentility for a feeling of suspicion not to have been engendered in society.

Mrs. Papendiek's father, Frederick Albert, came over to England with Queen Charlotte and she married Mr. Papendiek, who was also not only a German but a member of the Household. She herself became later an Assistant Keeper of the Wardrobe and reader to her Majesty. Meantime she brought up her family with a care, thrift, and elegance which called forth the admiration of the Queen and of all her circle at Kew and at Windsor. In the pages of her delightful journals edited by her granddaughter, Mrs. Delves Broughton, we follow with absorbed interest the competent manner in which she met the perplexities of life as lived with an insufficient income on the fringe of the Court.

If Queen Charlotte was frugal minded, she certainly exacted the extreme of economy from the Household, whose perquisites were cut down and who were expected to live with every sort of inconvenience. We may look with envy at the little houses on the Green at Kew; their charm and elegance are priceless in a conventional age of flats and three-storied houses indistinguishable from their neighbours. But for our consolation we may remember the embarrassments of their original possessors, the heavy road which separated them from London, the many journeys on horseback or in lumbering coaches which they must take to follow the caprices of their Royal masters. At Windsor Mrs. Papendiek, perpetually separated from her husband, did not fare much better, and it is no wonder that she enjoyed her visits to her father's apartments at St. James's Palace.

For many years after her marriage she kept only one servant, and all the arrangement of the table as well as the superior cookery fell to her share, which, as Mr. Papendiek, after the manner of husbands, always liked to ask a friend in without warning, was no sinecure. Mr. Papendiek, accustomed to Court fare, was by no means satisfied with the first dinner which his young wife provided for him— a knuckle of veal in soup, with parsley and butter, and a rice pudding. It is not appetising fare, but has a distinctly Teutonic flavour which might have recommended it to the bridegroom's palate. It did not, however, nor did he dissemble his views, and henceforward Mrs. Papendiek was careful to prepare one good thing at the top, with "makes-up at the bottom" as well as confectionery and pastry.

Her trousseau was simplicity itself, and a striking contrast to that of Lady Macdonald some twenty years earlier. She had two white dimity jackets and petticoats, handsomely trimmed with muslin frills. Her fawn-coloured silk of two summers' wear and a puce satin were "vamped up." She had two or three ordinary gowns and morning wraps, a "Manchester cotton," which was a stripe of cotton and wool mixed, and a narrower one of satin. She also had a new white lustring to be made up at pleasure, a print with aprons, a hoop, a horsehair petticoat, a white hat, a black bonnet and some caps. Further, she had a pelisse, or great-coat of Bath coating, a black silk muff, and Quaker bonnet. Her white fox-skin trimming was put upon a white satin cloak in which she was married; and, like everybody else in those days, she was provided with a black silk cloak trimmed with lace. Mr. Papendiek's present of a pair of diamond cut-steel buckles for her black satin shoes must have made a dainty finish to what, if not a magnificent, was at least in its details a sufficiently charming wardrobe.

Mrs. Papendiek was an interested and skilful manager of her clothes, and we hear much of them and of the prevailing fashions. The puce satin is turned and re-turned for Royal birthdays, concerts, and other occasions; but we notice that, whatever the simplicity of her wardrobe, her head is always solemnly dressed by the famous Mr. Kead. Competent as she was in all else, she was no more able than the Stuart ladies to do her own hair except for the seclusion of home life; and after all, which of us who does not possess a skilful maid is not glad enough, in the twentieth century, to resort occasionally to the coiffeur? When Mrs. Papendiek had unexpectedly on one occasion to spend a night in town, she found in the room prepared for her paper for curling her hair, combs, powder, "and all that paraphernalia," but no night raiment! Evidently by night, no less than by day, the head was considered of the first importance! We read of the charming muslin frocks and caps, hats and pelisses, she made for her pretty children, many of them out of the materials of her modest trousseau. We learn that in 1768 hoops were discarded in favour of a horsehair petticoat, and that a handkerchief of muslin or gauze, supported by a network of silver called a "titonier," was worn over the bodice, and as we know from the portraits of the period, the pretty muslin cap tied under the chin was universally becoming. In 1788 the King and Queen visited the glove factory at Worcester, and the fashion came in for the long gloves tied above the elbow, "to preserve the arm in beauty for womanhood." These were made of light grey with smooth white insides, and also of brown York tan, which latter the thrifty Mrs. Papendiek always chose for herself and her children.

While Mrs. Delaney was teaching the Princess Elizabeth to paint flowers from nature, and the Princesses were covering the furniture at Buckingham House with their own artistic endeavours upon white velvet, another "work of ingenuity," as such genteel employments were then called, had come into fashion in the making of artificial flowers. Everybody in polite society, both male and female, carried a nosegay, but the price which these cost, according to Mrs. Papendiek, who excelled in the art, must have been prohibitive to those who were not well off. The material and instruments for making a full-blown rose with buds, leaves, wire, and silk amounted to about £12 12s.! The ladies also made pillow-lace, paper mosaic work, dried flowers and ferns, and collected shells and fossils; indeed, there was no end to their ingenuity.

Before leaving this most pleasant and informing chronicler of her own time we must notice her entertainment of her neighbours. There was no money for lavish display, but we may be sure that Mrs. Papendiek applied her intelligence and power of management to the best advantage on these occasions. When her babies were born, her caudle chocolate and cake were always ready and of the best. She tells us with some compunction that it was the custom of the day for each visitor to place 2s. 6d. in the saucer as a *douceur* for the nurse. It was on one of these caudle visits that her "Papa" presented her with six nankeen double-handled cups and saucers, which were great treasures to those who could not afford to collect china.

Accustomed all her life to the society of intelligent people—as a girl she had been one of those who hung on the wisdom of Dr. Johnson, and was constantly at the Thrales—Mrs. Papendiek would naturally seek out the best she could find among the other members of the household and their friends at Kew and at Windsor. Her informal musical parties were well attended, and we may safely conclude that she did not

THE FAMILY MAID.
By George Morland.

eat her cold chicken alone afterwards. On one occasion, New Year's Day, 1788, she actually achieved a small dance. Her large kitchen, hung with lamps and decorations, was put into requisition as a ball-room; tea and refreshments were served in the common parlour, cards were in the drawing-room, and the front parlour and side room were set aside for the supper, which, according to the custom of those days, was prepared at home. The supper did not differ greatly from what it might be at a similar festivity in the country to-day. The *épergne* on each table, with pickles and preserves, wet and dry, is certainly no longer seen, nor would mulled beer, negus, and punch be served; but the variety of cold dishes, poultry and game boned in aspic, tipsy cake, jellies, pigeon pies, savoury patties, etc., need startle no modern housewife, though she would probably think it unnecessary to have a round of beef and a fillet of veal on the side table.

By the middle of the eighteenth century the education of girls, though not very comprehensive, was once again being regarded more seriously. It certainly began early enough. Little Charlotte Papendiek at five years old could stitch a pocket, read prettily, had begun to write and was supposed to be learning her notes and "gamuts." Her mother, at eight years old, had been sent to the famous school at Streatham recommended by Mrs. Montague. Here the young ladies learnt not only the usual accomplishments, for they were little more, English, French, geography, music, embroidery, and dancing, but they were also initiated into the mysteries of housekeeping, by being allowed to help to give out the stores. At Mrs. Roach's, where little Charlotte was now to be educated, the terms were only £20 a

year, but here there were parlour boarders who paid
a little more for the privilege of being allowed to take
their meals with the governesses and join in any company there might be out of the schoolroom, and these
were mostly the daughters of rich merchants who wished
to show their gentility by spending a little more money
than their neighbours.   There were others, again, of
smaller means, who paid half the fees and gave some
instruction, and were equivalent to the pupil governesses
we still hear of.

The curriculum of these schools was certainly limited,
but meantime women's minds had greatly expanded.
The Blue-stockings had been at work, and in the stultifying atmosphere of a Court life Fanny Burney was
writing her inimitable pictures of the society of her
time.   In 1775, the same year which lost to England
the American colonies, was born one whom some of us
may think even greater than Miss Burney—Jane Austen,
the incomparable and friendly satirist of the middle-
class life of a rather later date.

The eighteenth century in England was a time of growth
in art, literature, and the drama, and there were great
and absorbing political interests.   Such things could not
leave the women untouched, and certainly most of the
charming faces which smile at us out of the portraits
of Romney, of Sir Thomas Laurence, of Sir Joshua
Reynolds and Gainsborough, with due allowance for
artistic embellishment, show no lack of intelligence.
There was another influence at work.   Jean Jacques
Rousseau had had a considerable following among the
ladies when he visited England.   This prophet from
Savoy certainly had honour out of his own country, and
was, perhaps, a pleasant antidote to the robust com-

mon-sense of Dr. Johnson. Anyhow, the ladies read his confessions and wept over them. They strove to follow nature, and thereby not infrequently reached the furthest limits of artificiality. Mrs. Boscawen is much interested in 1774 to find her daughter, Mrs. Leveson, nursing her own child instead of sending her to some good woman in the country for the first year or so of her existence, as was the custom with women of fashion. Other ladies made a farce of following her example, much to the detriment, occasionally, of the " bantling " ! History does not relate whether the infants' clothing was also affected by Jean Jacques's teaching. Hitherto the baby girl had been put almost immediately into stays, for, as Mrs. Delaney remarks, " If a good air is not settled from the beginning, it is as difficult to be attained afterwards as good manners if neglected ! " But this was surely as severe an outrage upon Nature in the name of gentility as ever a wet nurse could be !

It was " Rider's British Merlin," " Bedeckt with many delightful varieties and Useful Verities," which the lady of the period most commonly used as her combined journal and account book. In this volume were provided tables of expenses and wages, a " computation of the most remarkable passages of the Times from the Creation to this present year," not to speak of admirable advice to the housewife suitable for each month.

In January there is a warning against taking cold ; a warm diet, warm clothing, and a merry wife are recommended. In March blood-letting should be attended to. In April physick is good, but " Pray to God for a Blessing." July was evidently a month when pestilence was dreaded. There are instructions to bathe in the river rather than in Baths : to keep the chamber window shut until sunset, and to perfume the chamber every morning with Tar. In December " Let a warm fire and a Cup of Nectar by thy Bath, the Kitchen thy Apothecaries' Shop, Hot Meats and Broths thy Physick, and a well-spread Table the proof of thy charity to thy poor neighbours."

The writer has been permitted to see several of these diaries, with the neat faded handwriting upon the yellowing leaves, pathetic reminders sometimes of a rather lonely existence. The diary of Miss Frewen, of Brickwall, which carries us into the nineteenth century, is restricted to her accounts and the bare facts of existence, family events, her callers, the weather and the briefest allusions to the advance of the suffering disease, of which she died a few days after the last entry. In the cover have been treasured some domestic notes, including a servant's character : " My servant Mary Turner has done my work very well. I believe her to be sober, honest, and cleanly. Why she leaves my place she does not tell me. I am with compliments, Mdme. Yrs. etc., 13 Feb. 1811." A further note states : " I hired Sarah Welsh from Lady Day 1811 for one year at £3. 10 for a month's warning or a month's wages. At same time let her have half a crown to buy her two shifts." At this time domestic servants were still hired in the country at the annual Mop or Hiring Fair, as in very remote districts they still may be, where the farm servants, each wearing an emblem of his calling in his hat—a shepherd wool, a wagoner whipcord, etc., were also congregated. The women stood rather apart from the men—red ribbons denoting a cook and blue ribbons a housemaid. When they were hired the emblems were exchanged for multi-coloured ribbons. It must not be inferred that a lady in Miss Frewen's position would have hired a servant in this fashion, but it is not impossible seeing that she advanced her 2s. 6d. to buy "shifts." Wages had evidently not greatly risen yet in Sussex. There is also a small dressmaker's bill :—

Miss FREWEN to WINARK & MARCHANT

						s.	d.
Making gown. ...	...	...	...	...	...	3.	0.
1½ yards Linein at 20d. ...	...	...	...	...	2.	6.
Tape ...	...	...	...	...	...		2.
						5.	8.

And lastly there are two or three recipes—one for Usquebach, a favourite drink of the eighteenth century : " Take quart of ye best Aquavitae one ounce of licorise with ye rine pilled off and sliced into thin pieces, half an ounce of raisons stoned, twenty cloves and three of ye largest mace, or stick of ginger sliced. All these ingredients continuing in ye Aquavitae one moneth then ye may drain it pure into another vestle." The spelling is almost as uncertain as that of her great-grandmother must have been, but there is a virile dignity about Miss Frewen's manner of expressing herself which suggests the lady who laid down the brick path with her own hands, and is in strong contrast to some of her contemporaries.

Mrs. Larpent knew no such reserve—on paper. Sixteen stout volumes of her close, neat writing have been preserved, in which she not only notes all the doings of each day, expresses her views upon the people she has met and the books she had been reading, sometimes with the most scathing criticisms, but also pours out her inmost thoughts and feelings which are always however of an absolute correctness. Nevertheless

Mrs. Larpent's journal is very racy reading. As the wife of the first dramatic censor she no doubt felt entitled to express her opinion freely upon all matters social and intellectual. We have one only complaint of her, and it is one that applies to all the intellectual ladies of this era, that, however excellent they may have been as housewives, they seldom considered domestic matters worthy of mention in their journals.

The expressions they used in conversation and in writing at this time are as sprightly as they are descriptive. Dissipations and parties were described by the most sedate ladies as "Raking." We hear of the "impertinent visits" after tea, which merely meant that people had a right to call without being invited. Mrs. Delaney complains of her mornings being "strangely dangled," and Mrs. Larpent perpetually refers to the "fiddle-faddle" notes and business which have squandered her time, with which every modern lady will heartily sympathise. Mrs. Larpent was her own housekeeper, and evidently a competent one, though, as we have said, beyond the careful keeping of her accounts, her work on her house linen, and on one occasion the turning out of some presses in the housekeeper's room, we hear little of domestic matters.

Mr. and Mrs. Larpent were probably the first people to possess what may be called a "week-end" house. This was at Ashtead in Surrey, and they went down constantly for a few days at a time, driving there and back. In London they lived in Newman Street. The manner in which this estimable lady spent her time is characteristic of so many others of her period that one or two of the entries in her diary are worth recording. Here is a London day :—

" Rose before 8, red an hour in *Lettres de Savory,*
etc. Breakfast. Taught George to spell, read and learn
Latin. Received Mrs. Planta (a daughter of Mrs.
Papendiek) for half an hour. All the rest of the morning
entering the House Accounts of the last month.
Dressed, dined, drove to St. James' Park and walked
there an hour, returned to tea. Mr. Trail came ; we
chatted, supt, to bed at 11."

They went out a great deal into society, which Mrs.
Larpent evidently dearly loved, though her strictures
upon other people's dress and manners are exceedingly
severe, and it was obviously not polite to admit that she
had enjoyed herself. If they were at home in the
evenings in London they sometimes played a rubber of
whist or Mr. Larpent " read loud " the *Rambler* or one of
the plays which he had been asked to license, and upon
which she does not spare her opinion. In the country
the programme was a little varied. " Rose at $\frac{1}{2}$ past
8, [this was uncommonly late—in the country it was
usually 7], prayed, red two chapters of *Mémoires du
Marechal de Richelieu.* Breakfasted with my family at
$\frac{1}{2}$ past 9. Walked half an hour. Taught George to
spell, to read short natural history (the Rational Dame),
and to write. Then John wrote out some geography.
This employed me above two hours. I then read for an
hour in Richelieu, dined at $\frac{1}{2}$ past 3, dressed.
Went at 8 to ye Xmas ball at Epsom, a thin
meeting. An odd set of company. No precedence is
awkwarder than that formed by the weight of money
bags. There was not one person of fashion there."

We can trace the influence of the day in the kindly
patronage which Mrs. Larpent extends to nature. She
does not dislike when she visits a farm-house " to see

21

Nature in all its varieties," and she loves "to view mankind in their various classes and professions." She was as fond of needlework as the other ladies : "I worked Tent Stitch all morning, a new job of work which interested me and amused my mind. I always find that work do so. The monotony and mechanism like the returning sound of water or any other sensation that marks time calms the spirit by fixing the attention. Then the glow of colours and shading please ye imagination." In 1798 netting fringe came into fashion, and so fascinated was Mrs. Larpent by this new " work of ingenuity" that she admits to having netted on Sunday and " did not spend the day quite as I ought."

We have only to dip into such a journal as Mrs. Larpent's—to read it all we should require a second span of life—to see how women's interests had widened by the close of the century and how much value they placed upon self-culture.

There is another point, however, which strikes us no less. In the middle of the century writing, dancing, and music constituted the chief part of a school curriculum. Grammar was quite neglected, and yet with what fluency these women who kept journals or wrote letters expressed themselves, and what a command they possessed of the English language, even while their spelling continued fanciful ! Mrs. Chapone at an earlier period in her Letters to her Niece, recommends her to write three or four lines as well as she can when she rises in the morning to offer to her friends at breakfast. She is not, however, to write more than six lines at a time, and that in perfection. Evidently if the rules of grammar as such were ignored, great importance was attached to ease and elegance of expression, and the command of language which did not pause to consider the rules of syntax, and yet never failed to convey the required meaning, survived among some of the elder ladies within our own memory. Not necessarily, however, be it noted, among those who had received the best education. In most cases it was the outcome of a mind receptive of the literary and artistic influences of the day, which had received no hint of a classical training, was free from the pains of accuracy, and was supplied with a good fund of self-assurance and a natural and pleasant egotism which convinced it that its interests and occupations were worth recording. The higher education of women with its lofty standard and use of the curb has successfully destroyed much harmless and informing garrulity in speech and on paper. Few women in these days have time or inclination to write gossipy journals. Nobody writes letters and nobody wants to read them. The social life of our times must be culled, if it ever is, from newspapers, from the bare stated fact of the printed word, at best from the columns of ladies' fashion papers largely composed by fashionable dressmakers. Let us hope that future generations, if they have time to take any interest in us at all, which is improbable, will not exclaim as we may do in reading the diaries of our great-grandmothers, " *Le style, c'est la femme !* "

CHAPTER XVII

THE HONOURS OF THE TABLE AND THE FOOTMAN'S GUIDE

"*L A table*," says Brillat Savarin, "*est le seul endroit, où l'on ne s'ennuie jamais pendant la première heure*." But to attain this rare hour of pure enjoyment many preliminary measures, according to this famous eighteenth-century epicure, must be taken.

Naturally the food must be of the best and the most carefully chosen which a Parisian kitchen could produce. The meal must be absolutely punctual; a tragic example is given in the *Physiologie du Goût* of what may occur if the gently encouraged appetite is not satisfied at exactly the right moment. And this is not all. The guests who approach the table must be in the right mental attitude to appreciate to the full what is set before them and to give of their best in return.

Gourmandise is indeed very far removed from gluttony. It is defined as a serious and discriminating and also ardent taste for those things best suited to the individual palate and digestion. Savarin had a profound but contemptuous pity for those benighted people who did not possess this refined and delicate quality, and could only eat to satisfy their appetites. In women he considered *Gourmandise* distinctly attractive. He thought there could be no more agreeable sight at the

table than "*une jolie gourmande sous les armes.*" Her
napkin is delicately arranged (under her chin, we imagine),
her eyes are brilliant, her conversation charming, all her
movements graceful, as she sips her wine and conveys
the carefully cut up morsels to her smiling lips. Only
a Frenchman, and a Frenchman of Savarin's period,
could conjure up so dainty a vision out of the commonplace circumstance of a lady eating her dinner. !

The amazing solemnity with which the whole question
of gastronomy is approached found small counterpart in
Savarin's contemporaries across the Channel. There are
innumerable cookery books of the close of the eighteenth
and the beginning of the nineteenth centuries in England,
and to these is usually added one modest chapter on
what are called "The Honours of the Table." The writer
possesses one very small and slim book belonging to the
reign of William IV. which is given over entirely to this
subject, but its most elegant recommendations pale
beside the precepts of the famous Frenchman.

In one particular, however, they are wholly agreed, and
that is that the hostess who receives her friends without
giving personal attention to the preparations for their
entertainment does not deserve to have friends at all !
There is no English equivalent to the *Payer de sa
personne,* merely "taking trouble" does not express it in
the least—it is far more than that. It is a quality to which
no money is equivalent, and one which the possession
of money too often discourages. It means the giving of
time and strength and intelligence to others for the
period required, and it is the most important and the
highest quality which any housewife, or for that matter
any woman, can possess.

In this faded little booklet on the "Honours of the

Table" we notice a great increase of elegance since the middle of the preceding century, but the standard of elegance has by now slightly altered. At what particular period the ladies ceased to lead the way into the dining-room in strict order of precedence is not clear. William III. is supposed, as we have said, to have introduced the Dutch fashion of gentlemen and ladies sitting alternately, but we doubt if this custom was followed to any great extent until much later in the century, probably soon after the accession of George III. Dinner parties, apart from formal banquets, where the sexes met were probably rare during the reigns of the first two Georges. The ladies appear on ceremonial occasions to have continued to do the carving, for in 1733 we read that the Countess of Hertford carved at the wedding of the Princess Royal to the Prince of Orange.

But by the time this little book appeared the nineteenth century had well begun, and the manners at table were more nearly akin to our own, with just those little differences which make them worth considering. The rules for "Conduct to the Observed" are almost as primitive in their details as those of Lady Rich's "Closet." The guest is entreated not to eat too quick nor too slow and not poke his nose into his soup plate. This vulgar habit is properly prohibited, but for a reason which recalls the false gentility of a past age—because "it has the appearance of being used to hard work"! Some of the mandates will hardly bear repetition, but among other things the guest must not eat greedily, nor lean his elbows on the table, nor pick his teeth *before* the dishes are removed, nor leave the table before grace is said. He must also be easy in carriage, not clownish nor bashful nor forward. He must command his temper and counte-

nance, affect not the rake or dandy, keep up outward
appearances and be not dark or mysterious. He must
also remember not to look at his watch, nor read a letter,
nor hum a tune in company nor stare in anybody's face.
" If possible," the instructions conclude, " take no snuff,
it may fall into your food and prove hurtful " ; and lastly,
" Pride not yourself on being a wag ! " It is to be hoped
that such maxims were learnt in the schoolroom, for the
guest who endeavoured to acquire them at the command
of society would have had enough to think about to
make him a very dull fellow.

To the young lady who must be the *beau ideal* of good
taste and good manners, the injunctions are scarcely less
detailed. " Never be afraid to blush, do not talk loud—
refrain from talking much, do not even hear a *double
entende*, avoid lightness of carriage, be discreet, affect no
languishing, dare to be prudish, dread to be cheap, study
dignity of manner—boast not of your appetite, nor say
anything that conveys an indelicate idea, be affable with
the men, but not familiar, be civil, but not complying, be
prudent but not too reserved, be careful not to be deemed
a coquette." The poor young lady who was thus bom-
barded with good advice of so confusing a nature, might
well in her dread of appearing a coquette have relapsed
into self-conscious smirking silence. But in an age
when it was still polite for a lady to turn pale and swoon
at an emotional crisis, the young girl trained from her
cradle to such gentility of conduct was probably not in
reality much more nervous than her robust sister of the
twentieth century, who is properly proud of her good
appetite, and enjoys a *camaraderie* with "the men"
which would send her great-grandmother from one
swoon into another.

The rules for conversation in mixed company were, we may conclude, honoured rather in the breach than in the observance, but no doubt the well-bred guest would have refrained from holding his friend by a waistcoat button while he talked to him, or from pinching him to make him admire a witticism.

We gather that by this time the fashion of drinking healths was considered vulgar, and there was another custom, innocent enough in our day, which was regarded with justifiable horror early in the nineteenth century. In a late edition of Mistress Margaret Dods' famous cookery book she observes that " when the third course is cleared away, cheese, butter, a fresh salad, or sliced cucumber, are usually served, and the *finger-glasses*, where *these disagreeable things continue to be openly used*, precede the dessert. At many tables however of the first fashion it is customary merely to hand quickly round a glass or silver vessel or two filled with simple or simply perfumed tepid water, made by the addition of a little rose or lavender water, or a home-made strained infusion of rose leaves or lavender spikes. Into this water each guest may dip the corner of his napkin, and with this (only when needful) refresh his lips and the tips of his fingers. Polite foreigners cannot reconcile the use of finger-glasses with the boasted excessive delicacy of the domestic and personal habits of the English." It is, perhaps, better not to inquire too closely into the reasons why Mistress Dods held the finger-glass in abhorrence, or the use which inelegant guests sometimes made of it for cleansing purposes.

In the middle of the eighteenth century finger-glasses or their equivalents had been looked upon with suspicion for the temptation they offered to Jacobites to drink to the king across the water ! Where Royalty were present it was the custom down to our own time for the other guests to be deprived of their finger-glasses for the evening. But Mistress Dods' reflections were quite unpolitical.

The quaint high finger-glasses with the lips or ears, as they are called, on either side had a further use, which she admits "partly carried off their indelicacy by giving them the apparent use of coolers of the wine-glass." The two wine-glasses for dessert were brought in inside the finger glass fitted into the lips, the water being added afterwards. These old finger-bowls were relics of the fine glass of the Georgian period, which, however, was now in greater houses being largely superseded by cut glass.

A fashionable dinner at this time was extended to three courses. Mistress Dods gives us a specimen :—

FIRST COURSE.

(at the top of the table)	Turbot boiled Lobster Sauce
(at the foot of the table)	Soles fried in two ways Fish Sauce

and on either side of the table

Soupe à la Reine
and   Soupe Brunoise

SECOND COURSE.

Turkey roasted with Truffles

Sweetbreads	Stewed Mushrooms	Currie in Rice Border
Cutlets or Tendrons of Veal	Haunch of Venison or Mutton Venison Sauce	Patties

and again on either side of the table

Chicken boiled
and   Ham decorated

THIRD COURSE.

Jelly	Roasted Pigeons	Small Pasty of
	Sauce Tureen	Omelet
	Macaroni Pudding	
	Trifle ornamented	
Tartlets	Cranberry Tart	Italian Cream
	Sauce Tureen	
	Grouse roasted	

and on either side

            French salad
    and   Dressed Lobster

Then follows a course of cheese, biscuits and butter, the inevitable grated Parmesan cheese in a glass dish, which in old-fashioned houses survived until late into the last century. Finally there was dessert, which consisted of ices at each end of the table, fruit, cakes of different kinds, and wafers.

Mistress Dods gives a variety of bills of fare for family dinners. The plainest of these must consist of five dishes, of which here is an unappetising example :—

	Pease Soup	
Potatoes browned	Apple Dumplings	Mashed Turnip
below the Roast	or Plain Fritters	or Pickles
	Roast Shoulder of Mutton	

or still worse

	Knuckle of Veal Ragout or with Rice	
Parsnips	A Charlotte	Potatoes
	Roast Pork or Pork Chops	Sage Sauce

Mons. Brillat Savarin, if these menus had been presented to him, would have wrinkled his delicate nostrils, shrugged his shoulders, and prayed to be delivered from the barbarous and unimaginative cooking of *ces pauvres*

Anglais. Family dinners, however, were permitted to those who could afford it to be more extensive. There were dinners of seven and eleven dishes recommended in this famous cookery book ; they ran to two courses and even occasionally to dessert, and they speak equally well for the good appetites and the absence of a nice discrimination in taste in our great-grandfathers. Quantity continued to make up for quality, and how such a meal as some of these could have been eaten between four and five in the afternoon passes all modern understanding. Apparently the side dishes were still allowed to grow cold in the waiting, the great idea being to have the table thoroughly well covered.

Flowers had been introduced as a decoration under the Regency, but did not appear on the ordinary dinner table until many years later. We hear of a dinner at Carlton House where the Prince's lady friends dabbled their fingers in miniature streams where real fish disported themselves and flowers drooped over the brim. But these extravagances, rather suggestive of the Stuarts, were over. Flowers when Mistress Dods was writing, if they appeared at all, were on a silver plateau which was to be covered with vases and crystal dishes filled with flowers, confections or crystallised fruits. We can imagine the formality of it, the handsome cut-glass vases and the porcelain vases of classic design with medallions or more probably adorned with landscapes hand-painted or in transfer. They would be small and expected to hold more flowers than they had any right to, and these would be short stalked and selected with geometrical correctness.

We have said that Brillat Savarin had no counterpart in England, but the editor of *Walker's Original*, published weekly in 1835, held quite as pronounced ideas upon the arrangement of a dining-room and the dinner table as ever were expressed by the French epicure upon the gastronomic pleasures. The door and the windows and the sideboard should all be in a certain position to suit Mr. Walker's fastidious taste. The kitchen, if he had his way, should open directly out of the dining-room, but there would of course be no noise in this Utopian establishment and no smell of cooking. Mr. Walker had evidently suffered from chilly entrées and puddings, and in a day of large and elaborate banquets he pleads for a small party, a small table, and few but well-chosen dishes. He regrets that up to his time no convenient mode of lighting the table save that of having the lamp or candles upon it has been discovered. We wonder whether certain modern modes of lighting a dining-room would have satisfied him better.

Flowers and decorations he would away with altogether. He would have in the centre of the table a basket of beautiful bread, brown and white, with a silver fork on each side that the guests may help themselves. While preferring a few simple dishes himself, of old-fashioned English cooking, Mr. Walker admits the advantages of a French dinner with its lightness and variety. In his absence of insular prejudice and desire for simplicity he was very much in advance of his age, and not least so in his wish to see champagne served immediately after the Madeira, as the only wine during dinner, since "its very appearance is inspiring," and the "sparkling" being "well adapted to give brilliancy and joyousness," would, he justly decides, be preferred by everybody! But he must have preached each week to a generation as deaf as the adder, for the cumbrous dinner dragged on its weary course, the mahogany groaned under a multitudinous number of rich and often untouched dishes, while the heavy wines were solemnly circulated far into the Victorian era.

It was about a generation later than the appearance of *Walker's Original* that the first sign of the revolution in the English dinner-table showed itself. The *Diner à la Russe*, where the carving was done on the sideboard, was first introduced into elegant circles soon after the Crimean War, but it was long indeed before the new fashion at all found favour.

In the matter of drinking wine, etiquette must be closely adhered to. The host must attend to the needs of his male guests, for apparently it was not the custom for the butler to hand the wine as a matter of course. The wine when asked for was brought in glasses on a silver waiter, and when finished with these were replaced on the sideboard. Here the butler or footman must exercise his memory, for if a second glass of the same wine were desired, the same glass might be used again for the same person. Otherwise it must be washed in a tub of water under the sideboard, for table glass was still expensive and comparatively scarce. As it was obviously unseemly for the ladies to call for wine, the gentlemen " must ask them in turn whether it is agreeable to drink a glass of wine," saying "Mrs.—or Miss—will you do me the honour to drink a glass of wine with me ? " They should then ask what kind of wine the lady preferred and call for two glasses of the same. " Each then waits till the other is served, when they bow to each other and drink ! " We can understand that such elaborate procedure would be extremely irksome to Mr. Thomas Walker, who would have liked the decanters to be within easy reach of everybody at the table, and must often have scandalised his friends by his outspoken sentiments on this subject.

The accompanying plans, taken from a little old book called "The Footman's Guide," published in the year of Queen Victoria's accession, gives a very good idea of the arrangement of a table in the early years of the nineteenth century. In this connection we may glance at the table silver which would be mostly legacies to the housewife from the preceding generation. The beautiful simple design of the silver of Queen Anne and the early Georges, often decorated only with the engraved coat of arms of the owner, would probably have seldom been seen on such a table. Adam's influence, though to be found in the silver, had not preserved it from becoming a great deal heavier and more florid at the close of the eighteenth century, a fashion which would probably have still been preferred in the years which followed. Sheffield plate, so eagerly sought after in these days, the housewife also had at her disposal and probably rather despised. This work of silver on copper was first invented by Bolsover in 1742, and the output only lasted altogether for about a hundred years. At first only small articles "in the toy way," such as buckles, buttons, and little snuff boxes with steel mirrors in the lid were produced. It was more than twenty years before larger pieces of table plate, salvers, coffee pots, tea urns, etc., were attempted. About 1780 an immense improvement was introduced into the designs by the familiar bead or thread edging which successfully concealed the copper where the two edgings of the silver plating met. It is at about this time that we hear of people having their silver table plate copied at Sheffield for common use, "so exact that they can't be distinguished" if the silver ones on a State occasion should run short.

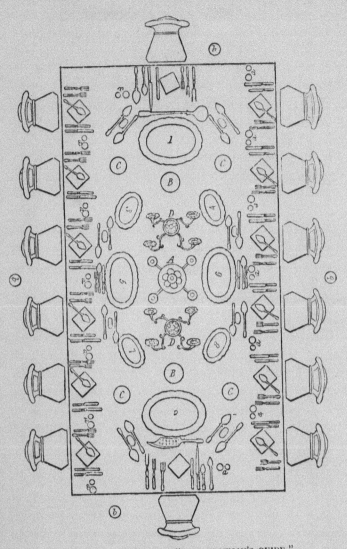

THE DINNER-TABLE IN "THE FOOTMAN'S GUIDE."

Plate I.

1. Soup.
2. Fish.
3. Vegetables.
4. Melted Butter.

5. Tongue.
6. Chickens.
7. Asparagus.
8. Fish Sauce.

A. Epergne.
B. Wine Coolers.
C. Water Carafts.
D. Branch Candlesticks.

a. 2 Wine Glasses to each person.
b. Attendants, or Waiters.

Silver forks were not common in the eighteenth century. In Mrs. Papendiek's circle they were not used at all, steel ones being considered sufficient. When Queen Charlotte sent her a wedding present of plate there were, as a matter of course, cruets, salt-cellars, candlesticks and spoons of all sizes, but as a great concession six large and six small knives and forks were added.

In the last period of its manufacture from 1800 to 1850, Sheffield plate like everything else became heavier and more ornate. The Empire influence from France made itself felt, not always with the best effect. Massive florid borders replaced the tiny bead edging, and Greek and Roman models, designed by Flaxman, became very popular. It is the specimens of the second period, the last two decades of the eighteenth century, or their faithful reproductions, that the collector of these days most usually prefers.

If we study these plans of the table we shall notice that the fish forks still had only three prongs, but the meat forks by now already boasted of four. These would be extremely solid, of a design familiar to us all as possessed by our grandfathers or great-grandfathers and engraved with the owner's crest or coat of arms. In the centre of the table is an elaborate *épergne* with its little glass dishes for dried fruit, olives, etc., and on either side are heavy branched silver candlesticks ; flowers are, however, still conspicuous by their absence. The day of specimen glasses or of sinuous green tins or shallow curved glasses creeping along the table, filled with a strange assortment of little blossoms planted in sand, was yet some thirty years distant.

There is no pretence at decoration in the folding of the napkin ; it lies flat and square upon the table, the soup spoon placed solidly upon it. At each side of the centre of the table stand the wine coolers, a decoration by the loss of which (unless they are filled with flowers) the modern table is in no sense improved. Miniature stands of the same shape for glasses were also sometimes in use to prevent the surface of the mahogany from being stained in the case of a full glass and a trembling hand! The clumsy cruet had taken the place of the charming pepper pots and mustard pots of an earlier age which have, however, fortunately returned to their full use and popularity on the table since oil and vinegar and other condiments of the cruet are no longer so frequently in request.

"The cloth being removed, and the table wiped clean" according to directions, we now have the plan for dessert. Here a silver cake basket may take the place of the *épergne*. The wine decanters are congregated at the bottom and the top of the table. A d'oyley and two wine glasses are presented to each person, and if the habit so severely censured by Mrs. Dods is countenanced a finger bowl is added. We can see the pretty shell-shaped dessert dishes and may make a fair guess at the others. Probably they come from Worcester, or Derby, or Coalport, and were perhaps made for the owner on his marriage, and are stamped with his coat of arms instead of the artificial landscape.

In all "respectable families" we are told in "The Footman's Guide," there will be a cut glass water jug and goblets, if not a whole service of the same. The handsome heavy cut glass of the period had superseded the plain or engraved or mirrored glasses of the preceding century. The glass of the Georges is once more greatly admired. We put our flowers into their capacious goblets

22

or their delicate fluted wine glasses, a base use they would have thought it, and we prize as treasures the covered sweet-meat or conserve jars with their charming cut surfaces and graceful lids.   The curiosity shops have windows full of what they call eighteenth century glass; it is pretty enough and may answer our purpose, but it has not the music of the old glass of our forefathers, that wonderful ring which the ordinary modern glass maker has not yet managed to reproduce for our deception.

But far be it from us to despise the services of cut-glass collected by our great-grandfathers, with the scintillating reflections beautiful as a diamond and the wonderful glow of the wine through the prisms.   Beautiful indeed must they have looked on the mahogany table, and fortunate are they who have been lucky enough to inherit or by other means to possess such treasures.   It is at this point, when the table is set out in all its bravery of glass and silver and delicate china, and when the wine has been once or twice offered, that it was considered expedient for the ladies to retire, and we may as well follow them !

Except in the case of family dinners, where the tea was sometimes made in the dining-room, it was usually taken up to the drawing-room accompanied by bread and butter, cake and biscuits, though it is difficult to believe that the ladies could have been in much need of such sustenance.   The gentlemen were beginning by this time to prefer coffee.

As the dinner-hour crept slowly on, supper naturally became of diminishing importance, and not being required until nine or ten o'clock was necessarily of the lightest. The housewife's ingenuity must have been greatly taxed to provide any dishes which were quite light enough.   It

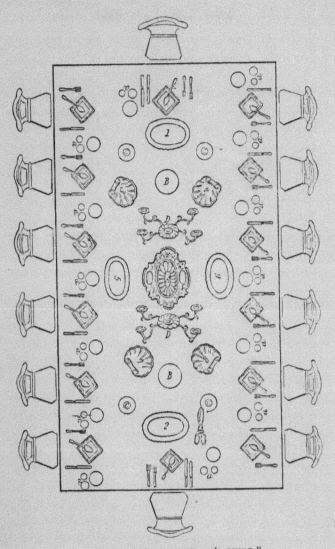

DESSERT IN "THE FOOTMAN'S GUIDE."

Plate II.

1. Pine Apple or Melon.	5. Apples.	A. Silver Cake Basket or Epergne.	a. Finger Glass and 2 Wine Glasses to each person.
2. Grapes.	6. Plums.	B. Wine Coolers.	
3. Nectarines.	7. Peaches.	C. Water Carafts.	
4. Figs.	8. Walnuts.	D. Branch Candlesticks.	

is indeed described in contemporary cookery books as a
"slight showy refreshment," and beyond this vague statement the author seldom commits herself. The footman,
however, is recommended to take it up to the drawing-room
and to have in readiness a large supply of "rummers"
and tumblers, decanters and wine-glasses, since it was
supposed the guests might again be thirsty. " Rummer " is
merely an old word for a glass of large dimensions, which
was considered convenient for beer or porter.

According to this little old, well-worn volume, which
though this late edition only appeared in 1837 speaks
to us from about a hundred years ago, the duties of the
footman where single-handed were as responsible as they
were varied. Besides waiting at table, he must clean the
plate, lamps, boots and shoes, the furniture, the marble
mantelpieces, the ugly gilt over-mirrors then coming into
vogue, and his master's clothes. For the care of the
mahogany dinner-table the instructions are naturally
minute. A little paste compounded of beeswax and
turpentine might be used, but arm-oil or elbow-grease
applied with a piece of wash leather are considered
greatly superior. On occasion a little *warm beer* might be
rubbed in and carefully dried off again.

An important part of the footman's duties was the
delivery of "complimentary cards" for his lady on her
arrival in town, and also of complimentary messages on
some special occasion. Here is an example cited of the
kind of message with which he was expected to burden
his memory from one young lady to another : "The
Honourable Miss Clare presents her compliments to Lady
Downshire, and avails herself of the opportunity of con-
gratulating her Ladyship on her attaining her eighteenth
birthday." Or it may have been a "lamenting" card,

or message for illness or some trifling circumstance such as the lady's absence when her friend paid her a visit.

Ladies, however, did not trouble to "call" much themselves, in the sense of the word in which we use it. They paid state visits, when it was the footman's duty to balance himself on the rumble behind the coach, and he is told that by leaning forward a little on his toes occasionally he will be able to ride the easier. He must not, however, scratch the varnish or injure the panelling with his nails or the top of his umbrella or his cane, to be held with the small end uppermost, "as idle, thoughtless boobies sometimes do." He must have money ready for the turnpike gate, of which there were still many in London, and he must be sure to hold fast by the holders with his disengaged hand, for fear he should fall if the horses suddenly started, while he produced the money with the other, and he is warned against a habit common to toll-men of dropping the money in the mud and pretending to be unable to find it !

He must also accompany his ladies on their shopping and visiting expeditions on foot. He must carry a small cane, and if any one insults them he must defend them "with all his courage and strength." If he has to accompany a sedan chair, he must walk ten yards in front of it to clear the way. The unmarried ladies were of course especially his charge, and must never be lost sight of for a moment. Indeed, the poor footman should have grown prematurely aged with his many responsibilities.

But this was not all. If the family desired to go to a watering-place for a short sojourn, it was his business to go and take the apartments, to see that they were properly furnished, to take an inventory of all the contents and make these his especial responsibility when leaving. If, on the other hand, his mistress wished to make a tour through the country in her own carriage, he must make himself answerable for her comfort at the inns, and even on occasions do her packing, not to speak of keeping her accounts.

The maiden lady of those days who possessed a footman of such varied capacities was indeed singularly blessed. We cannot but ask ourselves, however, how many footmen lived up to such an exalted standard, suppose that the flunkey of that time ever found himself single-handed and not one of a small regiment, as was much more frequent.

Even the footman, however, must sometimes be prepared to descend from his high estate. "Some families, even of respectability," he is told, "stop occasionally at boarding-houses." Here he must be prepared to face his trials bravely and to exercise his best ingenuity to overcome discomforts and difficulties. We can imagine that the powdered, silk-stockinged gentleman would have felt a right to be disgusted with the shifts and con-trivances necessary to procure what he would consider his own self-respect and the social position of his mistress demanded in such base surroundings. At least it cannot be said that this particular footman did not work for his living! A change had indeed come over the scene since the days of good Queen Anne, when he and his fellows filled the galleries at the theatre and the lobby at the House of Lords, and vied with one another in insolence, dishonesty, and idleness.

With the accession of Queen Victoria, the moment seems to have come when we must ring down the curtain upon the housewife. A great and glorious era was to begin for the Englishwoman, and one in which house-wifery and the cares of domestic life were not to be among the least of her serious avocations. But in the earlier years of Queen Victoria's reign, domestic life did not probably differ greatly in its details from that of which we can get a very clear idea from the little book just quoted. The gradual rise in wages and the decrease in many of the expenses of life, owing to the use of machinery and the improved facilities for locomotion and the extension of trade, all helped in a slow develop-ment towards the state of affairs which we know to-day.

The latter years of Queen Victoria's long reign are within the memory of most of us, and are at all events too near our own time to be approached in the impersonal fashion with which we have treated the more distant periods. There is another reason for not pursuing the housewife farther. The early and mid-Victorian eras do not lend themselves as a worthy pictorial background, from a domestic and interior point of view, to the charming and intelligent women which they produced. Taste in decoration and furniture was at its lowest ebb. A clash of styles had resulted architecturally in no style at all. The spacious dignity of the early Georgian drawing-room had vanished. The handsome and beauti-ful furniture was stowed away in attics to make room for the gaudy and much decorated and often gimcrack chiffoniers and consoles, twisted and deformed settees, and chairs and couches. The Victorian housewife, no less than Nature, abhorred a vacuum ! Pictures, china, knick-knacks of every sort and description, good, bad, and indifferent, many of them products of the famous Exhi-bition of 1860, crowded her walls, her mantelpieces and her cabinets, and her flimsy little tables, a trap for the unwary. The graceful mirrors of the previous age were replaced by atrocities in heavily gilded frames, which as we have seen it was one of the duties of the luckless footman to preserve from flies. But we need not search further in this retrospective scene of horror. We have at least partially emerged from it, and if there is still much room for improvement in the modern drawing-room, the housewife has at least learnt to value the past, and year by year she is, we hope, acquiring that more difficult art of discrimination.

But, on the other hand, what the Victorian housewife lost for us in one department, she no doubt gained in another.

The dinner-table of the twentieth century, both in its light and graceful decoration and its carefully chosen menu, may compare very favourably with any of those which preceded it. The modern mistress of a house—housewife we can hardly call her—no longer knows how to preside in her own kitchen, where she would certainly not be welcomed. The still-room and the malt-house have for her no existence. But if she is worthy of her position, she has applied her excellent brains and education to running her establishment upon the best and most comfortable basis, to the choice of competent servants and to the composition of wholesome and attractive dinners. The Pudding Age we have left, not so very long, behind us. The stew-pot and the twice-cooked dishes, highly coloured with cochineal and saffron, we have ceased to find attractive. We prefer a few flowers to the Warners and Subtleties of our ancestors and flying birds and skipping frogs would be regarded as an insult.

A *Soufflé* has taken the place of a *Quelquechose*, and a *Carbonado* would find no congenial situation upon our tables; while clear soup is generally preferred to pottage. A sirloin of beef and plum pudding and mince pies, the two latter only making an annual appearance, are among the few and respectable survivors of old English fare. We have attained to a simplicity which is delusive, for it ·may be extremely elaborate in its conception and can certainly be costly. But whether costly or the reverse, it must always be dainty and appetising, and conceal the fact that it is sufficiently solid and nourishing to satisfy a healthy British appetite.

The reign of science may have come into the kitchen, but the brain and the imagination of the mistress must be there also. The lady who carefully composes her list of orders to be transmitted to the tradesmen on the telephone has not finished. The personal touch, the *payer de sa personne*, is as necessary, if much less arduous than it was in the ages behind her, and can alone make her hospitality worth having.

INDEX

UNWIN BROTHERS, LIMITED, THE GRESHAM PRESS, WOKING AND LONDON.

Printed in March 2019
by Rotomail Italia S.p.A., Vignate (MI) - Italy